# Praise for Robert Wainwright

'... a skilful portrait of a woman who cut a London dash but remained a quintessentially Australian country girl.'
*Australian Women's Weekly* on *Sheila*

'The charm of Wainwright's biography is that he makes us see what an engaging, admirable and sometimes heroic quality it is to be a life-enhancer like Sheila.' *Daily Mail* on *Sheila*

'As social history Sheila Chisholm's life is fascinating ... it's undeniably enjoyable to read of all that glitter and gold.'
*The Spectator* on *Sheila*

'Nothing short of impressive ... Wainwright has revived a legend.' *The Lady* on *Sheila*

'While it is nigh impossible to capture what she was really like, her beauty and her boldness shine through this fascinating tale.'
*Sydney Morning Herald* on *Sheila*

'Muriel Matters's name is apt: she certainly does matter ... [a] highly readable biography.' *Daily Mail* on *Miss Muriel Matters*

'A splendid family drama spanning four generations.'
*Weekend Australian* on *Rocky Road*

'Wainwright's extensive research reveals an extraordinary story that is far more bitter than sweet.' *Herald Sun* on *Rocky Road*

'undeniably compelling' *Sydney Morning Herald* on *Enid*

Robert Wainwright has been a journalist for more than thirty years, rising from the grassroots of country journalism in Western Australia to a senior writer with the *Sydney Morning Herald,* where he was a three-time finalist in the prestigious Walkley Awards. His career has ranged from politics to crime, always focusing on the people behind the major news of the day. He is the author of, among others, *Rose: The unauthorised biography of Rose Hancock Porteous*; *The Lost Boy*; *The killing of Caroline Byrne*; *Born or Bred?* (the story of killer Martin Bryant); the bestselling *Sheila*; the award-winning *Maverick Mountaineer*; *Miss Muriel Matters*; *Rocky Road*; and the critically acclaimed *Enid: The scandalous life of a glamorous Australian who dazzled the world. Nellie* is his fourteenth book.

# Nellie

## The life and loves of Dame Nellie Melba

# Robert Wainwright

ALLEN&UNWIN

SYDNEY • MELBOURNE • AUCKLAND • LONDON

First published in 2021

Allen & Unwin
83 Alexander Street
Crows Nest NSW 2065
Australia
Phone: (61 2) 8425 0100
Email:  info@allenandunwin.com
Web:  www.allenandunwin.com

 A catalogue record for this
book is available from the
National Library of Australia

ISBN 978 1 76087 825 2

Internal design by Lisa White
Set in 12.5/18 pt Minion by Post Pre-press Group, Australia
Printed and bound in Australia by SOS Print + Media

10 9 8 7 6 5 4 3 2

*To my mother, Rae*

# CONTENTS

# PROLOGUE

**25 March 1919**
**London**

Philippe sat at the desk beside the window, barely noticing the hotel room's opulence. Staff had drawn the heavy curtains for the night but the faint *clop* of harnessed horses could still be heard in the street outside, mingled with the *chug* of early-model cars and overladen buses taking office workers home.

London was beginning to reopen in the lee of the Great War, the world at an uneasy peace as the terms of Germany's surrender were thrashed out in what would become the Treaty of Versailles.

But Philippe's mind was elsewhere this night, head bowed in concentration and pen poised over a sheet of hotel stationery, excited and yet uncertain about what he should write.

He was normally a man of supreme self-belief, even though others had prevented him from attaining what he considered his birthright. Philippe d'Orleans, 'pretender' to the French throne, had lived most of his life in exile from his Paris home, a fate he regarded as worse than a prison sentence. He was locked outside rather than locked within.

Philippe was used to writing about complex political affairs but the task tonight was different and deeply personal. Although the words he chose would have no public consequences, they would determine what might happen next in an important relationship that had been lost and only now rediscovered. Other than the title he would never officially bear, this loss had been the greatest disappointment of his life.

Finally, he scrawled a dateline at the top of the letter—*From the Ritz Hotel, Piccadilly.* It was unnecessary given that it was here, in the city's most famous hotel, just a few hours before that he had met the woman he once adored and even wanted to marry. But formality was the way of the world for both of them—a blessing and a curse—he a king without a crown and she in the twilight of a stage career that had shone like few others. And he wanted her to know that he had sat down to write immediately after she had left, the feelings still warm and unsettling.

They had first met thirty years ago. They were young back then; he was a wilful prince with thick blond hair dusted with faint rust, pale blue eyes and a square jaw and she was a striking, powerful soprano taking the London opera by storm with her golden trill and feisty colonial spirit. Their affair had risked all,

2

burned brightly and was then extinguished before the flame could take hold.

It all seemed so long ago and yet this afternoon those same feelings had returned. They were both older, of course, each successful but worse for wear, physically and emotionally, from life's rigours and uncertainties. He still had the bearing of a man used to an active life but a waxed moustache and pointed beard flecked with grey hid a middle-aged chin while she had arrived at the hotel wrapped in chinchilla that only served to enhance the inevitable widening of a once lithe frame.

But the changes only served to confirm that their love was more than just lust, and that behind the tingling pleasure of their reunion there had been regret, on his part at least and he hoped on hers. What might have been if not for the demands, antiquated rules and expectations of others.

Both had married others and neither relationship had lasted. She had one child but he had no heirs and his title, for what it was worth, would pass to a nephew when he died.

Who could say if their union might have been different if it had been allowed to flourish and settle, but if his feelings these long years later were any test, then the answer was surely 'yes'.

Their meeting today had been all too brief, barely enough time to confirm with a touch of hands that the passion they had held for each other so many years before had not disappeared. But there was so much more to say, to express and to explore. He wanted to see her again, not to reignite the fires of their brief love affair but to re-establish their friendship. Tomorrow they would dine together and talk, he hoped, as he finally put pen to paper.

My dear Nellie,

What can I tell you of the tender emotion that I have felt
again after so many years? It seemed to me that it was
yesterday that I said au revoir to you and that I found myself
near to you the same, in spite of the age I then had nearly
thirty years ago. I was so happy to find you in spite of your
sufferings, moral and physical the same Nellie who has never
changed and who remains in my life, sometimes so sad,
the only constant and faithful friend whom—even in the
delirium of death that I so closely escaped—my soul and
heart reached across space. For you know me and understand
me! In spite of all the world has done to separate the one
from the other, I am satisfied because the confidence you give
me is my recompense. Thank you again for the few moments
in which you have really made me happy in evoking the best
years of my youth that I have relived through you and with
you. I count the minutes that separate me from the moment
when I will see you tomorrow evening. I hope for longer than
this evening? I have so many things to say to you that I cannot
write. But that tomorrow evening will come of themselves
from my lips when I am near to you. I do hope you will give
me time to tell you all that I have in my heart. Meanwhile, my
dear Nellie, I kiss most affectionately your pretty hands and
am always your old Tipon.

The letter was delivered to Nellie the next morning as she prepared to move into a house she was renting barely a kilometre from the hotel, just behind St James's Park and within sight of Buckingham Palace, where she had been a regular visitor during the reign of Victoria and her son, Edward.

She had arrived in London the previous week, making the icy journey across the Atlantic from New York for an unexpected return to the concert hall in which her fame had been cemented and celebrated across the world.

Queen Victoria's grandson, George V, had asked that she perform at the reopening of the Covent Garden Opera House to celebrate the end of the war. The building had been shuttered and used as a furniture warehouse during the years of conflict and, although its paint had faded, gilded stalls dulled and curtains worn, it was time to reawaken the city's cultural heartbeat. And Nellie Melba, the supreme soprano of her day, was the person who would headline its revival.

But it was not the upcoming concert that had dominated her thoughts in the days since her arrival but the man whose infatuation with her had threatened to wreck her career at the very moment it was set to triumph. Despite the furore that followed, she had never once regretted their liaison, rather she had mourned its demise. There were few people who knew the details or the depth of their affection.

She had long known that Philippe lived in a great house named Wood Norton at Evesham on the edge of the city, but something had always stopped her from making contact. She was not sure why. After all, the scandal that had surrounded their affair was long forgotten and, for those who did remember, hopefully understood and forgiven.

Things were different now; this was a time of rebirth and revival.

Perhaps that was the driving force behind her decision to contact Tipon, a nickname she'd given the Duc d'Orleans, as he was then known, to hide their liaison. Given all the heartache and loss around her now, how could she deny herself the opportunity of a rekindled friendship?

A few days after she got off the boat in Liverpool, Nellie sent a short telegram to Philippe. It was succinct, but written with all the eagerness of a lovestruck teenager.

*At the Ritz. Can I see you?*

He replied almost immediately, as eager as she to meet again. There was a risk, of course, that the encounter might have been disappointing; a cordial acknowledgement of a past that had no future. Instead, Philippe had felt strongly enough to write immediately after their meeting and express his love for her and the impact she'd had on his life. She had felt the same, otherwise she would not have sought him out.

The risks were too great during their affair to write anything to each other except the simplest note, and certainly nothing with tender yearnings in case it fell into the wrong hands. The missives were all destroyed. Perhaps that was why this letter meant so much, and why it would remain among her most treasured papers and souvenirs of a life so full of adulation.

Philippe must have followed her career, read of her operatic triumphs and perhaps even attended performances as he had when he pursued her, because he had known of her sufferings behind the public facade of success, not just for him but for her son. His words made clear that he had also treasured her discretion and loyalty over the years.

They would dine together tonight and talk more.

A few weeks later she would write her own letter, not to Philippe, with whom she would stay in contact, but to her fans through *The Times*. The Covent Garden performance was a great success and she had been overwhelmed with letters, telegrams and floral tributes. A letter was her only means to acknowledge the response, as she wrote:

> It is physically impossible for me to acknowledge these
> individually; but to everyone who has expressed sentiments
> of appreciation and affection I am now and forever indebted.
> Will they please accept my warmest and most heartfelt
> thanks? I will not attempt to convey in words my feelings of
> gratitude. My heart is full, and I can only say that my joy at
> being once more in England is indescribable.

It was not that simple of course. Nellie's feelings for the great city and its part in her life were much more complex, just as she was a woman who appeared to be as supremely confident as her celebrated voice and yet had always harboured doubts and anguish about her place in the world.

# 1

# OPPOSITES ATTRACT

Helen Porter Mitchell was an unusually naughty child; incorrigible, unreasonable and unmanageable, incapable of behaving even by accident. These were her own words, an unkind self-assessment delivered much later in life, possibly as a means of justifying why her parents did their utmost to prevent her from pursuing a career as a singer.

Her father, David Mitchell, was a God-fearing man who would have regarded his oldest daughter's voice as a heavenly gift, and yet he could not abide the notion of her taking the stage professionally. It was one thing to sing at a charity concert for the church or the local school but entirely another for a woman to warble for money—'shilling entertainments'—much less in costume and grease paint. That would be promiscuous and lacked respectability before God; and his Nellie, as Helen would always be known, would not be a part of it.

9

When she was an eager teenager, Nellie decided to hold a drawing-room concert to raise funds for the repair of a cemetery fence at the local church. She wrote to friends asking them to donate and attend the concert, even creating and pasting colourful posters on walls around the neighbourhood advertising the show, but when her father heard about the event he wrote to each of the invited guests asking, as a personal favour, that they stay away. When Nellie stepped out onto the makeshift platform there was an audience of just two. She sang anyway but never forgot the experience.

Neither time nor her success would dull her father's hardline view. Many years later, when she returned to Australia as the most famous soprano in the world, Nellie sang in Scots' Church, Melbourne, which her father had built. It was a magnificent homecoming and yet, afterwards, when she asked her father if he had liked her singing, his only response, delivered in his gruff Scottish burr, was 'I dinna like your hat'.

And yet her father was her hero; a strong and dependable rock but impenetrable and unyielding.

David Mitchell had arrived in Melbourne penniless and yet he made a fortune, hewn from his learned skills as a stone mason. He was responsible for many of Melbourne's most enduring structures, including the Royal Exhibition Building.

He met dark-eyed Isabella Dow, the daughter of a business associate, at church one Sunday in 1857 and they married a few months later. They would start a family immediately but, tragically, their firstborn, a girl, and then a boy would both die in infancy. Nellie was their third child, born on 19 May 1861.

The Mitchells watched anxiously over her and celebrated with prayers when she reached her first birthday.

There would be another seven Mitchell children, roaming around a large, turreted house called Doonside, built by their father in inner-city Richmond, but Nellie's heart lay at the end of an 80-kilometre stagecoach ride out of the city to an old cattle station known as Steel's Flats, which was beyond the town of Lilydale.

It was here that she thrived, happy fishing or swimming alone in the nearby creek, exploring bush tracks and gullies beneath towering eucalypts filled with raucous birds or clambering into the foothills of the ranges behind the homestead; her wanderings limited only by the endurance of her pony and her imagination.

Nellie was a contradiction, a young woman who was happy in her own company and yet someone who needed affirmation. She was stung by criticism but ultimately used it as a driving force to succeed.

But it was her father she so desperately sought to please. 'If he was a stern master then I was a willing pupil,' she would later write in her memoir. As much as she looked like her mother, it was her father after whom Nellie took; they were both resourceful, fearless and determined but also stubborn and quick to anger—character traits that would serve her well but also have consequences.

She could never say from where her abilities came. David and Isabella Mitchell were both musical but neither was more than accomplished, and certainly far from extraordinary. Nellie would sit beside her mother's feet as she practised the piano and on her father's knee as he played the harmonium.

Singing seemed as natural as breathing, her constant humming around the house an irritation to her mother but, in retrospect, an unintentional vocal exercise that helped develop her famous trill.

Nellie was six years old when she performed at a Sunday school production and just eight when she sang in public for the first time, at a fundraising concert in the Richmond Town Hall in which she accompanied herself on the piano and earned several encores. An enthusiastic reporter from *The Australian* newspaper observed: 'She is a musical prodigy and will make a crowded house whenever she is announced again.'

Nellie's parents were hoping for 'docility'—for their daughter to conform to the expectations of the time that young women should stay quiet and not express an opinion—but they only succeeded in entrenching her rebellion and forming an enduring sadness about being misunderstood. She hated the strict boarding school she was sent to, especially as it was so close to home she could see her father riding to work.

Those memories would never fade: 'A girl should not be brought up too strictly,' she remarked in an interview in 1910. 'Particularly, she ought to be allowed to choose what she will do with her life.'

Although she found school distressing, it was the music program at the Presbyterian Ladies' College, East Melbourne, that set her on the pathway to success. It was here she found her first singing teacher, Mary Ellen Christian, a concert contralto who had studied at the Royal Academy of Music in London. When she left school, Nellie continued studying singing with Pietro Cecchi, a tenor who had studied in Rome's Academy of Music. The foundations had been laid.

❧❧

Nellie's mother died in October 1881 at the age of forty-eight. It wasn't unexpected—she had been ill with chronic hepatitis for some time—but, even so, her death from liver failure came as a shock.

In her last days, she had made Nellie promise to take care of the youngest child, four-year-old Florence, known as Vere. Not simply to watch over her but to protect her *as a mother*.

In the bleak months that followed the funeral, Nellie, aged twenty, felt the weight of that solemn vow. The sight of Isabella's body being lowered into the ground in a coffin and covered with dirt was haunting. But death was also a beginning, and there were consequences for the living; her little sister had become a responsibility in a life that, until now, had none.

Nellie's response was to move Vere's cot into her own room, to tend the child as one would a newborn baby. It was as if she could not let Vere out of her sight lest something happened and yet, despite her attention, one evening barely three months later Vere fell ill. It was too late to call a doctor, so Nellie put the feverish girl to bed and hoped her temperature would subside by morning.

Unable to sleep, she listened with increasing concern to Vere's wheeze, clearly the girl had an infection in her chest.

As she finally began drifting off to sleep, Nellie was disturbed by the sense that a third person was in the room. Unable to rid the notion, she sat up to see what she thought was a dark figure near the fire. In her anxiety and drowsiness she pictured her mother wearing the simple black dress in which she had been buried. Nellie watched, transfixed, as the spectre moved slowly across the room and stood over Vere's cot where it raised its hand and pointed at the child before making a sweeping motion and disappearing. Nellie raced to the cot where Vere was asleep, peaceful and cooler to the touch. Was it possible or the hallucinated vision of a stressed mind?

The next morning she told her father what had happened, including the appearance of his late wife's apparition. David Mitchell, on his way out to attend to business, dismissed his daughter's concerns with a wave of his hand and insisted that she delay calling a doctor to tend Vere until he returned that evening.

But he was tragically wrong. The little girl's condition worsened through the morning, her raw throat causing her to gasp for breath. Nellie waited, hoping her father would return so they could call the doctor, but by the time David Mitchell returned, his young daughter had choked to death.

Nellie was distraught. She had failed her mother, and her sister who had died in a horrible fashion. The funeral and Vere's tiny coffin being laid next to their mother only heightened her shame.

She would later recall her father's condescending words when she pleaded for a doctor: "'Tut, tut girl. Get those foolish notions out of your head." By the evening it was too late. My sister died at four o'clock. These are the facts, unadorned. I do not seek to explain them.' It was as close as she would ever come to criticising David Mitchell.

A renewed pall of doom settled over Doonside. Nellie, who now shared home duties with her sisters Anne and Belle could not shake the sense of shame over the deaths of her mother and Vere. 'Death on my youthful horizon shocked and bewildered me,' she would write four decades later, the memories still powerful.

David Mitchell, normally so unemotional, could see the impact the losses were having on her. There was nothing he could do to bring back his wife or youngest child but he could save his oldest.

He had taken a contract to build a mill for a property at Marian, 24 kilometres inland from the township of Mackay in northern Queensland. He decided to take Nellie on a business trip north for several months, leaving the other children to the care of staff. The change of atmosphere might lift her spirits, he thought. It was a decision that, in a perverted way, would be her making.

Mackay, built low and spare at the edge of mangroves, had a population large enough to justify three newspapers, six schools, two banks, a hospital, library and a dozen hotels to slake a tropical thirst. Nellie would describe the town as barbaric, despite there being a thriving social and cultural community into which she soon fell, joining an amateur company as a pianist and second-string singer. Her first two performances were to raise money for a cricket club and another for the local church. She was well received by audiences who flocked to the town's wooden theatre but considered inferior to a local girl named Julia Wheeler.

But, by the end of the year, Nellie had become an indispensable performer, 'rapturously encored' according to one report in the *Mackay Mercury*, which concluded: 'This lady has firmly established herself as a favourite and no amateur concert is likely to be held without her assistance.'

The applause only confirmed to Nellie that she desperately wanted a career on the stage, as she intimated in a letter home to Cecchi. The letter also revealed a competitive streak that would be both a blessing and a curse: 'I had great success at two concerts I sang at, so much so that all the ladies up here are jealous of me. I was encored twice for each song, and they hurrahed me and threw me no end of bouquets.'

❧

The sunshine of Queensland had thawed Nellie's spirits, as David Mitchell had hoped, and she settled into Mackay society with its endless rounds of tea parties, riding and boating trips, even writing home about the fun she was having flirting and then fending off the eligible young men of the town.

At age twenty-one, Nellie Mitchell was handsome rather than pretty, with dark, almond-shaped eyes and a fine-lipped mouth that seemed lost between a long, distinctive nose and prominent oval chin. Her hair was usually worn tied up with tight curls splashed across her forehead, hinting at her mother's Spanish heritage, as did her light-olive complexion and shapely figure accentuated by a tiny waist.

She was a young woman whose attractiveness came as much from her personality, with a magnetism that radiated the sense that she was someone with whom to be reckoned. She possessed a mind of her own at a time when women were supposed to be meek and complacent. It lent credence to a story that she once stripped off to swim nude in the Yarra River with the boys of Richmond and another story that, during a particularly tedious church service, she played 'Can't You Dance the Polka?' on the organ instead of the requested hymn.

She enjoyed the attention in Mackay and took none of it seriously, although there was one young man she couldn't shake off. Charlie Armstrong was rangy, good-looking and strong in the lean manner of someone who has lived an outdoors life, with ice-blue eyes and a shock of blond hair bleached almost white by the sun. He had a demeanour to match; an authority that made men wary and women feel protected.

He was the antithesis of his background, the youngest son of an ageing Irish baronet who was in his mid-sixties when Charlie—his thirteenth child—was born. The baron died when the boy was aged five. It was little wonder then that Charlie's early adult life was spent wandering from job to job, trying to find his place.

At the age of seventeen he was sent to Australia to work on the family station outside Brisbane. He thrived in the bush where his skills and bravery were admired and no quarter was expected or given. Along the way he had picked up the nickname Kangaroo Charlie, which some linked to his ability to stay aboard a bucking stallion until its snorting fury had calmed, while others attributed it to his devastating boxing skills, able to dispatch opponents with calm ring craft rather than brutal thuggery.

Either way, it was clear that he and Nellie came from different worlds. Nellie was the oldest child of a self-made man and Charlie the youngest of an entitled baronet; Nellie was a city girl who wanted to ride in carriages and dreamed of singing opera while her beau was a rodeo-loving country boy whose interest in music began and ended with music hall ditties. But there was an instant attraction between them, perhaps not only a physical desire but a shared spirit of independence, and an impulsiveness that could lead them into trouble.

Charlie was looking for a change, away from the loneliness of campfires, rough sleeping and the company of men. The vivacious girl from Melbourne was fun but prickly at times, akin to a wild horse that he now wanted to tame.

David Mitchell was not quite sure about the relationship. Yes, Charlie Armstrong came from an aristocratic family but what good was that in Australia where a man needed drive and skills to get ahead? From what he could see, Charlie had plenty of drive but precious little when it came to skills, beyond breaking horses.

Perhaps he could also see that his daughter and Charlie were too alike to be a good match. He had already witnessed them lose their tempers and worried at what might happen if they were both angry at the same time. Although he had doubts, there was no sense in refusing the young couple. By November 1882 Charlie had proposed and Nellie had accepted. And on 22 December, they were married in Brisbane.

# 2

# 'I MUST MAKE SOME MONEY'

Two months after the wedding Charlie Armstrong punched his new wife in the face. They had been arguing in their bedroom at Doonside about money. He wanted Nellie to hand over her purse but she had refused. His response was to lash out. To make matters worse, Nellie was pregnant.

Even in the context of nineteenth-century misogyny it's impossible to minimise the brutality of such an attack and the impact it would have had on Nellie, physically and psychologically. Once a man had hit his wife it meant that he was capable of doing it again. In future when they argued—which was frequently—Nellie would automatically brace herself for the next blow.

It came soon enough, only this time the violence was in public. They were out driving a buggy one afternoon when Charlie lost his temper and began whipping the horse. Nellie tried to intervene and grab the whip but she was struck in the face with the butt end. Still angry, Charlie pulled to a stop and forced her to watch as he flogged the horse. She almost fainted at the sight. Years later she would recall the incident with some distress, not only for the poor animal but also the clear implication that it could have been her.

It was a pattern of behaviour that would continue as the months went by, their disagreements quickly turning into arguments. They were both hot-headed individuals who refused to retreat from their point of view, but it was only Charlie who descended into physical violence. Far from the charming individual he appeared to be, Charlie Armstrong was an entitled man who believed his wife was a possession for him to control. When that was challenged, he felt he had every right to respond physically.

Charlie became more and more frustrated with city life, struggling to find work while Nellie resumed singing lessons with Signor Cecchi and wondered why she had made such a rash decision to marry.

It was no surprise that Charlie returned to Mackay a few weeks later. He had gone with David Mitchell's blessing who, despite his new son-in-law's lack of management experience, had appointed him to run the Marian sugar mill.

Nellie followed him a month later, bound for Sydney where Charlie was supposed to meet and escort her to Queensland. But he was delayed so she waited a fortnight before deciding to continue on alone. While in Sydney she had found an enthusiastic audience, performing at several private parties and a concert: 'They all call me the Australian nightingale,' she told Cecchi proudly in a letter.

To compound her misery, Nellie was seasick on the voyage from Sydney to Mackay, a combination of Pacific swells and morning sickness. It started raining a few days after she arrived and didn't stop for six weeks. She sought refuge in a boarding house while her new marital home, a tin-roofed cottage being built alongside the mill, was finished.

There were moments of joy, linked mainly to the arrival in town of a travelling opera company that filled the local theatre for a week with performances from *Faust* and *Il Trovatore*. Nellie longed to join them onstage but could only watch from the audience. It felt like a prison.

Any social fun was spoiled when she almost drowned during a boating trip with Charlie and a friend. Their yacht was hit by a squall off Mackay and capsized, leaving them clinging to the hull until help arrived. She was five months' pregnant and lucky not to lose the baby.

It would be September before she and Charlie moved into the cottage, just in time for the birth of their son. George Nesbitt Armstrong was born on 16 October 1883 and named after Charlie's older brother who was a doctor in Melbourne.

It was not an easy birth, and the months afterwards would be made worse by the sapping heat of a tropical summer and living in a five-room timber cottage alongside a thumping sugar mill. Tempers frayed quickly here. Charlie was annoyed by the nurse hired to help take care of baby George while Nellie recovered her health, and before long he had confronted the woman's husband which, as usual, ended up in a fist fight.

It was the smell of mould that Nellie would remember most, the acrid rot and puffs of powdery mildew every time she sat at the piano to play in a bid to drown out the drumming tattoo of tropical rain on the iron roof of the house.

What was she doing here, in the middle of nowhere, married to a man she hardly knew whose chief love was breaking horses and fighting? All she wanted to do was sing but there was no audience out here in the bush, save the mill workers who mistook her voice for the whistle sounding a return to work.

Her clothes, cumbersome and restrictive at the best of times, were heavy and damp in the muggy heat. Even the mantlepiece crumbled one night when Charlie rested his elbow on it.

Insects flourished, buzzing and scurrying in the lamp-lit gloom, and reptiles nestled in the humid darkness beneath the marital bed. Bathing meant a walk to the nearby river, past trees writhing in green snakes, where she washed quickly to avoid leeches that clung to and puckered her skin. At the back of her mind was the giant crocodile that was said to live just upstream. By the time she walked back to the house, she was wet from the humidity again.

The cottage's broad veranda seemed to provide some relief from the cloying heat, although there was little to watch other than the lush tropical jungle growing in front of her. She was lonely out here, far from the energy of Melbourne.

'I am very unhappy. There is no music; there is no nothing,' she told Cecchi in one letter, adding that the couple had found

22

it impossible to live off Charlie's meagre income. Even her husband could see the problems that lay ahead and consented to her trying to establish a singing career to keep the family afloat. She wanted Cecchi to organise a touring group.

'My husband is quite agreeable for me to adopt <u>music</u> as a profession,' she wrote, underlining the words that she wanted to emphasise.

> I do not mind telling you that times are very bad here, and we are as <u>poor</u> as it is possible for anyone to be. We have both come to the conclusion that it is no use letting my voice go to waste up here, for the pianos are all so bad it's impossible to sing in tune to them. Not only that, the heat is so intense that I feel my voice is getting weaker every day. So you will understand that I am anxious to leave Queensland as soon as possible. <u>I must make some money</u>.

The letter made clear that, although he was a wealthy man, David Mitchell had not stepped in to help his daughter and grandson, despite the fact that it was he who had sent Charlie back to Mackay with the promise of a meaningful job. Whatever he was paying his son-in-law to manage the fledgling mill it was not enough. The couple would have to make their own way.

Signor Cecchi immediately replied to Nellie's desperate letter, telling her to come back to Melbourne as soon as she could. On 12 February 1884, Nellie boarded a steamer with baby George and headed back to Melbourne, alone.

Nellie had no intention of ever returning to Mackay, even when Charlie followed her south, hoping to lure her back with promises of better times ahead. When the discussions turned to arguments he left again, hoping that time might change her mind if her attempts to begin a singing career failed.

David Mitchell hoped so too, unsure what was worse for his daughter—a bad marriage or a stage career. Even so, he accompanied her to her first concert on 17 May, where she was the only amateur performer in a charity event at the Melbourne Town Hall in front of two thousand people. Despite last-minute nerves, she sang an aria from the Verdi opera *La Traviata*.

Two days later, she spent her twenty-third birthday poring over newspaper reviews, including a critic from *The Australasian* who described her voice as 'one picked out of ten thousand', adding that the concert 'will never be forgotten on account of the delightful surprise afforded by Mrs Armstrong's singing and everybody who heard her will desire to hear her again, and everybody who did not hear her is at this moment consumed with regrets at not being present'.

It was the moment she realised that her voice was special. But what did that mean outside Australia? How good was she?

'I had never heard a great singer in my life, never been to an opera,' she would later write. 'I had no possible means of comparing my own voice with the voices of singers who had already made their reputations. But still, I felt the people of Melbourne could not be after all so very different from the people of Europe, and if I could have this success before them,

24

surely I could at least command a hearing in other places. To go to England was my ruling ambition.'

Despite the bouquets and kind words, the next four months produced few engagements, and in early September she relented to Charlie's continued entreaties and made the long journey back to Mackay, where she found her husband had moved into a hotel.

Nellie decided to make the best of it and offered to organise a charity concert for the district hospital. The gala event was scheduled for 20 October but her hopes of gaining social acceptance in the town were dashed six days beforehand when Charlie's fists got him into trouble yet again.

⚭

Charlie Armstrong delighted in his reputation as a fighter, so much so that he had offered £100 to any man who could best him. The rumour had gone around Mackay like wildfire but no one had taken him up on the offer until a man named Michael Ready was reportedly keen. But the challenge never materialised.

A few weeks later Charlie spied Ready in the billiards room at the back of the Wills Hotel. 'Is it true you want to fight me?' he demanded. 'Come outside and I'll thrash you.'

Ready shaped up, Marquess of Queensbury-style, to his opponent. 'If you want to fight then I'll give you plenty,' he managed, adding, 'but not outside, in here.'

Ready was foolish enough to drop his guard for a moment and Charlie struck him with a punch to the jaw that sent Ready staggering backwards against the billiard table. The older man regained his balance, grabbed a cue and rushed back at Charlie. Charlie easily ducked and caught Ready with another blow, this time to the stomach.

It became obvious that Ready was no match for a trained boxer like Charlie Armstrong. Finally, swollen and bloodied and backed up against a wall, Ready dropped his hands in submission. 'You wouldn't hit a man with his hands down, would you?'

'No, I wouldn't,' Charlie replied.

But Ready had been humiliated and wanted revenge. 'You bastard. I'll kill you, and if I can't then I'll get a man who can.'

Charlie ignored the threat and went to a nearby hotel where he continued drinking. Around eight o'clock that night he was finally on his way home, when he heard a shout. 'There he is. There's Armstrong.'

Charlie looked up to see Michael Ready and five or six men. Outnumbered, Charlie and his pal were chased up the street to the Wills Hotel where they sheltered until the local constabulary was called and calmed tempers.

It might have been the end of the matter but Charlie demanded a court order to ensure that Michael Ready kept the peace. The Mackay courthouse was packed on 17 October to hear the case. A dozen witnesses gave evidence of the one-sided contest. The magistrate ruled that Charlie had started the fight and couldn't expect the court to protect him from the man he beat up. Besides, he was more than capable of taking care of himself. The case was dismissed.

Three days later, Nellie was the star at her own concert before a full house at the arts theatre, singing half-a-dozen songs to encores and praised for 'devoting herself heart and soul' to organising one of the town's most successful charity events. But she did not stay for the plaudits. A few hours after singing her last song, aptly titled 'Goodbye', she and George once again boarded the steamship bound for Melbourne. This time there would be no going back.

3

# 'YOU WAIT AND SEE'

Her marriage was in tatters but Nellie's dream to sing profession-ally was soon realised, initially with appearances at the Melbourne Liedertafel, a choral club that held regular concerts, and a smat-tering of one-off events including a concert above Allans Music Shop in the city, held to advertise the arrival of a new piano. It was hardly the attention she had imagined but it was a start.

Not that she was under any illusions about the road ahead. Success in the professional world was not about polite applause at afternoon tea parties but discipline, struggles and knock-backs. Success was earned. She was her father's daughter, whether he approved of her choices or not, and her day began at 6 am with scales, and she was unapologetic at waking the rest of the household.

Her breakthrough came in June 1885 when she was offered £20 a week to join a tour of Melbourne and Sydney. She was not the star of the show, rather she was support for a virtuoso violinist named Johann Kruse, a hometown boy who had struck it big in Germany. The month-long tour would not fill her coffers but it would instil her with the confidence that she was on the right path. She followed the experience with several concerts in Ballarat and then a tour of Tasmania, all of which sharpened her desire to go overseas.

'I would give ten years of my life to be able to get to Europe to have a trial,' she told a female friend in a letter. 'I feel certain I would have some success for I am so anxious to get on. I work like a Trojan now, so what would I do if I had a proper trial. I do not want to boast, dear, but since I have been singing with Kruse I have made a great name for myself. All the papers say I am the first concert singer in Australia.'

That was true of the Melbourne newspapers although the Sydney critics had been more reserved: a clear, well-cultivated voice 'worth respectful attention' summarised their response as they questioned the depth of her voice and her acting ability. But by the end of the concerts they had warmed to her potential: 'The lady improves in the impression she has made on the public with every performance,' the *Sydney Morning Herald* concluded.

The tour also highlighted a complexity in Nellie's life—her relationships with men. She was a married woman—billed on concert flyers as Mrs Armstrong—and her father had seen fit to send her sister Annie to Sydney to act as a chaperone. To be seen in the company of men, however innocent it may have been, could be viewed by others in the wrong light, and yet Nellie didn't seem bothered by what others may think.

She met Jack Moore and his friend Arthur Hilliger at a house party in Darling Point the evening before her first performance at the Theatre Royal. Both men were infatuated with the song-stress, Moore so much so that he bought tickets to eleven of the twelve concerts and 'was allowed to escort her back' from the theatre to the hotel each night 'where the supper parties were full of fun and friendliness', as he would recall four decades later.

'As she and I were nearly of an age, and both in our early twenties, it was natural that she should talk freely about her hopes and expectations,' he wrote for the *Sydney Morning Herald* many years later. 'It was to be the prelude to something very much greater, and indeed the future Melba one evening after the concert as we walked together, declared frankly her intention one day to be a real prima donna—with the world at her feet. I laughingly remarked that it was well to aim high, and she retorted: "Well, you wait and see; give me time"—or words to that effect. Her poise and self-confidence were in evidence then; and her determination and initiative were as refreshing as her voice was beautiful.'

Arthur Hilliger also had eyes for Nellie, who enjoyed the attention, as she had the young men of Mackay before being swept off her feet by Charlie Armstrong. David Mitchell would have been outraged had he known that his two daughters, one of them married, had accompanied two young single men on a beach picnic to Narrabeen.

Nellie was keenly aware of the dangers of flirting, even if they were just friendships, as she wrote to Hilliger after returning to Melbourne: 'I have not heard anything of my husband for such a long time. I am rather glad, for when he writes, it is only to insult me . . . I am awfully unhappy. If I could see you I would tell you my troubles but I dare not put it in black and white.'

Her chance to travel to Europe would come unexpectedly in November when her father was appointed one of Victoria's representatives at the 1886 Indian and Colonial Exhibition in London, created to stimulate commerce between England and her colonies. David Mitchell had no intention of taking any of his children, the youngest of whom had just turned ten. Instead, he planned to sell Doonside and move them to a sheep property he had bought at Camperdown, almost 200 kilometres from the city where, overseen by staff, they would be safe from the city's temptations while he was absent.

The other children seemed to accept their fate but Nellie was having none of it. She was twenty-four and not only was her father denying her a chance to get to Europe but he was effectively killing her singing career in Melbourne. She began pestering her 'pig-headed' father who eventually yielded and agreed to take Nellie and George, as well as Nellie's sisters Annie and Belle.

The proviso was that Nellie had to pay her own way and that Charlie would have to go with them. Although he had harboured doubts about the union, David Mitchell wanted them to try to make the marriage work, if only for the sake of his grandson. Charlie, perhaps surprisingly, agreed to go to London; it would be his first trip home in a decade.

For the next three months Nellie took every opportunity to work so she could raise the funds she needed to make the trip to London, appearing several times a week at concerts in Melbourne and travelling across Victoria from Ballarat to Bendigo and Hamilton.

Back in Melbourne she risked her father's wrath by taking a paid position as a soloist at St Francis' Catholic Church in Lonsdale Street. Clearly aggrieved, David Mitchell made a point of driving Nellie in the family carriage on a Sunday to St Francis' where he would set her down in view of the crowd before taking the rest of the family to Sunday service at Scots' Church in nearby Collins Street.

Nellie spent Christmas in Sydney where she sang for the Sydney Liedertafel and performed Handel's *Messiah* with the Philharmonic Society before striking further north in the New Year to sing in Grafton, accompanied by Jack Moore, where poor crowds and torrential rain ruined their takings. To compound matters, the journey back to Sydney was marred when the steamer ran into a sandbank, hurling Nellie against an iron bulwark.

Still nursing bruises from her sea voyage, Nellie travelled across the Blue Mountains with a concert troupe to the town of Bathurst, only to be disappointed again with poor attendance. But one final performance at a benefit concert back in Sydney restored her confidence when she was presented with a gold star in front of a big audience that included Lord Carrington, the Governor of New South Wales. The inscription read: 'Honour to Mrs Armstrong. From friends and admirers'. They believed in her.

By the time she returned to Melbourne there was little time to prepare for the voyage, a few weeks during which she would sing at a handful of benefit concerts, including a rousing fare-well on 6 March which raised £67.

But her success would be tarnished by a last-minute conflict when Pietro Cecchi, her teacher, promoter and confidant, asked to be paid £80 he believed was owed to him for lessons. When Nellie protested that she couldn't afford the fees it led to a confrontation during which she flung the money at his feet. It would leave an unfortunate stain on their relationship and sully memories of his undoubted important role in her development.

There was one last task before she sailed. Nellie couldn't just walk into the homes of famous teachers in London and expect to be received, let alone granted an audition. She needed letters of introduction, and even those would not guarantee her entry. Lady Loch, the wife of the Victorian Governor, was happy to provide her support, as was Alfred Cellier, a London composer who happened to be visiting Melbourne and wrote letters to several colleagues including Wilhelm Ganz, one of London's most influential musicians, and Arthur Sullivan, the composer half of the light opera duo Gilbert and Sullivan.

Nellie had also asked for support from Madame Pinschof, wife of the Austrian consul who had sung opera in Vienna and Zurich and suggested that Nellie go to Paris and seek out her former singing teacher, Mathilde Marchesi.

When the steamer *Bengal* sailed on 11 March 1886 Nellie had no idea that it would be sixteen years before she would return to her hometown.

In late March, a few days out of Colombo, Charlie lost his temper and punched Nellie so hard that she was knocked to the ground and lost hearing in one ear for several weeks. It happened again a week or so later as they approached the bottom of the Suez Canal. This time she fled to a cabin shared by her sisters and refused to talk to Charlie again for the rest of the voyage.

It seems improbable that David Mitchell would not have been aware of the altercations and his daughter's injuries, although Nellie probably hid them from him, as she did with friends back in Melbourne. A letter written home to a supporter would make no mention of marital problems, instead describing a fun-filled journey with half-a-dozen concerts and balls, deck sports and music.

Their domestic problems were brushed aside when the *Bengal* docked in the grey gloom of Tilbury on 1 May. They had plans to travel to meet Charlie's mother, who had been ill, before settling in London so Nellie could begin her hunt for a teacher and mentor.

First though, Nellie attended the opening of the Colonial and Indian Exhibition at the Albert Hall where she heard the French-Canadian soprano Emma Albani sing. It was the first time she understood the quality of singers with whom she would have to compete for roles if she wanted to succeed. Although she found Albani's voice magnificent, her self-confidence was not dinted; it was even buoyed further a few days later when she heard the Swedish star Christina Nilsson and was disappointed. It was only a few weeks later when she heard the Italian diva Adelina Patti, the queen of Covent

Garden opera, that she realised the mountain she had to climb.

Nellie would remember the tulips in Hyde Park—golden, crimson and yellow—as she made her way through central London to appointments she hoped would pave the way to stardom. She was nervous, an unusual feeling for someone instilled with so much hopefulness, but the buzz of the city, with its vast shops and crowded streets, was reassuring. She felt she had made the right decision.

She had an appointment to see Arthur Sullivan, who was enjoying immense success with his latest production, *The Mikado*. He was tinkling at his piano when she was shown into his Westminster apartment, as she would later recall in her memoir. 'What would you like to sing?' he asked, politely enough.

When she asked if there was anything he would like to hear, he simply waved away the question. 'One thing is as good as another,' he replied dismissively. He seemed to merely be going through the motions, doing a favour for a friend rather than having a sincere interest in a new young singer.

His expression had not changed when she finished 'Ah! Fors' e lui' and waited patiently for his judgement. Finally he sighed. 'Yes, Mrs Armstrong. That is all right. If you go on studying for another year there might be some chance that we could give you a small part in *The Mikado*—this sort of thing.'

In one short sentence, Arthur Sullivan had washed away the armour of confidence she had so carefully constructed in her head. *All right?* It was about the most depressing assessment she could imagine.

Over the next few days she suffered similar knockbacks from composer Hubert Parry, teacher Alberto Randegger and piano maker John Brinsmead, all of whom had various excuses for not taking her on.

She had one chance left. Wilhelm Ganz was a German-born violinist who taught at the Guildhall School of Music and was a friend and sometime accompanist for Adelina Patti. He was also a successful composer whose most recent song, 'Sing, Sweet Bird', had been among Nellie's repertoire during her Melbourne and Sydney concerts. Ganz was clearly thrilled with her rendition. 'I am enchanted,' he declared, offering to arrange a concert for her.

Nellie couldn't help writing to Pietro Cecchi to express her excitement, in which she admitted having started writing letters to her old teacher several times but stopping each time because of their disagreement over money. But after the second of the Ganz concerts, she could not hold back any longer.

'You will be pleased to hear that I have already sung twice in London, and had the greatest success, splendid critiques, and everyone predicts a great future for me. Herr Ganz has taken a wonderful fancy to me, and declares my voice is more like Patti's than any voice he has ever heard.'

Nellie Armstrong was a young woman in a hurry. She was given an encore in her first performance at the Prince's Hall in Piccadilly on 1 June and praised by critics for her 'favourable impression', then sang the next night at a theatrical fund dinner where the critic from *Musical World* described her as having a 'high soprano voice of fine quality'.

But it was not enough to be praised for her performance; her biggest delight was the 'fearful rage' backstage of a more seasoned singer named Antoinette Sterling, who was furious that Nellie had stolen her limelight. A competitive streak, born of the instincts learned from her father and the struggle to be recognised in a man's world, would be a hallmark of Nellie's career; one that was seen negatively by some—the behaviour of a diva. By her supporters, however, it was regarded as a necessary element of a performer, to be the best.

A third concert would pass unnoticed but Ganz had grander plans, inviting Carl Rosa, the owner of one of the city's best-known opera companies to meet and audition Nellie. But when she arrived at Ganz's house for the interview, Rosa failed to show up. He had forgotten the appointment, having noted the time in pencil on his shirt cuff and then sent the shirt off to be cleaned.

Nellie, angry and disillusioned, refused to accept Ganz's apologies. She had been treated poorly but had one more option. She had already posted the letter from Madame Pinschof and had received an invitation to be auditioned by Mathilde Marchesi. If London didn't want her then Paris might. It would be the last roll of the dice.

# 4

# THE AUDITION

The resplendent footman at 88 Rue Jouffroy d'Abbans opened the door and looked down at the woman who'd rung the bell. It was not unusual to find young ladies at the door—dozens arrived each week for their singing lessons—but this one was different. She was alone.

The footman looked more closely, slightly suspicious. The lady was well dressed and clear faced, her bold features attractive rather than pretty. She stood tall and there was a sense of purpose in her eyes as she tried to make herself understood in broken French. An Englishwoman, he thought. It was only when she fished a letter from her purse that he understood she had an appointment to see Madame.

Letter in hand, the footman disappeared inside, leaving the would-be visitor waiting in the September sunshine. When he reappeared ten minutes later he had good news, or so he thought;

the letter had the desired effect and Madame had consented to meet the young lady and to hear her sing—but not today. She would have to come back at ten o'clock the next morning.

Much to his surprise, the young woman seemed to greet the news with disappointment. Had she misunderstood? he wondered; after all, not everyone who knocked on the door got to see Madame.

The footman was right; Nellie was trying hard not to cry. The *come back tomorrow* response had been deflating; another rejection, it seemed, and this time without even having sung. She bit her lip as she walked back to the hotel, determined to regather her composure.

Thankfully, morning had traded disappointment and misfortune for anticipation and opportunity. She had never wanted anything more, Nellie told herself as she scurried back to Rue Jouffroy, arriving on the doorstep a full twenty minutes before the scheduled appointment. The same footman led her into a hallway dominated by a gilt mirror hanging above a grand white marble fireplace where she sat, hands on her lap, and waited, listening to the sound of voices coming from a room behind two grandly panelled doors.

When they finally opened, a prim, grey-haired woman walked in and stood expectantly in the middle of the room. It wasn't Madame's physical stature that alarmed Nellie but the fact that this woman in black represented her last hope of a singing career. Her father had made that plain the week before when she had pleaded for money to travel to Paris and meet the great teacher. 'Very well, but this must be the last time,' he had said with a condescending pat on the head, insisting it would be his last, indulgent contribution.

The realisation that her dream could die at this moment gripped Nellie's heart. This was it. Mathilde Marchesi seemed to grasp the situation; she smiled and the ice was broken. But her fleeting smile disappeared as she sat beside Nellie and asked about her background, her family and her singing experience. After all, she had a business to run and she needed to know if this girl's family could afford her fees.

Satisfied, Marchesi led Nellie into the larger room where three other women sat together on a sofa against a wall; the disembodied voices she'd heard. Nellie was not the only aspiring singer seeking the famous teacher's attention.

Nellie tapped her foot nervously on the lacquered parquet floor. It made a dull noise as if absorbing the sound. She scanned the room, which was heavily draped so not a hint of sunlight or outside noise could penetrate. A glittering chandelier was suspended from the ceiling to counter the darkness, casting flickering shadows across photographs and portraits of men and women she assumed to be Madame's famous pupils. Potted ferns placed on tabletops tried in vain to soften the sombre tone. A collection of mahogany stools and chairs were scattered as if an imaginary audience was seated to listen in while framed former pupils watched from above. This was where she taught. This room was the heart of the *Ecole Marchesi*.

Madame sat at a piano in the centre of the room, a square wooden platform to her left where students were positioned, facing the empty chairs. One by one, the other hopefuls stood and sang for their lives. Nellie listened intently. She couldn't hear anything that caused her concern. If these women were good enough to audition then so was she. Her heart beat with excitement; there was nothing to be afraid of here.

At last it was her turn. She stepped onto the platform and turned to face Madame, who appeared uninspired by what she had heard from the other three women and unconvinced that Nellie could do any better.

'What would you like to sing?' The request was sharp, her earlier soft, welcoming smile now a mask of seriousness. Impress me, it said.

Nellie, who would recount the scene in her memoirs, tried to sound confident. 'I shall sing the aria from *La Traviata*.'

Marchesi said nothing, turned back to the keyboard and began to play the accompaniment to 'Ah! Fors' e lui' in which the opera's heroine, Violetta, laments about the love of an admirer that threatens her place in society.

As she sang, Nellie could not help but glance across to see if there was a response from Madame. There was none, the *professeure* was expressionless but clearly listening. Then she stopped suddenly and spun around. 'Why do you screech your top notes. Can't you sing *pianissimo*?'

Nellie froze, terrified by the brutal response and unable to respond. 'Sing,' Madame commanded as she turned back to the piano and struck a top B—the note on the keyboard at the higher end of the vocal range for a soprano.

Nellie took a deep breath. This was her last chance; if Mathilde Marchesi refused to take her on as a pupil then the dream was over and she would have to return to Australia and the life of a housewife in nothern Queensland.

She sang, this time as softly as she could.

'Higher,' insisted Marchesi pressing the high C key. Did this young woman have the vocal range to be successful? Did she have the purity of sound to be worthy of attention?

Nellie gently coaxed the note from her throat. 'Higher,' Marchesi repeated and played high D. Nellie's confidence had grown and she dared another glance as she reached quietly for the next note. This time she detected a sparkle of anticipation in Mathilde Marchesi's eye as she pressed the key for high E and finally high F. Nellie's pitch in response to the challenge was perfect.

Madame stopped playing again and left the room, leaving Nellie standing on the platform, unsure what had happened. Was she being rejected? The other three singers who had sat and listened to her performance tittered among themselves, which suggested that she had failed.

Madame was gone several minutes and gave no explanation when she returned, accompanied by an older, white-haired man who settled on one of the empty chairs while the teacher sat back at the piano and insisted that Nellie sing again, as if to confirm that what she'd heard was true. The mood in the room had now completely changed, the sniggering trio were silent as Nellie repeated the notes perfectly. Nellie felt it too; never had a scale been sung with such joy.

Marchesi took Nellie by the arm and led her back to the hallway where she had waited with trepidation for the audition less than an hour before. Now it was the teacher's turn to be apprehensive. She motioned for Nellie to sit beside her on a sofa, clasped her hands and looked her would-be protégé in the eye.

'Mrs Armstrong. Are you serious about this?' she asked quietly.

'Yes,' Nellie replied, almost whispering in her earnestness.

Marchesi sighed. '*Alors*, then you can study with me for one year. If you are serious then I can make something extra-ordinary of you.'

The way she stretched the word *extra-ordinary* seemed to emphasise that Madame truly believed Nellie had the raw, innate talent to succeed. It was the first time she had heard anyone confirm what she held in her own heart: 'I realised that she meant what she said, and I felt at last I had begun,' she would recall.

It was months later that Madame told Nellie what had happened when she had dashed out of the room during the audition. In her excitement at hearing Nellie perfectly pitch a high F she had rushed upstairs to find her husband, Salvatore, who was in his room reading a newspaper. She burst into the room and snatched the newspaper from his hand.

'Salvatore, *j'ai enfin une etoile*,' she cried into his ear.

'Salvatore, *I finally have a star*.'

⑅

Singing came naturally to Mathilde, the youngest of three daughters of wealthy Frankfurt merchant Johann Graumann and his wife, Catherine. She lapped up the encouragement from those around her, sang her heart out in church and relished being entrusted with the lead role in school concerts. Soon she was being paraded in front of house guests, her parents' pride in her talent tested on occasions when she refused to sing because she did not like the guest. Like Nellie, Fraulein Mathilde Graumann had a mind of her own, and was only willing to sing for people she believed would appreciate her performance.

By her early teens she had decided to pursue a life in music but in 1838, when she was seventeen, her father lost his fortune in a calamitous business deal and the once powerful family was now destitute. Her life of privilege had ended in a moment, and with it her prospects of marriage.

While the family mourned its loss of position and wealth, Mathilde spied an opportunity. Rather than being expected to marry and have children, this was her chance to pursue her dream of a professional life in music, or so she thought. Her father disagreed, believing that a professional career would not bring credit to the family. Instead, he organised a governess position for her in Vienna. Luckily, Mathilde's sister Charlotte stepped in and offered to give her sister her own savings so Mathilde could take singing lessons from the best teachers in Vienna, befriending composers like Felix Mendelssohn, Franz Liszt and Gioachino Rossini.

But Mathilde was dissatisfied with the instructors in Vienna, and struggling to make an impact on the professional stage. She was advised to seek the help of renowned Spanish vocal teacher Manuel Garcia who was based in Paris and who, in his desire to understand the vocal cords, had invented the laryngoscope.

There was a striking similarity between Mathilde's first meeting with Garcia and Nellie's audition for Mathilde four decades later. Without the great man's approval, her dream was over. He made her sing scales several times, just as she would with Nellie, but his acclaim of her voice afterwards would be far more mooted; Mathilde's voice was 'of good compass' but it would take several years to bear fruit.

She was devastated. Her savings were gone and relatives back in Frankfurt had showed no interest in helping provide financial support. Her father, who had recovered financially, went even further and demanded a written confirmation from Mathilde that she would abandon any plans for a theatrical career. The most he would tolerate was his daughter singing in concert rooms.

'I felt I possessed all the necessary qualities of a good dramatic artiste, and now I had to relinquish my cherished dream,' Mathilde would write in her autobiography. 'It was a dreadful disappointment but I did not lose heart.'

In 1851 she met Salvatore Marchesi, a scion of Sicilian aristocracy who had abandoned his heritage and embarked on a career as a baritone. They fell in love, married and began travelling, mostly following Salvatore's contracts with theatres, concert halls and opera companies.

Mathilde took private commissions, still hoping for a breakthrough, which finally came in 1853 when she was offered the chance to fill in for the prima donna of an Italian opera company performing in the German city of Bremen, playing Rosina, the female lead in Rossini's opera *The Barber of Seville*.

It was a moment of triumph she would always remember, the audience that night rapt in her performance as she would later recall: 'I was received with such enthusiasm that I had already pictured myself a star of the first magnitude in the theatrical world; but the determined veto of my husband kept me from the stage then and for all time. The fates were certainly not propitious to a theatrical career.'

And that was that. The desire and promise of a lifetime had been reduced to a single night and the recollection of her greatest performance to a single paragraph. After struggling for so many years, it was not her voice that betrayed her but a father and a husband who believed that a woman's place was not onstage. Her hopes had finally been crushed.

Mathilde had accepted the inevitable; that her career as a performer was over. Instead, she would embrace being a wife and mother and revel in the appreciation of satisfied pupils and their parents as a quiet, satisfying alternative to the loud applause of an adoring audience.

Ecole Marchesi was born, and now she had found not only a unique voice but a young woman whose life story and struggles echoed her own. She was determined that Nellie Armstrong would succeed where she hadn't.

# 5

# THE HOUSE OF WOMEN

Nellie had rushed back to London in excitement after being accepted by Mathilde Marchesi, her dream alive, at least for the time being. When she arrived at the house near Hyde Park where her family had been staying, she found her father preparing to return to Australia. David Mitchell's company workshop in Melbourne had burned down and he had to get home to take back control of the faltering business.

Annie and Belle would go with him but Charlie Armstrong would remain in England, at least for the time being, as he had just taken a commission as a lieutenant in the Prince of Wales' Leinster Regiment.

Mitchell's response to Nellie's breakthrough was less than enthusiastic, his mind distracted perhaps by news of the fire but also his obvious disappointment that she had succeeded where he had presumed she would fail. He was trapped;

47

having sponsored Nellie's trip to Paris he could not now withdraw his support for her lessons. Instead, he agreed to provide a modest stipend after which she would have to fend for herself.

Her husband's reaction was far more shocking. A month earlier, when Nellie had announced her plans to go to Paris and seek an audience with Mathilde Marchesi, Charlie had made his displeasure known by lashing out and kicking her under the table during dinner, causing her to limp.

This time he couldn't disguise his rage, drawing his sword from its scabbard and waving it in front of her face, pondering aloud if he should just kill her. Nellie ran screaming from the room, hysterical, but would later dampen the incident by passing it off as 'a jest'. In reality, she feared her husband and his increasing potential for violence.

Back in Paris, Ecole Marchesi would become a sanctuary of sorts, a place where she was embraced and where the doubts disappeared. It was a house of women, the few men who sought lessons shuffled off upstairs to be taught by Salvatore while his wife wrapped the rest of the house in her steely resolve.

The basis of Marchesi's teaching was an Italian opera vocal technique known as *bel canto*—translated simply as beautiful singing—which emphasised sound and technique over expression and performance. Its best exponents were able to shift their voices almost seamlessly from low through middle to high registers and sing rapid-fire runs and trills to decorate vocal lines. It was a favourite in the eighteenth and early nineteenth centuries but had long waned in popularity by the time the Marchesi school opened in 1861. It had been replaced by weightier, more intense and powerful sounds.

But Madame railed against what she called 'the modern system of shrieking', annoyed by the 'feverish impatience' for results. Singing was an art that would suffer if traded for quick business returns, she would argue. Give it time to mature, like a good wine, and savour the product.

At her school, beginners were only allowed to sing melodies for five minutes at a time and for a maximum of fifteen minutes a day. In her experience, too many singers burned out early because their vocal cords were strained by excessive use.

Singing time was gradually lengthened as each student's voice grew stronger. In between, their training was mainly a series of exercises, including scales, which aided their development of vocal range. When they weren't singing the students were attending lessons in languages, deportment, musical theatre, acting and even mime.

Madame prided herself on being able to speak a dozen languages and insisted that to sing properly, a vocalist needed to be able to enunciate each language perfectly, hence the need for classes in French, German, Italian and even Russian.

But Nellie Armstrong was unique. Marchesi would say later that she had been charmed by the pure tones of Nellie's voice when she auditioned, but it was clearly an understatement because, almost from the moment she arrived at the school, Nellie was treated differently from the other students.

Madame fussed over her new pupil, worried when she arrived one morning, sneezing and wet after walking through the rain. 'Have you washed your hair?' Nellie would recall her asking after she had dried off and presented herself in the teaching room.

'Yes, I washed it two days ago,' she answered, puzzled by the question.

The older woman wagged her finger at her protégé. 'Well, you shouldn't. A singer never washes her head. She cleans it with tonic and a fine tooth comb.'

Nellie laughed off the suggestion but took Madame's concerns to heart soon afterwards when her teacher implored her to give up her one luxury, riding horses through city parks, because the jolting was bad for her vocal cords.

Nellie came to regard her teacher as her protector. 'Not only was she my artistic mother, she was my guide and sponsor in other things as well.'

But there was a deeper connection, even if neither of them were conscious of the link; a disturbing similarity between Madame's story of battling society's expectations and male dominance to chase a dream and Nellie's experience in chasing the same elusive desire to sing onstage.

Marchesi saw herself as a mother figure to a young woman who had lost her own maternal guardian. She even signed one of her letters to Nellie as 'your very loving old mother' to which Nellie replied as 'your loving daughter'. They had also both lost children to disease. Three of Mathilde's children had perished young and Nellie had watched her sister Vere, for whom she held responsibility, die at four years old.

But it was Nellie's voice, even with its nasal twang and distorted vowels that required rounding, which inspired Marchesi to pay her special attention. The famous teacher realised that Nellie could be her crowning glory because she possessed a voice that, in her own words, 'resembles a bird more than a human creature'. Nellie wasn't just a star to be discovered, but potentially her greatest star.

Just a month after Nellie began lessons, Madame took her aside, sat her down and opened the class register she kept on her desk. Scanning the list, she announced, 'Mrs Armstrong, I find that I have no room for you in either my first class or my second.'

Nellie was shattered. What did she mean there was no room for her? How could she have lost her place at the school so soon after being accepted? She leaned forward and grasped her teacher by the hand. 'Please, please do not send me away,' she pleaded.

Madame smiled at the misunderstanding. 'I am not going to send you away. You are going into the opera class.'

There was one complication though. Mathilde's daughter Blanche was two years younger than Nellie and, although she had initially played the violin, it was perhaps inevitable that she would choose to sing and strive to build a stage career as a mezzo-soprano—a dream that had eluded her mother for so long.

Initially, Blanche had no shortage of encouragement or parental approval; quite the opposite in fact, as she would recall with embarrassment how her mother, joyful tears running down her face, extolled her singing in front of classmates, on one occasion even halting a student halfway through a song: 'Stop. Stop. Do not sing that song,' she cried. 'Take it away. My daughter sings it, and you will never be able to sing it like her.'

But all that changed the day Nellie Armstrong arrived and asked for an audition. There had been many students over the years who had needed Blanche's mother's attention, some of whom would become opera stars of varying brightness, but this woman from the other side of the world was different—she was a rival, in age and ambition.

Blanche had been at the centre of the operatic world all her life, surrounded by famous singers and composers and blessed with a strong and well-trained voice but she knew immediately that she couldn't compete with the newcomer whose voice she would describe as a diamond set in brass.

At first the pair were friends, Nellie even confiding in Blanche about her private fears over Charles Armstrong and his mad fits, but as the months went by and Nellie's true potential became obvious, the pair moved further and further apart.

Blanche's resentment festered when Mathilde Marchesi no longer cried in joy when her daughter sang. Instead, she was consumed by her new star, Nellie.

# 6

# THE DRESS

'Mrs Armstrong.'

The sharp voice made Nellie stop at the top of the steps. She turned slowly to face Madame Mathilde Marchesi. Her teacher, severe in her usual black, stood in the doorway, arms folded across her chest, hugging a grievance as if she were shivering against the cold. Her pale, pinched face matched her mood.

Nellie was perplexed. She had been attending Madame's classes for a while now and had been making good progress. And yet today it was clear that her teacher was upset, but why? The lesson had gone well, she'd even earned praise, which was not easily forthcoming from a teacher who staked her reputation on being demanding. What had she done wrong?

Madame slowly unfolded her arms and pointed an accusatory finger at Nellie's body. 'You will *never* wear that dress again.'

Nellie followed the line of the finger to the bodice of her dress; thick woven serge in blue and white stripes. The outfit had seemed so smart when she bought it the previous year in a city on the other side of the world, but under the older woman's withering stare it felt heavy, ugly and tattered.

Nellie blushed, embarrassed not by the dress so much as the admission she was about to make. 'I am sorry, Madame, but it is my only winter dress, and all I have to wear when it is cold.'

Madame, her arms folded once more, remained unmoved by the explanation, disbelief etched on her face. 'Why do you only have one dress?'

Nellie's voice dropped to a whisper. 'Because I have no money to buy another.'

The teacher made a clicking noise with her tongue, as if considering this revelation and whether it changed anything. It did not, she decided finally. 'Nonsense. You have a rich father. Go and order another dress and put it down to him.'

With that Madame turned away and closed the door. Nellie Armstrong was dismissed, her shame complete. She paused a moment, wondering whether to go back inside but thought better of it, and walked out into the cold night air of Paris. She had to get home where her young son was waiting.

The street was noisy with the uneven rumble of iron-rimmed carriage wheels on cobblestones mixed with shouts from passers-by, on their way to one of the many theatres or to meet friends. Despite the cold, the cafes and restaurants in the fashionable 17th arrondissement were doing a brisk trade in the early evening.

It was a forty-minute walk from Madame's splendid apartment to her own, a tiny nook in a street behind the Arc de Triomphe. At this time of the year, it was already dark by four o'clock in the afternoon, the gas lamps illuminating the icy slush that had been piled like a garrison of snowmen by street sweepers.

December had been particularly cold, blue skies and frequent snowfalls keeping temperatures below freezing, something to which, as an Australian, she was unaccustomed. Nellie walked quickly to keep warm, the ugly dress now a comfort as she dodged past strolling couples.

Paris was where she wanted to be, not for its cafes and wide boulevards and rooftops that were already inspiring artists like Vincent van Gogh, who would begin experimenting with impressionism by painting Paris street scenes that same year; nor for the wonder of the Eiffel Tower, whose giant iron foundations were about to be laid in the frosty ground of Champ de Mars. As she would reminisce years later:

I suppose that most girls who arrived in Paris for the first time, especially if their vision had been practically bound by the Australian bush, would have been delighted by the magic of the city in which they found themselves. But when I arrived in Paris, I saw nothing of the boulevards, the gay laughing crowds, the glittering shops—my mind was bent on one thing, and one thing only—singing to Madame Marchesi.

She pondered her predicament as she walked along Avenue de Wagram towards the River Seine. There was no sense writing to her father; David Mitchell would not entertain sending money for a new dress, not unless she agreed to return to Australia, which she would not do.

He had already made it clear that he believed her dream to become a professional singer was a folly that would wither and die as the winter cold set in and she ran out of money. That conversation was three months ago and her nest egg was almost spent, but her desire to sing was stronger than ever. Most of the money had gone on rent as well as a nursemaid, clothing and food for George who had turned three years old not long after their arrival in Paris. Her own needs came last, hence the single winter dress. At times she even went without meals in an effort to ensure that she had enough money to meet Madame's teaching fees.

On reflection, it had been obvious for several weeks that her teacher was unhappy that she had worn the same dress day after day. Nellie had sensed the disapproving stares but, because nothing was said, presumed that Madame had accepted the situation.

Tonight's clash had taken her by surprise because it served to highlight her impoverished situation and the sense that her father may have been right. Nellie was, for all intents and purposes, alone in the world. At least, that's how it felt.

Despite being estranged, not only from her husband but also her immediate family—at least in the sense that there was to be no more financial or moral support—Nellie was determined to succeed. Privation only fed her desire.

She was still pondering her situation when she reached her lodgings at 12 Avenue Carnot. The place had been recommended to her by Madame although Nellie doubted that her teacher had ever been to the property, let alone inside. From the exterior it looked like most central Parisian homes: a tall, elegant, pale stone structure that looked identical to the neighbours on either side of the road.

But the interior layouts of each building differed greatly and in this part of the city, considered an 'unfashionable quarter' despite being just a few steps from the Champs-Élysées, families were crammed into tiny spaces. Nellie stopped short of calling it a garret but the accommodation was basic, and a far cry from the luxuries of her large house in the inner suburbs of Melbourne.

Nellie hitched the worn hem of her dress and climbed the five flights of stairs to the top of the building. Inside the modestly furnished room George was being cared for by two elderly women, the Hyland sisters, who lived in one of the other flats and who had taken it upon themselves to watch over and tend to the young mother and her child.

It seemed odd that two 'dear old Irish ladies', as Nellie called them, would be spending their final days in Paris but they had proved a Godsend, as she would recount in her autobiography many years later.

'I do not know how I should have pulled through. Their kindness was inexhaustible. I remember that once when I had no money with which to pay my rent, the elder Miss Hyland came up to me and said: "Do let me lend you five pounds. I know that one day you are going to be famous, and then you will repay me. Till then it does not matter."'

George was an anxious child, unsurprising given the numerous changes in his short life. Each night, Nellie hugged him tight and told him stories of her own childhood to calm him and ease her own misgivings. Despite her determination to stay and succeed she wondered if she had done the right thing for the boy. Maybe she should have been the dutiful daughter and gone home with her father and sisters—and Charlie.

The next morning, Nellie put on the same dress before she returned to her teacher's house. A sleepless night of worry had only confirmed in her mind that Madame's demand was unreasonable, and one to which she would not bow.

Nellie ignored the horse-drawn omnibus that could have eased the journey, just to save money. The walk was even less joyful in the daylight, the street now filled with workers scurrying as best they could through a fresh covering of snow. Her square-heeled laced boots were slippery on the icy surface and the brass bell on Madame's door was cold through her gloves.

Nellie had been hoping her teacher might also have realised how harsh her demand was and quietly accepted the situation. Surely she could not expect Nellie to have been able to buy a new dress overnight.

But she was mistaken. Mathilde Marchesi, her face like thunder, was not used to being disobeyed. 'I told you not to wear that dress anymore,' she barked as Nellie walked into the parlour.

Rather than being cowed, Nellie held her ground. 'I told you, I can't afford one, and it is very cruel of you to talk about it at all.'

Madame seemed flustered at Nellie's resoluteness and started waving her hands furiously. 'I cannot possibly continue teaching you while you are wearing that ridiculous dress. It is an eyesore. You must get a new one.'

Nellie had not considered the possibility that she might be dismissed. The threat of losing her position changed everything. Bursting into tears, she fled from the room but, as she reached the front door, Madame once again called out for Nellie to stop. This time, though, her voice was pleading. 'Nellie, Nellie. I am so sorry. You must not go. Run to Worth's now and buy yourself the most beautiful dress you can find. I will pay. I will pay.'

Now it was Mathilde Marchesi who was afraid of the consequences of her actions. Nellie sensed the older woman's fear and composed herself. She had come too far to start backing down: 'No, dear Madame. Either you must put up with me in this dress or I cannot come anymore.'

Madame Marchesi shrugged and kissed her prized student. It was a price worth paying.

# 7

# BECOMING MELBA

Life was changing quickly. Barely three years ago Nellie was watching the monsoonal rain wash down the sides of a tin-roof house in northern Queensland, a newborn baby at her breast and wishing she could get back to civilised Melbourne, and now she was being touted as a future star of the Paris Opera.

But who was she or, rather, who had she become?

She was no longer Helen Porter Mitchell, the dutiful eldest daughter of a wealthy Melbourne businessman, nor Mrs Helen Armstrong, wife of a handsome, charismatic but domineering man. When she arrived in Paris she had adopted the mantle of Nellie Armstrong, single mother and struggling would-be singer, but Ecole Marchesi had transformed her into someone new; someone independent and powerful. Someone who didn't have to depend on others and was able to strive to be the best she could in a society that frowned on such female freedom.

60

She had always been single-minded, rebellious in a way, such as her insistence on marrying Charlie when her family had doubts. The marriage was a mistake, she knew in hindsight, but lust was blind to flaws and she loved their son. But for every misstep there had been a bold leap of faith in her own ability. She wouldn't be here, in Paris, if she had bowed to professional rejection or to family displeasure. And so she would continue to follow her own instincts, wherever they might lead.

Mathilde Marchesi sensed the change in her protégé. Nellie had a strong will, like her own, but Mathilde had made compromises and suffered because of it. If Nellie was to succeed where her mentor had failed then she needed a unique identity that embraced her new home in Europe, where most English names, like Armstrong, were considered as dull as the London weather.

It was not the first time Madame had suggested a stage name for a student. American Emma Wixom had arrived on her doorstep a decade before, talented and determined like Nellie. 'I am an orphan. Will you be my second mother?' she'd cried. Marchesi took her in and, after three years of lessons, Emma had made her debut at Her Majesty's Theatre in London under the name Emma Nevada, a nod to her home state and a name that neatly straddled the old world of Europe and the new world of America. She was now a star of the Milan and Paris operas.

One evening Madame and Nellie sat down to consider her options. Nellie resisted at first, perplexed by the idea that her name could be a handicap. When she finally relented, Nellie was insistent that she wanted to retain a sense of her Australian heritage so they needed to find a name from places important to her childhood. Two of the obvious choices were Richmond and Victoria—the suburb and state where she was raised—but none provided the pizzazz for which Madame was searching.

A third alternative, the city of Melbourne, was too long and conveyed nothing of France or Italy, which Madame preferred. But what if they took the first half of the word and added an 'a'—the feminine ending to an Italian noun—to create the surname Melba.

Helen Mitchell became Nellie Melba, and the first opportunity to use her stage name soon arose at one of Madame's musicales to be held at the Marchesi house. Nellie had attended a soiree the month before as an audience member and was eager to participate, particularly as the guest of honour this time was Ambroise Thomas, director of the Paris Conservatoire who wielded enormous influence in the city and beyond. Thomas was also a composer who had written the opera *Hamlet*, based on the adaptation of the Shakespeare play by French writer Alexandre Dumas.

Nellie implored Madame to allow her to sing at the upcoming soiree. Even though she had only recently entered the opera class, this was the opportunity to voice her arrival, she argued. Marchesi agreed and Nellie began learning the aria 'Pale et Blonde' from the scene in which Ophelia kills herself in grief over the death of her father at the hands of Hamlet. The song is interpreted as being about Ophelia's despair about her lack of identity and helplessness in a life dominated by men—an issue faced by Nellie herself.

There was little time to prepare and rehearsals were not without their problems as Madame drove Nellie, who was now spending eight hours a day at Rue Jouffroy, to learn the intricate trills that were a feature of a 'mad scene' aria, a dramatic feature in operas of the *bel canto* era.

One day Nellie fled the classroom in tears. Madame followed, aware that she had pushed too hard. 'Come back, come back; you know that I love you,' she cried. 'If I bother you it is because I know you will be great. Come back and sing as I wish.' Nellie dried her tears and returned to the classroom.

The day of the concert arrived and Nellie mounted the tiny stage in the classroom where she had stood only months before to audition for Madame. This time the chairs in the room were all taken, the room full of men who held her future in their hands. She almost lost her nerve when she noticed the white hair of Ambroise among the audience. This was yet another moment in a seemingly endless series of moments in which she could fly or just as easily fall. She chose the former, lifted her eyes to the ceiling and filled the room with a voice that none of the men present could rightly ignore.

Madame was also in the habit of inviting media to her concerts. Newspapers such as *Le Figaro*, *Liberté* and *Le Gaulois* often sent critics to review the performances. Several reporters were present this day and recorded the enthusiastic response after Nellie's performance, including the writer from *Liberté* who noted: 'Among those who received the greatest applause from Madame Marchesi's numerous and distinguished guests, we must mention Mlle Nellie Melba, an Australian, possessing a full, expressive voice, who sang the mad scene from "Hamlet" in such a way as to win the most flattering praise from Ambroise Thomas, who was present.'

Nellie Melba was on her way to stardom.

§⏛§

It seems remarkable that, until this point in her life, Nellie had never been to a performance in an opera house. That changed one night in late 1886 when Madame arranged for her to attend a first night performance of the new opera *Patrie!* at the Palais Garnier, the opera house commissioned by Napoleon III. The performers included soprano Gabrielle Krauss, another of Madame's former pupils, who was heading towards the end of a glorious career at the Paris Opera.

In the entrance of the gilded foyer, Nellie gazed in awe at the 18-metre-high ceilings, which were decorated with painted scenes from moments in music history. Beneath them hung a trail of chandeliers that flashed and dazzled along the length of a room designed to be the society drawing room of Paris.

This splendored mesh of Baroque, Palladio and Renaissance architecture was beyond anything she could have imagined as she took her place in her stall alongside a society friend, Mademoiselle Mimaut, in an auditorium that held two thousand people. The hubbub fell away as the great curtain was raised and the orchestra began to play. Nellie leaned back in her seat, eyes closed and engrossed in the first notes of the chorus, trying to imagine what it would feel like to be on the stage. This was the world that she wanted, to sing in front of thousands of people with all the glamour and adulation it entailed. She could die happy if it came to pass.

Nellie wasn't the only one with the same thought. At the end of the first act, Mademoiselle Mimaut turned to her and smiled. 'It won't be too long before you are singing here too.'

Nellie laughed out aloud at the prospect. 'What an extraordinary thing to say,' she answered, unwilling to admit to her earlier contemplation.

It seemed that fortune was on her side because, a few weeks after her trip to the opera, an opportunity presented itself when a man named Maurice Strakosch, called into 88 Rue Jouffroy to see Salvatore.

At first glance Strakosch appeared an unassuming man; small and balding with a receding chin and a habit of peering with a squint. But Strakosch was one of Europe's most successful musical entrepreneurs. He and Salvatore were good friends and the pair sat upstairs, chatting and drinking coffee and smoking cigars while Nellie began a lesson downstairs.

As he was leaving, Strakosch paused on the staircase to listen. The door into Madame's classroom was ajar and he could hear Nellie singing the aria 'Caro nome' from Verdi's opera *Rigoletto*.

Fearing that Strakosch had been offended by Nellie's relatively untrained voice, Salvatore offered to shut the open door but Strakosch stopped him. 'But no. I must have that voice. Tell me who it is.'

Salvatore shrugged. Although his wife was excited at Nellie's prospects, he was less impressed. 'It is only a young Australian whom my wife thinks may have a career,' he offered dismissively.

Strakosch thought otherwise. 'She may be young or old, beautiful or hideous but I must meet her.'

With that he pushed open the doors and introduced himself to a startled Nellie who, at Madame's nod of approval, agreed to sing several more songs. Strakosch needed no more encouragement; he took her aside and penned a management contract.

It was a cunning play by the Czech-born impresario who had begun his career as a pianist, a child prodigy whose playing career never achieved any great heights. At the age of eighteen he had met an Italian tenor named Salvatore Patti at a music festival in Vienna and found a new calling as a manager, successfully piloting Patti's career and that of his superstar daughter Adelina, considered one of the greatest sopranos.

Maurice and his brother Max now managed a stable of other singers and were opening up new markets, particularly in America, that generated huge profits, and big money for their superstars.

He could see instantly that Nellie Melba, young and raw, was an opportunity to be snapped up, and immediately offered her 1000 francs per month—roughly £40—for the first year which would double in the second year. By the third year she would get 4000 francs a month and so on.

Nellie was agog. The money sounded like a fortune, especially for someone who was struggling to pay the rent each month. 'I felt made for life,' she would recount many years later.

But she was selling herself short. Strakosch knew that if Nellie was half as good as he thought—and he was an expert judge of talent—then she was worth much more than he was offering. Adelina Patti, whom Nellie idolised, could command up to 25,000 francs every night she walked onstage. As the pair chatted he sugared the deal with charm, peppering her with praise and insisting that he could make her as great, or greater even, than Patti.

'In fact, he said I will take her place,' Nellie wrote excitedly to Arthur Hilliger in Sydney.

There was another, even more important, catch. Under the terms of the contract, Maurice Strakosch would effectively own Nellie in a professional sense because he would decide where, when and what she sang. And his decisions would be based purely on his own financial reward.

After fighting so hard to establish her independence and be free of men who directed her life, Nellie was about to agree to a contract that could effectively keep her captive for the next decade.

Mathilde Marchesi, perhaps ignorant of the implication or swayed by the excitement of such an early offer, stood by and watched her sign the document. They would both soon regret it.

The contract prompted media attention back in Australia, with *Truth* newspaper reporting that 'Mrs Armstrong, nee Mitchell, has been engaged by Maurice Strakosch, the celebrated impresario, for a term of five years.' The article also announced that she had changed her name. Nellie Melba had been introduced to the Australian public.

Nellie's excitement was punctured in the last days of the Paris winter with the sudden arrival at 12 Avenue Carnot of Charlie Armstrong. Her spectacular progress and the potential for paid work was not the news that Charlie wanted to hear and, once again, he resorted to violence to display his displeasure, seemingly unafraid of being discovered beating his wife. In his mind the aggression was justified, he was punishing her as he might punish a disobedient cattle dog. Nellie's continued defiance enraged him, and there was no room for George to hide in the small flat as he listened to his mother's cries. If the Hyland sisters heard they were not in a position to come to her aid.

Nellie was dressing one night to attend a dinner party hosted by an important social figure when Charlie vented his anger, kicking her legs and punching her arms as she held them up defensively in front of her face, until they were bruised. As he delivered the punches, he told her how he intended to maim her so she couldn't dance or go on the stage.

Nellie was relieved when he left a few days later to return to England but knew it would not be the last time she would face his jealous wrath.

Despite her fears, she told no one of his violence towards her. To admit as much would be embarrassing socially and achieve nothing. Prosecutions were virtually unheard of and it might even have harmed her chances of being hired. It was best to remain silent and cover any sign of the beating.

Even Madame, in whom she confided about her home life and concerns about George, could not have known about the violence, otherwise she would not have made such tender references to Charlie in later letters. 'Tell Charlie that he is my son-in-law because you are my daughter and that I kiss him as such'.

Instead, Nellie set her mind to learning as many opera roles as possible while her new manager searched for a suitable place and production in which she could make her debut.

Nellie realised the importance of not only her singing lessons but also language classes. After all, if she wanted to perform at the Palais Garnier one day then she would have to sing in French and, although her French had improved since her arrival, she still spoke and sang with the inflections of a foreigner.

Madame was eager to push Nellie's credentials and included her in the program for several more of her in-house concerts, as well as arranging an invitation for Nellie to sing at the Salle Érard, a music venue in the 2nd arrondissement at which her old friend Franz Liszt had announced his genius as a pianist.

It was here in March 1887 that Nellie experienced for the first time the rapturous applause of a Paris audience, the men calling '*Brava*' while the women clapped with gloved hands and waved lace handkerchiefs. The crowd recalled her four times and those still mingling outside an hour later cheered as she got into a car that took her home.

So excited was she that a neighbour at Avenue Carnot was awakened in the middle of the night by a light tapping on her door. She opened it to find Nellie standing in a white frock with tears running down her cheeks. 'I had to tell someone,' she said, apologising for the intrusion before telling the story of the performance and how she was mobbed by admirers, including an ageing French general who kissed and embraced her while insisting she was already 'one of the great ones'.

When the famous opera comique theatre Salle Favart was burned down in May 1887 killing eighty-four audience members, Ecole Marchesi was chosen to provide singers for a matinee charity concert and Nellie sang an aria from the Italian opera *Lucia di Lammermoor*. Taking a risk, Madame sat down to add a cadenza to the end of the piece, a flourishing trill to show off her student's birdlike voice and flexibility.

The risk paid off, Nellie's performance was acclaimed by the correspondent for the art and literary magazine *Gil Blas* with the caveat that she still needed to work on her pronunciation. A critic from *Le Journal Des Arts* was particularly effusive, describing her as 'a delicate Australian beauty with a vibrant, natural voice and extraordinary flexibility'.

There was another surprise. A few weeks after the matinee concert two men turned up at Ecole Marchesi. Alexandre Lapissida and Joseph Dupont were musicians turned theatre managers who jointly operated Theatre de la Monnaie in Brussels. They were keen to audition Madame's best students in the hope of recruiting singers to join the Belgian Opera company.

The men listened politely but seemed unimpressed by any of the singers Madame offered before asking to hear 'the Australian' who was now being discussed around the city as a potential star.

At first Madame resisted their request. Nellie was not available, she argued, because she had already been engaged by

Maurice Strakosch. But Lapissida and Dupont persisted and eventually Madame relented and called for Nellie who sang the mad scene from *Hamlet* that had been so well received in her first appearance in December.

The two men nodded and smiled to one another and asked Madame to speak to them privately in the adjoining room. Nellie was left alone, unsure who the men were and wondering what was happening. She could hear the muddle of low voices in what was clearly a serious conversation. Eventually the door opened and Madame appeared and beckoned Nellie to join them.

'These gentlemen wish to engage you,' she said.

Nellie hesitated. 'But, Madame, my contract with Monsieur Strakosch?'

Madame waved away her protests. 'Strakosch is a great friend of mine. He will perfectly understand. I will arrange everything.'

Still confused, Nellie sat down with the men and listened to their offer. She would be paid 3000 francs a month and her costumes would be provided without cost. It seemed surreal. Just weeks ago she had been astounded by Strakosch's offer of 1000 francs, and that had now been tripled. Her hand trembled as she signed the contract that assured her of a debut on the professional stage.

# 8

# 'YOU ARE THE STAR'

Mathilde Marchesi demanded fealty. It was never stated, merely implicit in her demeanour and her expectations of students. She had invested in their lives and she would bathe in their success. She would later plaster their letters of homage through her memoir like flowered wallpaper.

Most were happy to give it, Nellie Melba among them. In June 1887, as she reflected on the events of the past few months, Nellie sent her teacher a heartfelt letter: 'Words cannot express the deep gratitude and love I feel for you, my darling Madame, but I trust that the career which your grand teaching and loving guidance has opened for me may reflect honour on you and your school. At least, this shall always be my first thought. Ever your loving and grateful pupil.'

The note said so much about their relationship and the pace at which Nellie had progressed since her hesitant audition barely nine months before. By comparison, most of Madame's students would train for at least three years before being invited to sing at a soiree, let alone onstage with an opera company of the prestige that Brussels held at the time. But with speed came risk and, inevitably, mistakes and misgivings.

In the wake of the generous reviews about Nellie's performances at the Salle Érard, and using her extensive contacts, Madame had arranged a special audition for Nellie at Palais Garnier. On a darkened stage and with a single gaslight flaring in her face she had faltered in a rare case of nerves. The directors were unimpressed. For Nellie, this only served to highlight her fortune of having been offered a contract by Strakosch but also made her question the wisdom of the subsequent decision to also sign with Messrs Lapissida and Dupont.

Despite Madame's claim that she would smooth things over with Maurice Strakosch, the matter remained unresolved, even when Lapissida announced that Nellie was due to make her debut in October singing the lead role of Gilda, the young heroine of Giuseppe Verdi's opera *Rigoletto*.

Nellie was unaware of the continuing Strakosch obstacle until one morning in mid-June when there was a loud banging on the door at 12 Avenue Carnot. At first she was apprehensive about answering because she was alone with George and the knock sounded threatening but eventually she opened the door. Strakosch stood there, purple with rage and breathless from having climbed the five floors, an exertion made worse because he had to walk with the aid of a cane.

He couldn't speak at first and angrily waved away Nellie's offer of a chair, as she would recall in her memoirs.

'I want no chairs. I want the truth. There is a rumour circulating Paris that you have signed a contract with the Theatre de la Monnaie. Surely it is not true.'

Nellie was surprised. 'Of course it's true,' she said finally.

Strakosch shook with fury, shaking his cane. 'But your contract with me. What of that? Is it nothing?'

Nellie was flummoxed. Madame was supposed to have fixed this. But it was clear that the impresario had not been told, let alone cajoled.

Nellie attempted to explain the sequence of events and that Madame had believed sincerely that, in the circumstances, Strakosch would tear up their contract.

'Do you mind?' she asked when she had finished.

It was Strakosch's turn to look surprised. The question was idiotic. 'Mind?' he screamed. 'Of course I mind.'

Nellie could not recall the exact words that followed but would describe the next fifteen minutes as a tirade as he railed against the wickedness of Madame Marchesi and Nellie's stupidity. He had treated her fairly and been repaid with ingratitude. With a final flick of his cane, he stumped out of the flat and down the stairs.

Madame waved away the incident and told Nellie to continue studying. In the weeks that followed Madame gave her husband the task of soothing Strakosch and imploring him to allow Nellie's debut to proceed but the impresario held firm. He could not waive the contract because it would set a dangerous precedent. And he was not interested in Salvatore Marchesi buying out the contract because he believed that Nellie was a future star who would earn her salary many times over.

Lapissida and Dupont were distraught. They had signed in good faith and expected the Marchesis to sort it out. Nellie was due in Brussels by the end of September, two weeks before her debut.

When Madame shut her school for the European summer, Nellie took George and headed for England where she would spend a few weeks resting on doctor's orders to quell a series of migraines. She was staying at the home of Charlie's mother, Lady Armstrong, in the town of Rustington on England's south coast between Portsmouth and Brighton. It meant George could see his father who was farming and training horses with his brother on a property nearby.

A few days after she returned to Paris in late August she wrote to Arthur Hilliger, a mixture of self-praise—'everyone tells me my voice is pure gold'; pride in her work ethic—'I sing five operas in Italian and five in French'; and envy—'I know not why the Australians are making such a fuss of [rival Australian soprano] Amy Sherwin'.

But beneath the bravado Nellie was plainly frightened. Whatever had transpired between her and Charlie while she was staying at Rustington was alarming, the threat of violence now palpable. And a recent, unconnected event in Prague had heightened her concern. A pianist named Margaret Elmblad, with whom Nellie had worked back in Australia, had 'blown her brains out' with a pistol after a quarrel with her husband. The details were still scant and the situation would end up being vastly different from her own but to Nellie it rang alarm bells. She wrote to Hilliger: 'Always be careful what you say in your letters because as you know my husband is frightfully jealous and I have not a very easy time with him.'

She repeated her concerns in a letter to Blanche Marchesi: 'My husband is going to arrive very soon. I am most awfully uneasy as you know how afraid I am of him when he has one of his mad fits on.'

❦

Nellie arrived in Brussels in late September, excited but apprehensive. Her debut was so close now but remained uncertain. As she settled into a rented house on the edge of the old city a letter arrived from Madame in which she told her pupil that formal introductions had been made in the city for her but also issued a warning.

'With regard to M. Dupont and M. Lapissida, I approve of their caution. One mustn't forget that the contract with Strakosch still exists. However they want to present you to the public of Brussels, not as a member of their company but as a rising star who gives imposing performances.'

Nellie read the letter carefully. So they were hoping to skirt the Strakosch contract by using a technicality. It did nothing to put her mind at ease.

The following day brought another worry. Charlie arrived unexpectedly early and found his wife in the house taking tea with a man. Emile Wauters was a well-known painter, known mostly for his portraits and historic scenes. He had been commissioned to paint Nellie for her debut but Charlie, ignoring the logic of the explanation, read the meeting as having a different intent.

The tensions simmered for the next day or so until Charlie became agitated and started hitting George with a book. Nellie intervened and he turned his attention on her, threatening her with a razor. It was a repeat of the sword scene only this time Nellie believed he was capable of harming her. She ran into her son's bedroom and closed the door. Charlie left for London the next day.

It seemed that events were conspiring against her, exacerbated a few days later when she went to the theatre for the first time to begin rehearsals. As Nellie stepped down from the carriage a uniformed man she assumed to be a theatre concierge moved towards her. 'This is for you, Madame,' the man said, thrusting a sheet of blue paper in front of her. She scanned the document: Maurice Strakosch had obtained a court order that prevented her from appearing onstage.

Her heart sank. The ruse had failed and with it any chance to make her debut. She rushed into the theatre to see Alexandre Lapissida but he could do nothing. Strakosch was refusing even to respond to the desperate telegrams Lapissida was sending each day, some pleading and others threatening.

Apparently, Strakosch had made his own arrangements for Nellie but it meant she would not debut for another year, scheduled to appear in a production of the Verdi opera, *La Traviata*, at the Teatro dell'Opera in Rome.

With barely a week until the opening, Nellie Melba's debut had been cancelled. She retreated to the house and drew the curtains. There seemed no sense in rehearsing but neither could she return to Paris, just in case Strakosch had a last-minute change of heart.

On the morning of 10 October, just three days before the opening, Nellie woke to the sound of a maid tapping at her bedroom door. Alexandre Lapissida was outside asking to see her. She could hear him downstairs, calling out to her, as she would recall. 'Put on your dressing gown. I have some exciting news.'

Brushing the sleep from her eyes, Nellie threw a shawl around her shoulders and followed the maid out onto the landing. Lapissida was pacing below, clearly agitated.

'Yes, yes, what is it?' she called out.

Lapissida looked up. Nellie could see the excited look on his face.

'Strakosch is dead. He died yesterday evening at a circus. I expect you to be at the theatre at eleven o'clock.' With that he left.

Maurice Strakosch had collapsed from a heart attack during a performance at the Cirque Fernando, a popular entertainment house at the edge of Montmartre which would become famous that same year because of a painting by Toulouse-Lautrec.

As callous as it seemed to celebrate a man's death, his demise meant that the contract was void. Nellie Melba was free to make her debut.

The rain set in early on 13 October 1887 and didn't stop. The heavy skies above Brussels darkened the streets that Nellie already considered dull compared to the spirit of Paris. Was this the revenge of Maurice Strakosch? she wondered.

As she paced and watched the sodden deluge outside her window, Nellie could only think of one thing—Australia. She had not felt the pang of homesickness since arriving in Europe—life had been too exciting for that—but today was different, the most important day in her life thus far, and she warmed herself with thoughts of sunshine on the soft green leaves of gum trees.

Nellie could still recall the image years later while writing her memoir and trying to sort out the jumble of vivid memories from that day. First there was the sight of Madame, dressed in black as usual, rushing to embrace her protégé followed closely by Salvatore who wore a large flower in his buttonhole.

Then there was the trip during the afternoon to the theatre with Lapissida for a final run-through. She stepped from the carriage into the rain and paused, amazed at the sight of the crimson letters on the billboard that proclaimed MADAME MELBA. It made her heart race.

'Why is my name so much bigger than the others?' she asked the theatre manager.

'Because you are the star,' he replied, wiping a raindrop from her cheek.

But as grey day collapsed into black evening she became despondent, self-doubt whispering in her ear as she sat in front of the dressing-room mirror, a dresser fixing her hair and makeup, surrounded by flowers from well-wishers. Was she really ready for this? The risk of her leap from amateur to professional with so little preparation was laid bare as it dawned on her that she knew nothing about something as simple as applying stage makeup. This was only the third time she had even been inside an opera house.

Nellie allowed the dresser to continue until she saw her attempting to place a blonde wig on her head. Suddenly her emotions welled up and she burst into tears. 'I hate the wig. It is not me. I won't have it.'

Joseph Dupont, who would conduct the orchestra, appeared in the mirror behind her. He'd been standing outside and heard the commotion. 'Let her use her own hair,' he instructed. 'It's much prettier anyway.' The dresser shrugged, put the wig down and began plaiting Nellie's natural tresses. Gilda, the young heroine of Verdi's masterpiece, could be a brunette for the night.

Her famous aria was not due until towards the end of the first act so the nerves had settled by the time she stood alone on the stage to sing 'Caro nome', in which Gilda reveals her young voice of independence and expresses her love for a man she believes to be a poor student.

It was the hush she noticed as she looked out across the auditorium with its gold-trimmed stalls. It hardly seemed human that so many people could be so absolutely quiet. They were waiting, holding their breath in anticipation of the voice they had all come to hear—her voice. She began to sing *sotto voce*, soft and understated as Verdi would have wanted and Madame would have demanded. The notes came naturally, sweet and patient. As they floated out over the audience it seemed to Nellie as if they had been sung by someone else.

The applause as she finished was thunderous, the room aflutter with white lace handkerchiefs. 'That cannot be for me,' she thought. 'They are clapping and cheering for someone else.' But when she was summoned to the royal box after the third act and curtsied for the Queen of Belgium, Marie Henriette of Austria, Nellie knew that the adulation was indeed for her. 'You are wonderful,' the queen said, smiling gently. Of all the praise that would follow, this felt the most genuine.

It was Madame who brought her back to earth, at the post-performance supper serving dishes named in her honour—Cote de Chevreuil a l'Australienne, Oranges Melba and Pudding Gilda among them. Amid the babble of voices, her teacher leaned across the table and wagged a knowing finger at her student.

'How is it that you forgot the two notes in the [last act] quartet?'

Nellie's face fell. 'Oh Madame, I hoped you wouldn't notice. I'm sorry.'

The message was clear: *You are not yet a diva.*

The reviews arrived the next morning, thick and sickly sweet. She sat reading them in the apartment. Outside, the rain clouds were lifting but she didn't notice as she devoured the words.

'Ye gods! What enthusiasm!' exclaimed the Paris daily newspaper *La Réforme*.

Barely will the music of Verdi have found a more complete interpretation than that given to it by Madame Melba. The voice of the eminent artiste is of an exceptional purity, ardent and vibrating, uniting brilliancy and power and sweetness and infinite charm which makes one abandon one's self voluntarily to the caresses of her beautiful voice.

*L'Indépendance Belge* declared it as the performance of the season: 'Nature has treated Madame Melba generously by granting her the precious gift of a voice full of seduction; pure and limpid, with sweetness that shines at will.' *La Patriote* predicted she would be known as La Melba within two years, *L'Étoile Belge* admired her Empress-like profile and *Le Menestrel* complimented her remarkable style and expression.

The compliments seemed never-ending but there was one warning shot. Buried beneath the praise, the *La Reforme* critic detected a flaw. Although Nellie could sing with astonishing ease, there was a woodenness about her acting: 'Madame Melba acts rather like an Anglo-Saxon,' he taunted. 'Her gestures are rather embarrassed and stiff, with something automatic about them, but one must not forget it is the first time she has appeared onstage. We are persuaded that in a few days, she will abandon herself entirely to the dramatic temperament which she possesses and which is reflected in her countenance.'

The news reached Australia a week later, most papers giving her just a few paragraphs as if not convinced of her talent or the importance of the achievement, as the *Mackay Mercury* noted: 'Many of our readers will remember this lady (Mrs Armstrong) when she lived at Mackay, and though many admired her voice, few thought she would be equal to taking a place among the first operatic artists of Europe. But the lady herself thought otherwise ...'

More pointedly, they seemed reluctant to accept her new persona. She was Mrs Armstrong or the former Nellie Mitchell, not Madame Melba, which the *Daily Telegraph* correspondent insisted was a stage name that should be abandoned when she sang in London the next season, missing entirely that Nellie had honoured her hometown.

13

Charlie Armstrong was not in Brussels to see his wife's triumph. He was back in London, attending a theatre more to his own liking. On Saturday, 15 October, two days after Nellie's debut, he had travelled to Earl's Court in the city's west to see the biggest event in town—Buffalo Bill's Wild West Show.

Famed American showman William F Cody, aka Buffalo Bill, had arrived in London in May with a troupe of two hundred cowboys and Indians to perform as part of the American Exhibition organised to celebrate Queen Victoria's fifty years on the throne.

It had been a stunning commercial and cultural success with up to twenty-five thousand people each day flocking to the makeshift stadium to watch, agog, at the display of horsemanship and precision shooting, trick roping, races, mock stagecoach robberies and re-enactments of famous prairie battles. So enamoured was the queen that she went twice.

But only one event interested Charlie—the challenge to stay on the back of one of the show's buck jumpers. Among the hundreds of horses Cody had brought across the Atlantic, he had included a dozen or so trained to jettison riders. At least half-a-dozen men, all good riders, had been thrown and killed during the tour in America.

Very few who accepted the challenge had managed to remain aboard long enough to win the money offered for such a feat of horsemanship. But Charlie Armstrong was confident and was calling himself Kangaroo Charlie. It was an attitude that would have appealed to a showman like Cody as he presented Charlie with his meanest buck jumper, a coal black stallion called Misery Mike. Charlie agreed on the condition that he could use his own saddle which had been made back in Mackay.

The attending cowboys were dubious, fearing that the unknown rider was in danger because his saddle, albeit with a crupper strap that kept it in place by tying it to the animal's tail, was shallower than the deep 'Mexican' saddles used in the show, which were designed to keep the rider in place. One cowboy named 'Buck' Taylor was concerned enough to speak up: 'Stranger we don't want to see you killed. No man ever rode Misery with a crupper.' But Charlie merely smiled.

A local journalist's account would find its way into the *Queensland Figaro and Punch* a few weeks later:

In vain the horse did all he knew to shift his rider. He kicked and jumped and bucked and played at various fantastic tricks, but all to no purpose. There was Kangaroo, and there he remained until the horse tired out and gave in. And Cody and the Injun and the cowboys—what about them? They came to scoff and laugh and remained to applaud, like big-hearted fellows that they are! But strictly entre-nous, they don't exactly hanker after any more Kangaroos who can take them at their own game.

Charlie, who later dismissed Misery Mike as 'soda water' compared to Queensland horses, collected his winnings from Cody who promptly invited him to stay and take part in the evening show, this time playing the role of an Australian bushranger attacking the stagecoach. It was a brief moment in the sun for a man who was longing to quit the cold of Europe and get back to the freedoms of Queensland—with or without his wife.

# COVENT GARDEN

Christmas 1887 was in sharp contrast to the yuletide of the previous year. Nellie Armstrong, the struggling music student wearing a fraying serge frock, had become La Melba, the celebrated opera debutante who could afford a second winter dress or a third or a fourth for that matter.

She had finished the year playing Lucia in Gaetano Donizetti's opera *Lucia di Lammermoor* to great acclaim and was now casting her eyes beyond Belgium at a possible debut at Palais Garnier in the summer, something she had considered impossible six months before.

Despite Madame's wishes that she return to Paris for Christmas, and to bring Charlie and George with her, Nellie decided to remain in Brussels. George would later recall the exhilaration of snowfall on Christmas Day and a rare, if brief, truce between his parents.

Charlie hated Paris but Brussels was bearable for short periods, particularly because he joined a sporting club where he won the foils championship in swordplay and pounded opponents senseless in the boxing ring.

He felt lost and emasculated in his wife's world of finery and flowers and despised the fact that his son was being brought up among the bohemian elite—'theatrical people' who spoke French rather than English. He clung to the hope that Nellie's foray into singing would be brief and she could be persuaded to return to him and Australia. His mother had told him to be patient; that things would return to normal soon enough. Divorce was out of the question. In the meantime his only recourse was to take his wife's money, which he believed was owed to him as her husband. So when Charlie returned to Rustington at the end of the year he took £200, almost the entire sum Nellie had earned in her first two months in Brussels.

Nellie dared not refuse him and was relieved to see him go, not only because of her fears of abuse but also because it meant she was now free to go back to Belgium and Paris where she could rehearse for her next performances, the operas *Lakmé* and *Hamlet*, which were due to open in March.

Madame was her comfort and safety net, and the two French composers of the operas, Leo Delibes and Ambroise Thomas, were at her disposal in France. She needed their help, given that she had never even seen the operas performed, and both men were eager for her to succeed. Thomas had been a supporter since she sang Ophelia's aria at Madame's soiree; and when doubts were expressed about Nellie's French pronunciation,

Delibes retorted that he didn't care in what language she sang his opera.

Nellie's engagement at Monnaie had been a resounding success, although not without its hiccups. The season of *Rigoletto* was followed by a role as Violetta in *La Traviata*. The press reviews were full of generous encouragement although somewhat muted compared to the initial adulation.

One critic dwelled on her inexperience in stagecraft. Nellie knew it was true but she still felt snubbed, and wept and fumed for a week before deciding that the only way to answer her critics was to work harder. Self-belief was Nellie's armour and she wore it with the fury of an operatic warrior. When it was challenged, pierced or rattled she sought to make the chain mail tighter and stronger.

After that performance in *La Traviata*, Nellie had raced back to Paris for three days of lessons with Madame before opening as Lucia in early December. It was a pivotal decision. Not only did her performance restore the media's initial judgement of her future but among the audience on opening night was a woman who would become as important to Nellie's career as Mathilde Marchesi.

Lady Gladys de Grey was just twenty-eight years old but already one of the most important patrons of the arts in London and of opera in particular. So impressed with Nellie Melba was she that she told Augustus Harris, manager of the Theatre Royal at Covent Garden, that he should engage her for the coming season because she had the perfect voice for the Italian opera he was planning.

Harris journeyed to Brussels to see and hear Nellie for himself after which he spoke to Alexandre Lapissida. There was a break in performances at Monnaie between May and September so an appearance in London wouldn't interfere with her contract. If anything, it would enhance her reputation and marketability when she returned to Brussels for the autumn season.

Nellie, egged on by her circle of friends in Brussels, was eager to accept the offer but Madame was furious, imploring her to return and sing at the Paris Opera during the summer. Otherwise, she warned in a terse letter, Nellie risked missing her moment.

Look my dear Nellie, your Brussels friends are quite simply a bit jealous! That's all! At the moment the whole of Paris wants you. The Press is very well disposed towards you. The Opera assures you that its doors are wide open to you, at last now is the most favourable moment for your debut. I beg you to give me the authority to arrange the business side of your engagement, as much for the money as for the duration of the time and you will be happy with my diplomacy.

Madame's logic seemed impeccable. Impressed by Nellie's successful debut in Brussels, the directors of the Paris Opera had decided to ignore her earlier disappointing audition. The dream of singing on the stage at Palais Garnier was tantalisingly close, the title role in Charles Gounod's *Romeo et Juliette* was on offer, but if she waited another year then it might disappear.

There was another consideration. The World's Fair was being staged in Paris in 1889, which would almost certainly snuff out the publicity surrounding a largely unknown singer's operatic debut. But if she sang in 1888 and did well then she would be welcomed back as a headline act during the World's Fair, which would include the opening of the Eiffel Tower.

'. . . The whole world will be in Paris and your reputation will be made.'

The offer must have seemed irresistible and yet, for once, Nellie would ignore Madame's advice. She was still under contract to Lapissida and Dupont and they were happy to let her sing in London during the summer, provided she return to Brussels afterwards and resume her commitment. After her experiences with the Strakosch contract, Nellie was not going to risk another legal confrontation.

She also had George to consider. Photographs of the time would reveal a wary four-year-old child dressed in a sailor's suit, nestled into the crook of his mother's neck and peering suspiciously at the cameraman. The comings and goings of his father must have been confusing but in England he could go to Rustington, where he seemed happy with his grandmother, while Nellie concentrated on her performance in London. It would also mean that George could see his father who was back tending horses at Littlehampton.

The *European Mail* was one of a number of newspapers which reported Nellie's engagement in mid-April:

Madame Melba, the new prima donna engaged by Mr Augustus Harris for his coming operatic season at Covent Garden, is the first Australian lady to achieve that high position on the

London lyric stage. Lately she has been creating quite a furore by her singing in Brussels, and it is said that Mr Harris had a stiff fight with M. Gailhard of the Grand Opera, Paris, before he succeeded in securing her services.

⁂

Augustus Harris was an ambitious impresario, a former actor who, although almost penniless, had taken over the lease of the vacant Theatre Royal Drury Lane in 1881 and turned it into a thriving business by staging pantomime and melodramatic dramas to packed houses.

At the end of 1887, aged thirty-five, he turned his attention to the nearby Royal Opera House, known more simply as Covent Garden, where his father had once been stage manager and his mother ran the costumes department. The theatre had been the epicentre of London culture for more than a century, the place where Joseph Grimaldi, the clown of clowns, had made his name, but in recent years it had fallen into disrepair and now faced closure.

Harris convinced a group of wealthy backers to take over the lease and allow him to produce grand operas—'to give them a decent burial or resuscitate them'. With the showmanship of a cultured PT Barnum, he invited the cream of European and American singers and musicians to put on an eight-week season of opera, among them Nellie Melba.

If she had stopped to consider the sense of occasion rather than her own ambition then Nellie might not have looked back on her experience with such bleak pessimism, beginning with her house in Bayswater at the north end of Hyde Park—'one of the gloomiest streets in London'. It was far from it, of course, particularly as spring was turning to summer when London becomes a riot of colour, window boxes bulging with geraniums and marguerites in reds, pinks and white and the streets jingling with the bells of hansom cabs.

Instead, it said much about Nellie's state of mind and her expectation of instant stardom. The 26-year-old singer felt alone in London, unlike Brussels where she had felt welcomed and cocooned by well-wishers who, in their enthusiasm, had filled her head with the sense that she was already a star after only a handful of performances.

The loneliness also brought back bad memories of her previous visit to the city when she had been rejected as merely adequate by teachers like Arthur Sullivan and Alberto Randegger, and dismissed by critics like Herman Klein from *The Sunday Times* as 'decidedly amateurish and mediocre'. For the first time since they had left more than eighteen months before, Nellie missed her father and sisters.

There was more disappointment in store when Nellie arrived by carriage at the theatre. By night, Covent Garden was an entertainment mecca, attended by women ablaze in diamonds and tiaras guided by men in white tie, but by day it had long been a marketplace, the cobblestone streets covered in wagons, tents and horses, the air filled with the stench of horse shit, rotting fruit and vegetables and the sounds of shrieking stall owners. The tents and wagons were gone by late morning when Nellie arrived but the smells and rubbish remained as she stepped carefully over cabbage tops and fruit skins to get to the stage door to meet Augustus Harris. Surely this could not be the home of opera in London?

Finally convinced that she was in the right place, Nellie was shown into a cramped office where Harris warmly greeted her. He was a large, ruddy man with a reputation for being a genial but shrewd businessman, nicknamed 'Druriolanus' because of his impact on the theatre scene as the so-called father of modern pantomime. He began by telling the young singer that she would make her debut on the birthday of Queen Victoria when there was an air of celebration in the city.

Nellie was pleased. It gave her a few weeks to refresh the performance of Gilda, the role she wanted to play to make her debut. 'I suppose it will be convenient for me to sing *Rigoletto*. I would much rather do that than any other part because it was *Rigoletto* that I made my European debut in Brussels.'

Harris seemed surprised by her pronouncement, then shook his head. 'No. I'm afraid Madame Albani has the right to do that role.' Nellie might have been queen of the moment at Monnaie but not here in London where Emma Albani, the great French-Canadian songstress had been the long-reigning prima donna.

Harris's surprise at Nellie's demand was understandable given that he had already announced in the press that Melba would play the role of Lucia, the part she had just completed in Brussels with great success. She should be pleased at the opportunity, he assured her. Although she begrudgingly conceded that Madame Albani had the right to choose, Nellie left the meeting wondering if she had made a mistake by not following Madame's advice to take up the offer in Paris.

Matters were made worse over the next few weeks as she realised she would also have to compete for publicity against a slew of well-established singers Harris had brought to London for the season, which comprised thirty-two performances. Nellie may have been billed as a star in Brussels, her name in lights on the front of the building, but in London she was a debutante who stood behind not only Emma Albani but established performers such as Alwina Valleria, Sigrid Arnoldson, Zelie de Lussan, Lillian Nordica and Minnie Hauk among the women and Jean Lassalle and the de Reszke brothers, Jean and Edouard, who were later immortalised by Sir Arthur Conan Doyle in his Sherlock Holmes classic *The Hound of the Baskervilles.*

Nellie found herself on the second rung of singers, booked to perform on less fashionable midweek nights and even matinee performances. As a consequence, her name was not mentioned in the press as much as she would have liked, her lofty expectations challenged before she had even set foot on the stage.

The Covent Garden theatre could house an audience of more than two thousand but on 24 May, the night of her debut, it was barely half full or, in Nellie's mind, half empty. As she looked out on the audience and the knots of people gathering in the freshly gilded stalls and boxes she felt a sense of general apathy. Even the members of the orchestra in the pit seemed only half awake. She had only rehearsed with them once, and that had been in haste because of the demands caused by Augustus Harris's packed program. She wondered if any critics had bothered to turn up.

Despite her mood, Nellie held no nerves and sang with growing confidence as the audience, which included several hundred seats bought by an Australian businessman, warmed to her performance. There were two ovations and an encore but she woke the next morning worried that it had gone unreported.

She was wrong. The critics had been there in numbers to hear her. The maid had stacked the papers next to her bed, *The Times* on the top whose long-time critic Francis Hueffer began by describing *Lucia di Lammermoor* as 'hackneyed and tedious'. He was not referring to the performance of the cast but the opera itself, as Hueffer was no fan of Italian opera and preferred the weight and drama of a Richard Wagner production. In fact, the only reason he attended was to see Nellie of whom he wrote:

That Madame Melba will in the end be successful there is little reason to doubt although the impression produced by her debut was not an overpowering one. Her voice is of the light soprano kind, pure in tone and of good quality. Occasionally, the artist forces it, when it assumes that somewhat indefinite quality which the French call *voix blanche*. But this is a fault which greater experience will remedy. Altogether Madame Melba proved herself to be a talented and well-trained artist who, for all one can tell, may be endowed with dramatic as well as vocal ability.

Given his prejudices, Nellie might have regarded Hueffer's view as high praise but she read it with rising indignation. She turned to *The Observer* whose coverage began well enough:

A successful debut was made by Madame Melba...who possesses a soprano voice of pure quality and considerable compass. As an actress she has much in her favour; a good stage presence, expressive features and genuine dramatic instinct, and it seems probable that with further study and experience she may reach a high position amongst her operatic contemporaries.

Further study? The implication that she was not the finished product was galling. She seemed to have already forgotten Madame's warning after her Brussels' debut that she still had a long way to go to reach her potential as a singer.

Over the next few days, almost twenty newspapers and magazines voiced an opinion, all of them positive although the praise felt faint when compared to the sugared awe of the Belgian media. It was clear that she had made a strong impression with her acting abilities—even though she regarded them as awful—but there was almost no comment about her voice. 'They seemed altogether to have forgotten that my job is to sing, not to act,' she would later reflect.

Augustus Harris attempted to bolster the young singer's confidence by inserting into the advertised program his own review of her performance: 'The house literally rose to Madame Melba, the occupants of the boxes and stalls all joining in the spontaneous ovation, and the triumphant and deafening applause.'

Then Madame Albani graciously stood aside for one evening performance on 12 June to allow Nellie to play Gilda in *Rigoletto*, the role she had originally wanted to play, but tragedy struck when she awoke on the morning of the performance with a hoarse voice, exacerbated by two performances the day before at a concert arranged to feature all the singers.

In any other circumstance a singer would have stepped down and rested but Nellie, determined to make her mark on a London audience, was not going to let an opportunity pass. Instead, an announcement was made about her condition and that she would go ahead despite the problem. It was a risk that might have backfired, as one critic would later note. After all, some in the audience were paying five guineas for a seat and Alexandra, wife of Edward, Prince of Wales, and their daughters Louise and Maud, were in the royal box.

The ovations should have told her that she had made the right choice but again she was disappointed with the reviews the next morning, dismissing the respected *St James's Gazette* which summarised:

> The Gilda of Madame Melba is particularly interesting, and though it was, naturally, in "Caro nome" that she gained her great success as a vocalist, her dramatic singing in the various scenes with the hunchback are very impressive, so that the naturally cold audience was aroused again and again to enthusiasm.

It seemed that she would not be content with anything less than unqualified praise, and when Augustus Harris asked her to sing a secondary role as a page in a production of Verdi's *Un Ballo in Maschera* she decided that enough was enough and asked to be released from her contract. Harris reluctantly agreed. Announcing her departure a few days later he declared: 'In a little time they will clamour for Melba above all others, and, by gad, they'll have to pay for her.'

But Nellie didn't hear his words. Having collected George from Rustington, she had rushed back to Paris where she was being comforted by Madame in the sanctuary of 88 Rue Jouffroy, vowing never to return to London.

## 10

# A DOCTRINE OF RIVALRY

Nellie Melba was a shooting star. Between the last months of 1886 and the summer of 1888 she had risen from an unknown student begging for a place at Ecole Marchesi to a debutante at both Monnaie and Covent Garden. Despite being an English speaker with only passable French and Italian, and a noticeable Australian accent when she sang, the directors of the Paris Opera were now offering her 6000 francs per month to perform at the Palais Garnier, thanks in no small part to Mathilde Marchesi.

Nellie's journey stood in stark contrast to the experience of her classmate Emma Eames who, despite being acclaimed as a singer with as much potential, until now had only appeared in soirees and private concerts.

Emma was the daughter of an international lawyer, born in Shanghai but raised in Portland, Maine, who had begun studying at Ecole Marchesi several months before Nellie arrived. She had watched the new girl being taken aside to be given private lessons while she remained in group classes. Although insisting that she did not begrudge her—'she had a liquid, perfect and divinely beautiful voice'—the decision to set Nellie Melba apart and above the other students seemed to be as much about Mathilde Marchesi's vanity and business acumen as it was about Nellie's career.

Unlike Nellie's mother–daughter relationship with Madame, Emma would struggle with many of her teacher's methods and attitudes. There seemed to be no room for individuality, even though the voices and skills of each singer differed. Emma loved the drama of acting as much as singing but Marchesi believed that movement detracted from the voice and insisted her students remain almost still. In Emma's opinion, it made the school a place for mediocrity rather than excellence.

Not that she would have shared this view with a woman whose response to dissent could be brutal, as she discovered one morning when her performance was criticised harshly. Emma trembled, which only made her teacher angrier. 'You are much too sensitive for a career,' she snapped. 'Unless you can become hardened you will never make one.'

Despite her misgivings, Emma had enormous respect for Marchesi's skills, energy and devotion to students, as she would reflect in her memoir published in 1927 while Madame was still alive:

[Madame] had intelligence and real German efficiency although no intuition. She had a head for business which, with

100

her excellent musicianship, gave her the position she occupied for so many years—that of owner, manager and teacher of the greatest school of her day.

Of all Emma's concerns, the aspect that was most troubling was Madame's belief that singers, having embarked on their stage careers, should regard all their contemporaries not as friends but enemies, and that the only way to succeed as a prima donna was to jealously guard their turf, often to the detriment of others.

I had always believed that the world was large enough for everybody, even other singers. One had enough to do . . . without wasting time on professional jealousy; and if one had a genuine gift and a real hold on the public, nothing and no one could take them from one. The thought that others might be jealous of me paralyzed and depressed me instead of causing me to rejoice, as it did many who seemed to regard it as a tribute to their art. For I dreamed, in my innocence, of working hand in hand with other singers instead of fighting them every inch of the way.

So in the last months of 1887 it was with a sense of relief and excitement that Emma ended her lessons at Rue Jouffroy and followed Nellie Melba to Brussels where Madame had sent introductions to Alexandre Lapissida in the hope that he might debut her at Monnaie. Instead, she spent the winter and early spring waiting with her mother for the promised opportunity to emerge.

She was befriended by François-Auguste Gevaert who convinced her to spend otherwise idle time learning another role, as Rachel in the French opera *La Juive*. At first she resisted, worried that she was not suited to the role, but finally agreed in the hope that it might lead to a breakthrough and convince Lapissida to give her a contract.

One day Nellie Melba, who was performing *Lakmé* to rave reviews at the time, and planning her debut at Covent Garden, came to visit. Emma found herself talking about her worries and the lessons with Gevaert. Nellie sat down at the piano. The music for the accompaniment to the aria Emma was learning was on the stand. 'I really should like to know how you sing, Emma,' Nellie said.

'I sang it, and with so much conviction evidently that when I had finished there were tears in her eyes,' Emma would recall.

Nellie sat quiet for a moment. 'Oh Emma, I had no idea you could sing like that.'

Another month passed before Emma realised the importance of the incident. There was still no word from Alexandre Lapissida about a role and her patience was wearing thin.

Then, one day in the midst of rehearsal, Gevaert stopped playing and turned to her:

You are absolutely inexperienced in the ways of the world and the theatre, and I feel that I should be very cruel and wicked if I allowed you to continue under a delusion. This singer whom you regard as a good friend, and who is, as you know, having an enormous success and making, as the French phrase goes, 'sunshine or rain' at will, tells you that she will resign if you are not allowed to sing. But at the same time she is telling the directors quite the opposite. As she has still two years to sing in Brussels, there is only one thing for you to do and that is to go back to Paris and look for something else to do.

It appeared that Nellie Melba had taken Mathilde Marchesi's doctrine of rivalry to heart.

Emma would have to wait another year to make her debut, enduring several more disappointments in the interim. Struggling financially on her return from Brussels she had been forced to take a contract in the Opera Comique, another wasted effort as she was instructed to learn three parts while management dithered about its production schedule. But at least she was being paid.

She was still waiting when the composer Charles Gounod inquired at Ecole Marchesi if there were any singers Madame thought might be suitable for the role of Juliet in his famed opera that was about to be produced at the Palais Garnier.

It was the role that Madame had suggested Nellie take instead of going to London. The production had been delayed for various reasons and recruitment had been difficult. Jean de Reszke, who would come to be regarded as the greatest tenor of his era, had been signed for the male lead but Gounod was struggling to find the right voice for his heroine. When he heard Emma sing, he knew he had his Juliet and agreed to support her case to the director of the Paris Opera.

The opera directors baulked at a debutante playing the lead in such an important performance and insisted that Adelina Patti, in the twilight of her career, be recruited to sing the part for the first six performances and ensure its commercial success, after which they were prepared to take a chance and let Emma take over.

It would be the middle of March 1889 before Emma would make her debut, just as the city prepared for the grand opening of the World's Fair. That night she calmed her nerves by pretending to be Juliet rather than Emma Eames playing the role of Juliet. It seemed to work as she sang her first aria but when the audience applauded it sounded like thunder and her heart dropped. 'I stood there on the stage and thought: "I have not been able to convince them that I am Juliet otherwise they would have kept silent. They are applauding Emma Eames, not Juliet."'

She woke the next morning to rapturous reviews, typical among them Auguste Vitu, the critic for *Le Figaro*, who gushed:

Twenty years old, tall, svelte, the figure and the profile of Diana, the nose fine and the nostrils quivering, the carmine mouth exhaling the breath of life, the face a pure oval lit by big eyes full of impudence and candour at the same time, the expression astonishingly mobile, the forehead high and crowned by a mass of blond fleece, the arms superb attached to the charming shoulders—such is Mlle Emma Eames . . . such is the new Juliet.

These would be the last reviews Emma would ever read in what, despite its halting beginnings, would turn out to be an illustrious career. Her decision was not because she thought that she was above criticism but that she believed the only valid critic was her own assessment. Only she knew if she had sung well or not.

While the Paris critics were fawning over a new star, the American press were clamouring for interviews with their countrywoman, despite her telling them that she had nothing to say because she had no experiences from which to draw. When they were gone she sat in her room, filled with flowers from admirers, and dreaded what was to come. Surely she would be found out as a fake.

Nellie had been in the audience and came to visit a few days later. Emma had looked perfectly beautiful onstage, she offered in congratulations, but had sung perfectly false all evening. Emma took no offence at the comment, which she read as another singer detecting an apprehension in her voice. 'Perhaps no remark could have borne better testimony to my vocal trueness. I immediately thought: "I wonder if I did", and felt more wretched than before.'

A few weeks later Emma fell ill and had to withdraw from a matinee performance. When Nellie volunteered to take her place the critics rushed to the Palais Garnier.

Nellie relished the attention and the chance to take the limelight from the woman she had decided was her chief rival, and would delight in the resulting reviews that compared the two performers, concluding that Emma Eames was the better dramatic actor but Nellie Melba was the superior singer. Nellie would keep them in her scrapbook.

It would not be the last clash between the two women as they continued to spar over the next three decades, separated by their different personalities—one supremely self-confident and fearless in protecting her position and the other envious and riddled with self-doubt.

## 11

# 'AN AUSTRALIAN GIRL' TAKES PARIS

The Eiffel Tower opened to the public on 9 May 1889. Built as the gateway to the *Exposition Universelle*, the World's Fair, more than twelve thousand people eagerly climbed to the top each day to take in the view across the great city.

Paris was abuzz and alive with optimism, the fair a symbol of modern France, which was celebrating a century since its Revolution altered the nation's social fabric forever. And now the tower had presented it with a landmark like no other.

The evening before the tower's opening, Nellie Melba made her debut at the Palais Garnier in front of a rapturous crowd of two thousand who demanded not one, but three curtain calls to acknowledge her performance as Ophelia.

It was the first time in at least thirty years that anyone could remember such an ovation before the Palais Garnier audience, which was notoriously difficult to please. As she stood on the stage, dressed simply in white and adorned only by a garland of white trailing daisies, Nellie knew that she had truly arrived.

It seemed that the Eiffel Tower and Nellie Melba were entwined, their foundations both planted firmly in the Parisian winter of 1886–87 and revealed, fully formed, a little over two years later to excitement, adulation and a touch of controversy.

When she was a poor student studying at Ecole Marchesi, Nellie would have been able to see the nascent tower as she walked home each evening, the black iron lace structure rising higher and higher from the Champ de Mars across the other side of the Seine. The tower was supposed to stand for only twenty years before being disassembled; instead it would remain in place, an icon, as would the name Melba.

Nellie woke the morning after her triumph to what seemed an ocean of praise. The papers were brought to her bedside at the Scribe Hotel, around the corner from the Palais Garnier, where she luxuriated in the worship, particularly the words of M. Vitu of *Le Figaro* who lathered his review with superlatives. It read in part:

> It was Ophelia herself who charmed all eyes and touched all hearts . . . That which ravished us was not alone the virtuosity, the exceptional quality of that sweetly timbred voice, the facility of executing at random diatonic and chromatic scales and trills of the nightingale. It was also that profound and touching simplicity which caused a thrill to pass through the audience with those simple notes of the middle voice—*Je suis Ophelie* [I am Ophelia].

Nellie would welcome the press into her hotel suite, even the British newspapers like the *Pall Mall Gazette* whose reviews about her Covent Garden performances had been so displeasing. But these were reporters, not critics, who arrived in wonder to tell the story of a young woman from Australia who had become a shooting star. Their accounts would trace her journey from childhood recitals to her lessons with Madame Marchesi, the delirium of Belgium and now the 'perfect triumph' of Paris.

Nellie was happy to oblige. After all, performance did not begin and end on the stage. This show for the media, she knew instinctively, was part of the process of being a star. It was expected of her as she draped herself across a chaise longue, dressed in a nightingale-blue negligee and surrounded by bouquets displayed in giant vases.

'She spoke so nicely of everybody,' the reporter Robert Sherard would later write. 'It was a pleasure to listen to her. In Paris it is malevolent remarks which one is usually called upon to hear [but] she seemed to have pleasant things to say about so many people.'

Nellie had every reason to be pleasant—she was 'intensely happy' about her debut, according to Sherard. The operatic world was now at her feet with offers of 30,000 francs a month to return to Monnaie and 150,000 francs to perform in Berlin and Madrid. She rattled off the names of royalty who had told her she was wonderful and pointed to a photograph from Charles Gounod on which he had inscribed 'To the pretty Juliet for whom I long'.

She laughed off any notion that she had secrets about preserving and strengthening her voice. 'I do nothing at all. I take care not to talk too much on the days when I am to sing in the evening but my voice is young and fresh and needs no artifices.'

And the trappings of her success? Nellie leaned forward from the sofa and plunged her hands into an ornate box on a coffee table in front of her. 'As for jewels, of which this world is so liberal when one has no need for its largesse, I have handfuls! See, here are the pearls, rubies and diamonds.'

One large bouquet of roses and lilacs next to the jewellery box prompted a rare moment of humility. It had been sent to her by a group of Australians in Paris, she told Sherard, and it reminded her of the importance to her of being Australian.

> Those who are disposed to be unkind about me here in Paris can only find against me that I am a foreigner. So I am. I am an Australian girl, and proud of it. I want always to associate Melbourne with any triumph I may have, and for that reason I have called myself Melba.

❊

Gladys de Grey was also a guest at the Scribe Hotel. She had written to Nellie soon after the young singer had fled London in the wake of her disappointment at Covent Garden, hoping to repair the damage by inviting her back to perform the next season.

It seemed an audacious invitation and Nellie, still miffed

at what she believed was a deliberate slight, was in no mood to accept, particularly with so many other options, including Germany and a new season in Brussels. She had written back, politely but stiffly: 'While I deeply appreciate your kindness, I was so badly treated in London on my first visit that I have determined never to venture on a second.'

That, she thought, would be the end of the matter. But Lady de Grey was persistent, writing again and this time dangling a royal lure that Nellie would find hard to resist.

> I did not tell you in my first letter that one of those who are most anxious for your return is the Princess of Wales. She was present for your performance of *Rigoletto* and she was deeply impressed by your singing. I know that things were badly arranged for you before, but if you come back I promise you that it will be very different. You will be under my care and I shall see that you do not lack either friends or hospitality.

Nellie was hooked. She wrote back, assuring her ladyship that she would consider giving London a second chance provided that the performances could be wedged between her contractual obligations at the Paris Opera.

And now Lady de Grey was here in Paris, eager to thrash out the details of a series of performances in June and July. She invited Nellie to discuss matters in her suite. Strangely, it was the first time they had met and Nellie would recall her initial impressions:

It was in the morning and the spring sunshine was drifting
into Lady de Grey's apartment, lighting up the gorgeous green
foulard dress which she was wearing. She was sitting at her
writing table, and as she turned around the sun illuminated
her lovely profile, making me catch my breath with the beauty
of it.

The attraction was instant, both women admiring the strength
in each other's characters. Standing almost six feet tall, Lady de
Grey cut an imposing figure. Although her husband, Frederick,
was on the board of directors at Covent Garden, it was she who
was the true patron of the arts, happy to use her influence and
circle of aristocratic friends to ensure boxes were filled during
the season. And her biggest drawcard was Edward, Prince of
Wales. Perhaps for Nellie it was worth giving London a second
chance.

Paris had also thrown Nellie into a new world of extrava-
gance. The loneliness of London was forgotten amid the
constant swirl of social engagements; dinner parties where
guests would find pearls in their soup plates and hostesses who
would splurge fortunes on flowers and artistes, such as herself,
to perform. It was not uncommon to spend £10,000, an obscene
amount of money for its time, on a fancy dress ball.

The excess both thrilled and appalled her. One 'celebrated
man' had a penchant for chicken but only for the 'oysters', the
small discs of dark meat on either side of the backbone. If he
was hosting a dinner for three people, he would have eight birds
killed and roasted to ensure he had enough meat for himself

while the guests could eat the remainder, the bulk of which would be discarded. He considered himself frugal.

Nellie was at a lunch one day where the tables were adorned with bowls full of peaches, ripe and pungent. In Australia they were grown in abundance but in Europe they were an expensive delicacy. To her astonishment, the luncheon host picked up a handful of peaches and walked to the window where he began throwing them at diners in the garden below. Other guests followed suit, laughing at the jape while the targets picked up the pieces and hurled them back. It was not the childish behaviour that outraged her but the sheer waste. After all, she was a woman crafted from Scottish Presbyterian roots.

It was one thing to have self-belief on the stage, where she controlled the moment and held the audience spellbound with her voice, but entirely another to be led into a world of wild celebrity, *fin de siècle* as she would describe the Belle Époque, where eccentric genius glittered and her lack of sophistication was laid bare. For a long time she would feel she was a spectator rather than a participant.

One evening, Madame Marchesi took her to meet the famed and flamboyant stage actress Sarah Bernhardt. When they arrived at the theatre Bernhardt was preparing for a performance of *La Dame aux Camelias*, perhaps her most successful role and written by her tutor Alexandre Dumas. The dressing room looked more like a macabre circus than a salon, Nellie observed as she cast her eyes across the heavily draped expanse with its confronting collection of animal heads adorning the walls and hides scattered over the floor. There was a stuffed tiger, a bear and a snake displayed alongside busts of mythological beings and of the actress herself. A giant bowl filled with goldfish was placed beneath a table.

When she emerged, Bernhardt leaped onto a box and began peppering Nellie with questions. 'You sing like an angel and I want to teach you to act like an angel as well,' she declared before launching into a review of the part of Marguerite from *Faust,* a role Nellie was due to play following the season of *Hamlet.* According to Bernhardt, there were points of character that Nellie had overlooked which could be dramatised by subtle gestures using her eyes and hands. It was a revelation.

Bernhardt's influence on Nellie didn't stop at acting. A few weeks later she visited Nellie's dressing room at Palais Garnier and took control of her new friend's makeup. 'Bah, you make up your face like a schoolgirl,' she cried, perched on the dressing table with a box of grease paints. 'You have no idea how to do these things. You are too innocent. Take a lesson from me, the wicked one!'

Taking Nellie's face like a painter would a canvas, she began splashing rouge and powder and touching precisely with lipstick and pencil liner in a lather of artistic inspiration. Any move Nellie made towards the mirror was met with a demand that she not look until Sarah was finished.

'Voila, now you may look, my pretty,' she finally said with a flourish.

Nellie, hesitant, looked into the mirror and was amazed at the change; her look was now able to convey the drama of her emotions almost without effort.

Theirs would be a lasting friendship, the singer drawn to the 'wonder and personality' of an actress with a powerful will and independence, just like her own, and whose reputation was built partly on her golden voice, despite the fact that she could not sing a note.

Nellie would write later:

I have heard many golden speaking voices in my day, voices that made words travel on wings, voices that seemed to give a deep and poignant meaning to even the most commonplace phrases, but no voice ever had the same effect upon me as Sarah's.

Through Lady de Grey, Nellie met Oscar Wilde, who was in the middle of writing his novel *The Picture of Dorian Gray* and about to meet his lover, Lord Alfred Douglas—a relationship that would define and destroy his life.

Like Sarah Bernhardt, Wilde's charisma and voice struck Nellie from the moment she walked into the room where he was reading poetry to a silent room. 'As long as that brilliant fiery-coloured chain of words fell from his coarse lips, one felt it would be an impertinence to interrupt.'

Wilde's greeting was haughty but engaging: 'Ah Madame Melba, I am the lord of language and you are the queen of song so I suppose I shall have to write you a sonnet'. The sonnet was never produced although he wrote her 'charming' letters and came to visit in Paris. If she was absent when he arrived, he would often wait in the drawing room for her return. She could tell how long he had been there by the number of cigarette butts in the fireplace, most of them puffed only twice, like a nervous habit, before being extinguished.

The last time she saw Wilde was in a Paris street a few years after he'd completed a two-year jail sentence for gross indecency, 'a tall shabby man, his collar turned up at the neck and a hunted look in his eyes'. She didn't recognise him and was about to pass before he stopped her. 'Madame Melba, you don't know who I am?'

Nellie shook her head.

'I am Oscar Wilde, and I am going to do a terrible thing and ask you for money.'

Nellie could hardly look at him out of pity as she reached into her purse and took out some bank notes which he almost snatched and wandered off muttering his thanks. He would die a year or so later of meningitis.

## 12

# THE DEVIL WHO LEAVES

Charlie Armstrong had been back in Australia for more than a year, angry and disillusioned after the Christmas in Brussels with Nellie and George. While his wife set Paris alight with her voice and immersed herself in society, Charlie spent the next year virtually alone in the bush, carving a horse stud out of a 100-acre (40-hectare) land grant at Plane Creek, a half day's ride south of Mackay.

After stocking the property with thoroughbreds and coaching horses shipped from Melbourne, Charlie had designed and built a house overlooking an unspoiled stretch of beach facing the Coral Sea. He seemed to think he might still be able to convince Nellie to give up the stage and return to Queensland.

It is unlikely that he read newspaper reports of his wife's success although one of his close friends, James Chataway, owned the *Mackay Mercury* whose coverage of Nellie's career invariably referred to her as Mrs Armstrong.

§⁞₿

London seemed a different place from a luxury suite at the Metropole Hotel. Nellie was no longer in a rented, backstreet house on the wrong side of Hyde Park but in the centre of the city, gazing down from her upper floor room reached not by stairs but an electric elevator. She watched the bustle of carriages and passengers around Trafalgar Square and beyond to The Mall and Buckingham Palace.

The Metropole had opened four years before, at seven storeys high and six hundred rooms it was the biggest hotel in Europe with amenities like ensuite bathrooms and in-room telephones. There was a ballroom and two restaurants. Its builder, Frederick Gordon, wanted to attract the continental travellers and American tourists as well as society ladies coming to the city to attend state balls, concerts and theatres in the West End. Other 'super hotels' would follow, including the Savoy which was about to open its doors.

There was a letter waiting for Nellie at the hotel when she arrived, after dropping George at Rustington where Lady Armstrong, still hopeful that her son's marriage could be saved, would have informed her rebellious daughter-in-law that Charlie was on his way back to England.

The letter was from Lady de Grey, clearly concerned whether her carefully managed arrangements had come to pass. Nellie sent an immediate reply. Everything was wonderful, she assured her sponsor who wrote again the same afternoon, the undated notes rushed by messenger between the hotel and Lady de Grey's Mayfair townhouse like a modern-day email exchange.

My dear Madame Melba, I was very glad to get your charming letter which shows you understand mine. My fear lest there should be any hitch in the arrangements made me perhaps over-anxious. But now all is satisfactorily arranged and I am delighted I went to see Mr Harris about it yesterday on his return from Paris and found it settled. Au revoir dear Madame Melba with all good wishes. Believe me. Yrs sincerely Gladys de Grey

The theatre arrangements may have been settled but London's weather intervened and sought to ruin Nellie's return a few days later when she appeared in her now familiar role as Gilda in *Rigoletto*. The theatre was only half full, attributed to the monsoonal rains that had descended on the city that afternoon.

If Nellie was annoyed, the reviews the next morning put her mind at ease. It appeared that London critics had taken heed of her Palais Garnier reception and had chosen to follow suit, as *The Times* reported:

Madame Melba has now justly earned the title of a great singer; she has gained at the Theatre de la Monnaie the experience and confidence which were all too lacking on the occasion of her former appearances in London. Even greater certainty of command over her fine voice will no doubt be acquired as time goes on.

Nine days later she would return in what would be a career-defining performance. Augustus Harris, as was his wont, decided to take a risk. This was a season of Italian opera and he chose to cast Nellie as Juliet alongside Jean de Reszke as Romeo. But the performance would be in French rather than Italian, the first time ever in England.

This time, the house was full and the reviews were all she could hope for as she and de Reszke clicked as a duo. Among the accolades was *The Standard* which reported:

Madame Melba seems absolutely incapable of a false intonation, and is almost unsurpassed in the purity and sweetness of her tones. Her shake is close and even, the few embellishments she introduces are almost invariably in good taste and in all she does, sincerity and dramatic force are conspicuous.

The one exception was the writer George Bernard Shaw, then a critic for the *London Star*, who was scathing: 'At one or two points in the balcony scene she sang with genuine feeling, and in the tragic scenes she was at least serious to do her best,' he wrote. 'In the first act however, she was shrill and forward, coming out with great confidence and facility which Mme Melba mistook for art.'

Perhaps Nellie did not read Shaw's critique because all her frustrations about London seemed to have vanished with that single performance. 'What a night it was,' she would later write.

> At last, at long last, there was a packed house. I had been so
> used to singing to poor houses during my three appearances
> in England that I wondered if I should have to wait till I was
> middle-aged before people came to hear me. And so, when
> I heard the roars of applause, and when I read the next day,
> the criticisms, I felt inclined to say 'It's been a fight—a hard
> fight—but London really is awake now.'

Her turn of phrase—'really awake now'—was an accurate reflection of a city at the peak of its charm and excitement. 'The Season' was now in full swing as the landed gentry locked up their grand country estates and headed back to the capital after the Easter parliamentary recess for several months of social excess.

In May came the *vernissage*, or opening, of the summer art exhibition at the Royal Academy where society women paraded their new dresses; likewise the Sunday Church Parade at Hyde Park and Derby Day at Epsom. In June there was Royal Ascot week, the commencement at Eton School, the gymkhana at Ranelagh Gardens in Chelsea and cricket at Lords. Queen Victoria, who had earlier hosted a series of debutante balls, opened the grounds of Buckingham Palace in July while Oxford clashed with Cambridge in the annual boat race.

Parties began with breakfast along the Thames which flowed into garden parties that drifted lazily into the late afternoon. Dinners came later, after sunset, before grand balls that wafted into the early hours. Not even the discovery of the body of a young woman slashed to death in a Whitechapel alleyway, reigniting fears of Jack the Ripper who'd held the city in a grip of terror the year before, could dull the revelry.

Nellie was almost giddy with excitement as Lady de Grey hosted a house party in her honour. It was held at the de Grey townhouse in Bruton Street, Mayfair, where Nellie was introduced to society icons such as the Duchess of Leinster, robed in white satin and sapphires; the recently widowed Lady Dudley, covered head to knees in turquoises; and the sharp tongue of the ageing Duchess of Devonshire, nicknamed the 'Double Duchess' because her previous husband had been the Duke of Manchester.

Nellie revelled in the company of arts patron Lady Ellen Beresford and marvelled at the brazen flamboyance of 'Daisy' Countess of Warwick who was in the early stages of an affair with the Prince of Wales. The prince's wife, Princess Alexandra, was also a frequent guest at Bruton Street.

It was a world of subterfuge that made Nellie's marital woes seem a trifle, the elegant silk of society hiding a dark underbelly in which three women, one of whom was having affairs with the husbands of the other two, could circulate politely together in the same room.

⊞

Nellie would be reminded of her marriage problems soon enough. At the end of the season she went down to Rustington where George had been staying with his father while she was performing. They were joined there by Winifred and John

Rawson, their old neighbours from Marian in Queensland who had helped Nellie cope when George was born and had since moved to London. Nellie's sisters Annie and Belle were also visiting so it seemed an opportune time to christen the boy. Winifred Rawson would be his godmother and his godfather would be his namesake, Charlie's older brother George, who also happened to be visiting from Melbourne.

Family diaries would record that the local vicar required the two godparents to renounce the devil and all his works on behalf of little George who watched, dressed in what appeared to be a kilted sailor suit. As the water drained away, the eager-eyed boy observed: '*Voilà, ç'est Diable qui départ*'.

The touching ceremony would soon be forgotten however as Nellie, Charlie and George left for Europe with Annie and Belle. The troubles began in Paris where an argument broke out in a hotel room when Charlie blamed his wife for losing his pearl tiepin. In a rage, he grabbed a razor and slashed his hat to pieces. Turning to Nellie he growled, 'That would have been your head if you had been there.' She fled to her sisters' room for safety.

By August they were in Switzerland, staying at the luxurious Hotel Beau-Rivage at Lausanne. Despite the placid mountain beauty of their surroundings, the arguments continued. Charlie now realised that his wife's career was too advanced for her to quit and, instead, began to sow seeds of mistrust between George and his mother.

He encouraged the boy to disobey her, on one occasion urging him to throw stones while his mother and aunts swam in the waters of Lake Geneva. It appeared relatively minor but Nellie feared it demonstrated a more serious intent; that if she didn't obey Charles then he was planning to take George away from her.

The arguments grew steadily worse until one night, during a row about money, Charlie threw a heavy candlestick across the room which hit her in the back. Much to her relief, he left in early September to sail back to Australia, taking £200. He would not return for eighteen months while she and George moved into a new flat on Avenue des Champs-Élysées.

## 13

# THE PATRON

Gladys de Grey physically matched her graceful name; tall and lithe with a raised-chin carriage of elegance and a touch of disdain. Her visage was made more exotic by Russian roots and, in her youth, she was a nineteenth-century supermodel of sorts, a so-called 'professional beauty' whose photograph was on sale to the public. The novelist Edward Benson observed: 'When she was there the rest looked a shade shabby. They wanted a touch of sponge and the duster.'

Gladys would marry twice, first to St George Henry Lowther, the fourth Earl of Lonsdale who owned three castles and a stable of thoroughbreds. His annual income of £120,000 enabled him to 'spend without thinking'. He travelled the world in one of two steamships, returning home in time for major race events and just long enough for his new wife to fall pregnant before he left to study the Gulf Stream off Mexico.

It is little wonder then that Gladys would find other amusements and friends, like the sultry actress Lillie Langtry with whom she would host lavish parties at the family home Crowther Castle in the Lakes District where, among other exotic creatures, she kept an emu. She was particularly famous for attending a party dressed as Cleopatra, wearing a dress made of gold and silver tissue encrusted with jewels, her hair twisted and decorated with clusters of pearls and a diamond ibis. A photograph, retained by the Victoria and Albert Museum, shows an Arab slave carrying the train. He was part of the costume.

When the earl died in 1882 at the age of twenty-six, apparently of a heart attack in a private brothel, Gladys was left with a two-year-old daughter named Juliet and the need to find a new castle. Three years later she married Frederick Robinson, known as Earl de Grey, whose wealth even exceeded Lowther's.

Earl de Grey was a noted sportsman, which meant he loved shooting birds, particularly pheasants who were blasted in their dozens each time he loaded up. He kept an accurate count of his kills which would number an astonishing lifetime tally of 556,000 (including 241,000 pheasants), adding fifty-two birds on the morning he keeled over and died from a heart attack.

Frederick paid less attention to his wife, who decided that the spectacular family estate, Studley Royal, in Yorkshire was too cold and too distant from the excitement of the capital. She would soon become one of the city's most prominent hostesses and a member of the so-called Marlborough House set, the inner circle of Edward, Prince of Wales, whose sexual antics—mostly with one another—became the stuff of legend.

She was also a central figure in The Souls, a group of aristocrats who had become disillusioned with politics. One of their members, the poet Wilfrid Blunt, described their aims as 'a group of men and women bent on pleasure, but pleasure of a superior kind, eschewing the vulgarities of racing and card-playing indulged in by the majority of the rich and noble, and looking for their excitement in romance and sentiment.'

At first Gladys established her townhouse in Mayfair, where she had hosted events such as Nellie's party, but she would later buy a house, Coombe Court, at Kingston-upon-Thames which would become the focal point of her various 'stunts', as she called them. She quickly established a reputation for parties attended by literary and artistic figures and a mix of aristocrats but no politicians.

Edward Benson attended many of the de Grey events, which he dubbed 'Bohemia in excelsis . . . bohemia in tiaras'. He once watched one of Queen Victoria's equerries apply makeup to the face of a drug-hazed Duke of Cambridge while no one else batted an eyelid.

Lady de Grey sat in the centre of the web in touch with it all. Seemingly rather effortless but appreciative, she was the initial and effective force. An apparent casualness was her chief weapon . . . in reality, she was taking endless trouble, though it looked (and she did it so easily) as if she was merely leading the life of pageantry that was natural to her.

But Gladys de Grey was not content to just host parties, and sit around drawing rooms discussing literature and playing cards. She became an essential component in Augustus Harris's desire to save Covent Garden. In his first season, Harris lost almost £16,000—the modern equivalent of £1.5 million—which would have closed most businesses. So when Gladys de Grey offered to step in with a group of financial backers, including her husband, he leaped at the second chance.

The strange thing about the arrangement was that Gladys was no great fan of opera, or of any music for that matter. Her enthusiasm seemed to come from the entrepreneurial challenge and a desire to control and manage her place in society. She loved the pageantry, taking delight in being able to fill the gilded boxes of Covent Garden for the opera season (and later the ballet) simply by talking among her friends and lauding the performance of singers like Melba—*her* star—and the de Reszke brothers.

The Prince of Wales, normally a fan of musical theatre, was frequently persuaded to attend with his wife and daughters. In doing so, he naturally brought other members of the Marlborough House set. And then their admirers would then follow, and so on.

But there seemed to be as much in the relationship for Nellie as for Gladys, who had recognised the star quality of the young singer and drawn her from relative obscurity into the limelight. And as time went on, the relationship grew from one of patron and star into a friendship of sorts.

Nellie was not alone. Oscar Wilde dedicated his play

*A Woman of No Importance* to Lady de Grey. It was a comment perhaps on her ability to fade into the background once the party began, for she sought influence and not the limelight. Her seamless parties were the product of weeks and months of planning and days of anguish, exhibited in the letters she had sent to Nellie when she arrived at the Hotel Metropole. Lady de Grey left little to chance.

Even in love and lust she was strategic and careful, and occasionally venomous. During her first marriage, she was so sure that her husband would not be home that she displayed photographs of her lovers on the mantlepiece. She took the opposite tack in her second marriage when she became one of the first people in London to install a telephone in her home, apparently because she realised that it meant she could call her men friends rather than write notes that could easily be found.

Among her lovers was Randolph Churchill, father of Winston, which upset Lady Jennie Churchill, even though she was also openly cavorting outside the marriage. Another was the journalist Harry Cust, editor of the *Pall Mall Gazette*, who had such a reputation as a womaniser that he was said to have fathered a number of children of society matrons, as author Anita Leslie noted in her 1973 book *The Marlborough House Set*: 'So much of the Cust strain entered England's peerage that from such a number of cradles there gazed babies with eyes like large sapphires instead of the black boot buttons of their legal fathers'.

It was hardly surprising then that Gladys had rivals for Harry's attentions. In his bedroom one day she found a cache of racy love letters written to him by Lady Londonderry, another powerful society doyen and wife of the sixth Marquess of Londonderry described by Benson as 'a highwayman in a tiara, trampling on enemies as if they had been a bed of nettles'.

At first Lady de Grey used the letters for her own amusement, reading out excerpts to friends during afternoon bridge games on rainy London afternoons, according to author Juliet Nicolson in her 2008 book *The Perfect Summer*.

After tiring of the fun, she sent the bundle to the marquess. Gladys arranged the delivery for an evening in which she knew that husband and wife would be dining alone together. The footman took the missives—held together by a red ribbon—to Lord Londonderry's end of the dining table. Not only did the letters reveal the affair but Lady Londonderry had made the mistake of mocking her husband to another man. After Londonderry had read the contents, his butler retied the bundle and took them to the other end of the table to the dismay of his wife.

The affair itself was tolerable but the fact it had been made public was unforgivable. Divorce was out of the question, given the potential embarrassment, so Lord Londonderry took the only other option—it would be a marriage in name only: 'Henceforth we do not speak,' he told her. It was a promise he would keep.

Lady de Grey's lust trysts went beyond Britain's shores, enjoying liaisons with men such as Henri Bernstein, one of Paris's leading playwrights, who counted the novelist Marcel Proust among his lovers. Bernstein enjoyed taking society women, including Gladys de Grey to Le Chabanais, the city's most infamous brothel, where he hosted 'fine suppers' while *filles de joie* posed in lewd positions around the table. These often occurred after a night at the opera. Edward, Prince of Wales, was Le Chabanais's most famous client, booking a suite a year in advance so he could arrive at any time and indulge in fantasies such as bathing in a Sphinx-themed copper bathtub filled with champagne.

It came as little surprise then that when she was confronted with temptation, Nellie Melba would have little hesitation taking a leaf out of her patron's handbook. The only question was whether she was capable of being discreet about it.

## 14

# TAKING A COLD HOUSE BY STORM

On a clear morning in the spring of 1890 a man with the splendid name of Wordsworth Donisthorpe stood at the second-floor window of a building on the corner of Northumberland Avenue and Whitehall in London where, with a homemade camera, he took the first known motion picture of the great metropolis.

The ghostly, flickering vision lasts a few seconds—just ten frames still exist—and yet it succinctly captures daily life around Trafalgar Square: a farmer's cart homeward bound from Covent Garden markets, footmen riding an ornate carriage and a sprightly hansom cab passing a horse-drawn omnibus filled with passengers. Milling pedestrians can be seen against a backdrop of a spouting fountain and the dome of the National Gallery. More than a century later, little has changed other than the modes of transport.

London was alight in that summer, according to the publication *London of Today: An illustrated handbook for the season* which reckoned that the biggest topic of conversation was the impending electrification of the city. A huge power plant was being constructed on the southern banks of the Thames which, when complete, would have the capacity to create energy for 2.5 million lights—'a marvel of the age'.

The handbook was in its sixth annual printing—a 500-page guide to the city and its trends in fashion, entertainment and social behaviour; where to stay, where to dine and, most importantly, where to be seen and how to dress. Its editor Charles Eyre Pascoe described himself as 'the readers' very humble and obedient servant' in an introduction that assured them he was on top of the city's changes.

London was flourishing, growing and opening up its mind and palate to new ideas and tastes. There were two new city hotels, the Savoy and the Albemarle, where 'light and airy' French cuisine was the rage and American bars with 'diamond-studded bar-tenders and gumbo' were challenging the 'time-honoured gloomy and primitive' English tavern, although a well-breaded cutlet with chipped potatoes and a glass of claret remained the city's most popular lunch fare.

There were scandals aplenty but there was also goodness in the air as the city's legal inns, Temple, Lincoln's and Gray's, opened their grounds on summer evenings to the children of the poor. Hyde Park hosted weekly church parades and the queen had consented to a carriageway along the western side of Buckingham Palace to link the park to Westminster.

Kate Reilly's dress shop in Dover Street was the place for ladies attending Ascot race meetings to buy their gowns while those who needed court dresses were given directions to Mr Van der Weyde of Regent Street. The Lyric Club in Coventry Street was the 'in' place, particularly for ladies who, when attending the theatre, were now expected to remove their bonnets so as not to impede the views of those behind them.

There was a myriad of entertainment venues, from the fireworks at Crystal Palace to parlour singalongs, flower shows, marching bands and the 'new' Madame Tussauds in Baker Street. But the Italian opera at Covent Garden remained a place for the well heeled. The cheapest seats in the orchestra stall gallery started at £1 while a seat in a grand tier box cost £7, the equivalent of a month's wages for a skilled tradesman. The reason, according to the guide, was the cost of the 'soprani first line', prima donnas who lived in glass cages:

To unlock the case requires a golden key which, according to a moderate computation, would require to be made of five hundred gold sovereigns. The singing bird being released, carols a song or two, and then back she trips into the glass case again. Another golden key must be wrought of another mass of fine gold before the glass case may be again opened.

In the last days of May, as Augustus Harris was counting record subscriptions for a season at Covent Garden and putting final touches to his ten-week program, his brightest golden songbird arrived in town. Nellie Melba, buoyed by a successful season in Paris as well as a four-night performance in Monte Carlo, settled into a suite at the Metropole Hotel with a view across Trafalgar Square almost identical to the scene shot just a few weeks before by Wordsworth Donisthorpe.

The next few months would be a defining moment not only in Nellie's career but in her personal life as she began preparing for the first of seven operas which Harris had designated to her, beginning with *Romeo et Juliette*, followed a week later by *Lohengrin*, then *Lucia di Lammermoor*, *Rigoletto*, *Esmeralda*, *Hamlet* and finally *Carmen*. The shortest break between operas was just six days and the longest a fortnight.

She had less than a week to rehearse for Juliet, the role which had established her reputation the previous year. Her first performance on 3 June was before a packed house including the Prince of Wales and his family, Gladys de Grey by their side. She was hailed by the critics as one of the finest Juliets. If her 1889 performance had announced her arrival then the 1890 rendition entrenched her as the new queen of Covent Garden, as the *Pall Mall Gazette* concluded: 'Melba is now permanently associated with the opera and its striking success in London.'

Of more concern was Harris's encouragement that she perform the role of Elsa in the Richard Wagner opera *Lohengrin*, considered a risk by Madame Marchesi because of its heavy style that would not suit, and possibly even strain, her prize student's vocal cords. But in typical Melba style she decided to go ahead anyway and a week later, with only a brief rehearsal with a lone pianist, she won more plaudits.

'Melba has taken a cold house by storm,' the *St James's Gazette* quipped.

§||§

Nellie's growing friendship with the Prince and Princess of Wales was a double-edged sword. It opened doors socially and drew crowds to the opera which, in turn, made her a better commercial proposition for Augustus Harris. But it also came with expectations, as she discovered in early July when she and her male co-stars, the de Reszke brothers, Jean and Edouard, were asked to perform in private for Queen Victoria.

If the queen had been in residence at Buckingham Palace then the royal recital, set for 4 pm, would have been easy to accommodate but Victoria was ensconced at Windsor, an hour or more from the city by train. The Covent Garden performance was due to begin at 8 pm so there was just enough time to make the return journey, provided there were no delays.

The brothers were not performing that night so they were in high spirits as the train sped out of the city while Nellie sat drumming her fingers on the window pane, watching as green fields replaced lines of houses. She was clearing her throat in anticipation of the performance ahead, excited rather than nervous by the prospect of singing before the queen.

The problems began when they arrived at Windsor Station. The royal carriage that was supposed to take them to the castle had not been sent, so they made the trip up the hill in a rickety old cab driven by a reluctant man who seemed unsure of the correct entrance. Time was ticking as they were shown into an anteroom where they waited for half an hour before a courtier arrived to explain that the performance had been delayed because the queen's eldest daughter, the Princess Royal, had not returned from an afternoon drive.

Instead, the queen would listen alone, the courtier said as he led them into the castle. The woman who stepped forward to greet them was unexpectedly tiny given her towering reputation, still in mourning black for her long-dead husband with smooth silver hair pulled back that accentuated her heavy eyelids. As she shook their hands and politely discussed their careers, Nellie could hear the glass-cased mantlepiece clock ticking away the seconds.

The trio played and sang for forty-five minutes; solos and duets and a trio from the last act of *Faust*. It was 5.30 pm when they finished, just enough time to make it back to London. Nellie's sigh of relief was interrupted by a noise outside; the doors were opened by attendants and the Princess Royal walked in, her face flushed. To Nellie's dismay, the queen welcomed her daughter into the room: 'What a treat you have missed. We must have more for you.'

They were forced to go through the program a second time, their anxieties clearly impacting the performance, Nellie thought, fearing it had been rushed. *Faust* had sounded like Ragtime. Finally, the message was relayed to the Queen who called a halt to the program and ushered them next door for refreshments, which they left untouched as they rushed back to the station, luckily just as a train arrived.

The performance at Covent Garden had been delayed

by fifteen minutes by the time they arrived back; the audience restless and Augustus Harris, who was in the orchestra pit, an anxious mess. There was pandemonium backstage as Nellie quickly dressed, with little time for makeup and less for warming her vocal cords as she hurried onto the stage. Although the crowd hardly noticed, captivated by her rendition of 'Caro nome', the critics could sense a tiredness towards the end of the performance of 'a very hungry Gilda'.

On another occasion, Nellie was attending a lunch with the prince when a message came through from Augustus Harris asking if she could stand in for another soprano who was ill. 'Certainly not,' she told the messenger. The Prince of Wales, who was sitting across the table, smiled. 'I am going to Covent Garden myself tonight, so please, Madame Melba, send back another answer.' She did.

There was a price to pay if the royals were denied, as Nellie had found out when she opted out of performing at a formal Buckingham Palace concert, complaining of a bout of laryngitis. A few days later she attended a party hosted by Gladys de Grey where the Prince of Wales, normally friendly and boyish, snubbed her.

'After his fashion, he looked all around the room, bowing to his friends one by one, but when his eyes reached my corner he glanced at me coldly for a moment and then looked away,' she would later recall. 'Not a shadow of a smile, not even a hint of recognition crossed his face. I felt absolutely miserable and, thinking that everybody had noticed the slight, I sat down on a sofa and wished I could sink through the floor.'

Still worried the next morning, she asked Lady de Grey for an explanation. Apparently, the prince had been told that she was seen near the Thames 'enjoying herself' at the very time she was supposed to be performing at the palace. It was a dangerous moment, and Nellie knew it. She arranged a doctor's certificate and asked to see the prince at his Marlborough House residence the next day to explain herself.

'Are you sure?' he pressed when she declared she'd been in her sick bed and not down at the Thames. When she produced the doctor's note he waved it aside, seemingly satisfied.

They met again two nights later at a dinner party hosted by the wife of a visiting American businessman. Initially she feared the worst until the prince invited her to sit at his table, announcing: 'Madame and I have had a little misunderstanding but we have made it up and we are going to be great friends. Madame Melba, I drink to you.'

Her reputation was safe, the damage repaired, although Nellie Melba's world was about to be turned upside down.

# 15

# PRINCE GAMELLE

For a man raised to be the King of France, Philippe d'Orleans had an ordinary beginning to life, born in the quiet town of Twickenham on the western outskirts of London in 1869.

The family had been banished from France following the French revolution of 1848 that ended the reign of Philippe's great-grandfather Louis Philippe I and brought Napoleon III to power. They would spend the next twenty-three years in exile before Napoleon was defeated in the Franco–Prussian war and the family was welcomed back into Paris. Philippe, now two years old, would grow up believing that his father would ascend the throne as Louis Philippe II and that he would eventually follow.

But it was not to be, as the family was forced into exile once more in 1886, returning to London and the protection of Queen Victoria. The young Duc d'Orleans, now aged seventeen, was enrolled at the Royal Military Academy Sandhurst where he developed a flare for geography and natural sciences, interests that would play a big part in his later life. He had much to offer if the generous assessment published in July of that year was vaguely accurate.

'The young Duc d'Orleans has grown much of late years,' it began.

His face is intelligent and full of resolution and vivacity. His dark eyes look you full in the face with manly frankness. He has a resolute and decided disposition. He is an indefatigable walker, an excellent fencer, swimmer and rider, and a remarkably good shot. He speaks correctly and fluently four of the five languages.

Philippe would spend fourteen months in India after graduating, attached unofficially to the King's Rifles as a staff officer to Lord Roberts, Head of the India office, during which time he was almost mauled to death by a tiger. The incident was detailed in a book he published four years later, a boys' own adventure in which he and his cousin, Henri, joined a hunt in Nepal.

On the last day, an enraged male tiger leaped onto the back of an elephant he was riding forcing him to jump for his life while the tiger tore the howdah, a riding seat, to pieces. Recovering his composure, Philippe managed to shoot the animal which later measured almost two metres long.

The incident was reported in Paris with delight, the young duke seen as a sportsman of some note, but the publicity would present its own set of problems. What was he doing serving as a sub-lieutenant in the British Army? It would be the first of many such questions about a young man with no real future beyond a largely pointless military career.

Desperate for a role in life, and to match his father who had distinguished himself by serving in the Union Army during the American Civil War, Philippe went to Switzerland to complete a course in military theory. It was a short-lived venture and on 6 February 1890—his twenty-first birthday—Philippe left Switzerland by train with his friend the Duc de Luynes and travelled to Paris—a city his family was still banned by law from entering.

Although he travelled in disguise to enter the country this was not a covert journey, quite the opposite in fact as he presented himself by name to officials and demanded to be signed up to perform his three years of military service, as required by law of all men who had come of age. The shocked officer hurriedly sent him off to the city mayor who wanted nothing to do with the issue and sent him back to the recruitment barracks.

When he was rebuffed a second time, Philippe retreated to de Luynes' apartment where he penned and had delivered a letter to the Minister for War which prompted a farcical game of passing the buck, first to the Minister of the Interior, then the Governor of Paris and finally to the Commissioner of Police.

Philippe was chatting with friends when the gendarmes came knocking just after 7 pm. He was arrested and confined in the Conciergerie, the converted palace that once held Marie Antoinette, where, as one journalist noted wryly, he dined on partridge, sole à la Joinville, asparagus and peaches à la Conde.

Philippe's court appearance a few days later created a media furore, partly due to his dandy attire of a frockcoat with silk lapels and a fur-lined overcoat, glossy hat and black gloves. He was also sporting a bamboo cane with a silver knob. The newspapers editorialised according to their political perspective.

The Orleanist organ *Le Moniteur Universel* insisted he should be released and the charges dropped:

> His Royal Highness obeyed a patriotic inspiration, derived from the traditions of his race, to pay a debt which he owed to his country. He acted like a Frenchman and the Royalists greeted his manly youth with confidence.

But *Le Temps*, a republican journal owned by the prominent leftist writer Edmund Chojecki, advocated for a prison sentence and congratulated the prince 'for having faith in the Republicans and showing he is not afraid of being poisoned during his imprisonment'.

Others stood in the middle. The *Journal des Débats*, one of the city's most influential papers, backed the government's decision to prosecute but expected that, after being found guilty, he would be pardoned and escorted to the frontier. *Figaro* and *La Presse* agreed.

Philippe revelled in the spotlight, writing to President Marie Carnot from his cell to insist he was a patriot and pleading with him to allow the 'grandson of a soldier of Jemappes to serve his country', a reference to one of the early offensives of the French Revolutionary Wars. But his poetic appeal fell on deaf ears and when he was brought back before the court three days later he tried again, this time before the judges and a packed room at the Palais de Justice.

I wish to serve my country in a regiment. Is that a crime? I love my country. Is that a fault? No, I do not believe myself guilty. I have no wish to defend myself. I cordially thank my counsel for their devoted attention to my case, but I ask them not to defend me. I have learned in exile to honour the magistracy of my country, and I shall respect its decision. I expected no clemency, but if I am condemned I am sure of acquittal on the part of two hundred thousand conscripts of my class who, more fortunate than I, are able to serve their country.

Despite further pleadings from his counsel, the court accepted the prosecutor's argument that the prince had been caught *in flagrante delicto*—red handed—and therefore deserved no mercy and he was sentenced to two years' prison. The court erupted at the announcement with cries of 'Long live the army. Long live the Duc d'Orleans' as the magistrates tried to restore calm. The crowd, still chanting, poured out into the street, the guards unable to stop them as they paraded through central Paris decrying the decision.

Overnight, Philippe had become a quasi-political hero. Crowds gathered beneath his window at the Conciergerie where working men doffed their caps to the man they now called Prince Gamelle, in reference to the drinking bowl used by common soldiers in the mess. They were probably unaware that inside, *le premier conscrit de France* was able to receive and entertain guests, order meals from the finest Parisian restaurants, which he and his friends ate from plates adorned with the Royal d'Orleans crest. He was even allowed visits from Princess Marguerite of Orleans, his first cousin with whom he had become engaged.

There were many in the Republican establishment who argued that the 'precocious pretender' was simply grandstanding and deserved to be punished but they could not explain why he would chance a prison sentence to make a political point and were worried that his cult status was making the royalists more popular.

The mood was helped by newspaper profiles. Stories emerged of his days at Sandhurst and his ability to adapt when he arrived: 'Full of life and good nature, he is a warm friend and a devoted brother,' gushed one reporter, quoting one of Philippe's Sandhurst friends. Newspapers in Switzerland also weighed in with glowing reports of his time in Lausanne, describing his diligence and quiet, studious ways and politely ignoring a romantic dalliance with a waitress at the local casino.

The French Cabinet called an emergency meeting while monarchist deputies demanded that President Carnot pardon the would-be king. As the weeks passed, shopkeepers began displaying his photograph in their windows behind gilt grilles to imitate prison bars.

But Carnot held firm and arranged for Philippe to be transferred to Clairvaux Prison west of the city where he spent most days in the prison garden and entertaining visitors. The prison director, a Monsieur Arnaud, was in constant fear of being accused of poisoning his illustrious guest or him falling ill from indigestion caused by the local snails fattened on grapevines that Philippe ordered by the dozen from nearby restaurants.

But for all the pampering, Philippe still felt the frustration of confinement, something he made clear the day a large bouquet of flowers from supporters was placed in his cell. Angrily, he kicked the flowers across the room yelling '*Tant de fleurs, et si peu de liberté*'—so many flowers, and so little freedom.

Carnot would hold out for almost four months before mounting public opinion finally forced his hand and on the evening of 3 June, Philippe was smuggled onto a train and escorted to the Swiss border near the city of Basel.

But the attempt to smother any publicity failed. By the time, the train reached the Swiss border in the early hours of the following morning, the newspapers had already been briefed and detailed accounts of the duc's fond farewells to his jailers published.

The prince, who later sent 1000 francs to be divided among his fellow prisoners on their release, handed out souvenirs to the guards and, after waiting in the station master's office because of a late train, gave him the pin from his neck tie that he had worn in captivity. Even Monsieur Morin, the police commissioner who escorted him to the border, was obliging as he turned his back while Philippe sent a telegram to his father telling him he was being released and was on his way to London.

He also dictated a statement to be released to the newspapers which read in part: 'The act of clemency restores me to the bitterness of exile. I do but change one captivity for another. My resolution remains unshaken, nothing will make me abandon my ardent hope to serve France. I will come and claim it. With you for God and France.'

His words and threats to return to France only fed the public mood. The government had overplayed its hand and given the young prince a public following that might come back to haunt them, as press baron Arthur Meyer, owner of *Le Gaulois*, wrote: 'The prince was thrown into prison. He had neither to refuse nor accept imprisonment. He endured it. He had neither to refuse nor to accept pardon. He endured it.'

*Le Figaro* went further: 'Clemency is an act of justice which arrives too late, and cannot diminish the deplorable effect produced by the pharisaical application of an iniquitous law to a spontaneous and chivalrous act.'

As the repercussions raged in Paris, Philippe boarded an overnight train for Luxembourg where he breakfasted with his uncle, the Belgian king Leopold II, and then crossed the Channel to arrive at Dover where he was greeted as a hero by family and friends.

The *Pall Mall Gazette* watched as the Comte de Paris rushed to embrace his son—'both appearing much moved by the reunion'—before the party moved to a local hotel and then London where they gathered at the family house. The duc's new home would be a house in Portman Square, Mayfair, rented 'for the season' although he was uncertain when his fiancée, Princess Marguerite, would join him.

On 9 June, just two days after his arrival, Philippe went to visit the Prince of Wales. The meeting was reported in several papers as a one-line statement, but even without details or content its purpose was clear—the British royal family was in full support of their French cousins. Edward was twenty years older than Philippe but he would become something of a mentor and protector in British society.

Their friendship was soon on show two nights later when Philippe joined the prince and princess at the Covent Garden opera. The star that night was Nellie Melba who was recalled three times after her performance of Elsa before being called to the royal box to be personally congratulated.

# 16

# A DIVA MEETS A DUC

Among the hundreds of pages of newspaper and magazine articles pasted into scrapbooks Nellie kept during her career there is an innocuous clipping from the *London Evening Standard* which reviewed a private concert at St James's Hall on the morning of 26 June 1890.

The story, which mentioned that Nellie sang to 'warm applause' and that Jean de Reszke had withdrawn citing a 'severe cold and hoarseness', seems out of place among the adoring performance reviews she collected, and yet she had inked it with a star to signal it was significant.

Most likely it was not because of the concert itself, held to raise funds for a pianist named Zoe Caryll, but because after the performance she had welcomed a royal admirer into her dressing room. It was Philippe, the Duc d'Orleans, who had been in the royal box at Covent Garden the previous week

149

when she was congratulated by the Prince of Wales.

Nellie may have been introduced to him on the night but, if so, it had been fleeting. Either way, it was clear that she had left an impression on Philippe and he had found an excuse to meet her.

The encounter did not end there, if the reports that reached the ear of the Prince of Wales were correct. After leaving the dressing room Nellie and Philippe spent the afternoon strolling along the banks of the Thames, deep in conversation. They were so engrossed they forgot, or did not even consider, that their meeting might be noted by others.

Both their photographs were sold from shops and street stalls, his for his youthful bravado and hers as 'the new prima donna of Covent Garden', as many critics were now calling her. Even if their friendship was innocent, as it was on that afternoon, it could easily be misconstrued by those with reason to gossip. After all, she was a married mother (albeit estranged from her husband) and he was a prince, engaged to a princess whose family would be outraged if he mixed romantically with a commoner.

There was obviously a physical attraction—Philippe was tall and square-jawed with a piercing stare and she radiated a confident, handsome if unconventional beauty—but even though there was eight years between them (he was barely twenty-one and she had just turned twenty-nine) the bond seemed to be driven by something more profound, as he would write many years later: 'You know me and understand me.'

It is not hard to imagine the conversation they might have

had as they walked, the weather a balmy 25 degrees Celsius, as Philippe regaled her with details about his imprisonment and the frustrations of living in exile from the country he loved, and she recounted her journey from the tropical rain of northern Queensland to the salon of Mathilde Marchesi and the stages at the Palais Garnier and Covent Garden. They both had faced fierce obstructers who sought to deny them their chosen path in life. Neither had been prepared to bow to convention and both believed they had been miscast as peacocks.

It is doubtful that their respective partners were mentioned or dwelled upon. They were too interested in each other and, besides, Charlie was back in Australia developing his horse stud and uncertain when or if he would return, and George was staying at Rustington, while Philippe's marriage plans were in some doubt because of a disagreement between the two fathers-in-law. Nellie's marriage was the product of hasty lust, now regretted, and Philippe's, if it went ahead, the product of creaking aristocratic tradition.

They parted company because Nellie had to get back to Covent Garden and prepare for her performance that night. She was singing the role of Gilda in a production of *Rigoletto*.

Nellie's summer had been thrown into confusion. An illicit romantic relationship had been the last thing on her mind when she arrived in London. If the weight of expectation at Covent Garden and seven operas wasn't enough, she was also being bombarded with invitations to sing for society. It was something she had normally refused or charged fees that would dissuade the inquirer.

But the season of 1890 was different. She was in demand, already negotiating a new contract that would double her nightly fee in London and she had finalised a trip to Russia where she would sing for the emperor, Alexander III. There was even talk of an Australian tour, a titbit seized upon by Australian media, which had suddenly realised that the young singer who had left Melbourne four years before had achieved her dream and become a star.

It was impossible to ignore the swathe of lunches, dinners and balls during the summer. Not only were there royal commands but she felt obliged to her friend and protector Lady de Grey, which invariably meant attending functions, often squeezed in between rehearsals.

Two days after her encounter with Philippe, she was one of the singers hired for a party for a visiting Australian businessman named Robertson who had paid an astonishing £5000 for the Covent Garden cast to perform for his guests. There was also a private concert hosted by the Rothschild family, and others at the home of Mrs Henry Oppenheim, the Duchess of Manchester and of course at Lady de Grey's Mayfair house.

Philippe would also have been on the guest list at some of these events; in fact, Nellie would make a fleeting reference to the attendance of the d'Orleans family in her autobiography, published in 1925, in which she wrote of the lavish society balls: 'The whole of the great families of Europe seemed to be gathered together—Bourbons [Orleans family], Marlboroughs,

Romanoffs, Rothschilds—in one immense procession of magnificence.'

The link between them frequently appeared to involve the Prince of Wales who prevailed upon Nellie (via an entreaty from Gladys de Grey) to sing at Marlborough House one afternoon before attending a ball to which the duc was also invited. It was almost as if the future king of England was aiding and abetting the liaison, which was hardly surprising given his own history of affairs with at least three women, including the actress Lillie Langtry.

Philippe seemed relaxed by his upcoming marriage to Princess Marguerite, who had still not arrived in London. Questions were being raised behind the scenes about the proposed union, not over Nellie, which was still a secret, but because his father had also married his first cousin and there was concern about consanguinity (as they were descended from the same ancestors).

Nellie, too, felt unabashed about the liaison. Charlie had abandoned her and George and there was no sense about when, or if, he would return. For the moment at least she felt free. She was a young woman used to adoration at a distance, roses cast at her feet by strangers and royal waves from gilded balconies, but she must have craved physical affection without the threat of a slap or a kick. How could she resist the attentions of a handsome man who was interested in her as a woman and her talents, and not likely to raid her purse?

Although they resembled one another physically, Philippe d'Orleans was the antithesis of Charlie Armstrong in manner.

Hotel Metropole staff, who averted their eyes, became accustomed to the sight of the athletic French prince as he became a frequent overnight visitor over the next few months.

Although many would demean his interest as merely lustful, it was clear that Philippe had a love of opera and knowledge of singing, as Blanche Marchesi would discover in 1896 when she met the duc after one of her rare appearances at Covent Garden. 'Had I not looked at the program I would have known after the second bar that I had a pupil of your mother, the great Marchesi, before me,' he told her. 'I detect her pupils immediately. Her method is striking and cannot be mistaken.'

Apart from their stroll along the Thames, the enamoured couple took to heart the lessons of discretion, particularly as Philippe was being watched closely by French journalists. Among them was Arsène Houssaye, a famed writer, theatre critic and self-described 'man about Paris' who noted that Philippe's parents, the Comte and Comtesse of Paris, had taken a box at the opera house for the season although it was their son who occupied it most nights.

'The young Duc was always there,' he would later write for *L'Artiste* magazine.

He seemed fascinated by her [Melba's] singing or by her beauty, I don't know which. No one supposed he was trying to make love to her, however. Nor was there anything to excite comment in his attendance and evident admiration. The Prince of Wales also went almost every night, and indeed she drew more eminent personages to the opera than Patti herself has done in recent years. Then she was invited to sing before the queen at Windsor Castle and of course after that it was the proper thing for everyone who was anyone to go and hear her as often as possible. And besides all that she was, and is, one of the best singers in the world.

Jacques St Cere, correspondent for *Le Figaro*, was intrigued when the prince began hanging around the cast members from the Covent Garden opera, noting that he developed a daily routine of fencing every morning with a baritone named Jean Lassalle, who sang alongside Melba in the opera *Esmeralda*, after which Philippe often ate breakfast with the de Reszke brothers. What was even more strange was that 'Le Petit Duc' had given the brothers lodgings at his house in Portman Square 'on an equal footing', an act which St Cere regarded as the prince demeaning himself.

But nothing appeared in print, at least not at the time. When St Cere's account was finally published the following year, he would pen a scathing review of Philippe's 'boisterous manner' and dress habits, observing:

I saw him one morning in grey coat, grey hat, pink cravat and a gigantic rose in button hole; very noisy, laughing loudly and drinking a glass of wine which was offered him. I watched him out of curiosity, wondering if I could find in him traces of a princely race and proof of a great origin. I saw nothing. While gaping at him I noticed that he had a bracelet of leather on his wrist and a watch in it, like a woman. That was enough.

Do what he may, he will never do anything serious. When one is descended from a King of France one acts and dresses accordingly, especially if one desires to play a political role.

As for Melba, St Cere dismissed the romance as an 'amusement' but acknowledged that, behind the scenes, the Comte de Paris was struggling to convince his son that he should go ahead with the 'political' marriage with Princess Marguerite, who was also his first cousin. 'When he met Mme Melba one day he thought no more of marrying the Russian grand duchess than the princess.'

❈

The workload of seven operas was taking its toll on Nellie physically, and as July rolled on towards August, Jean de Reszke began to notice a 'ping' in his co-star's vocal cords which had begun to impact on her performances.

Nellie initially dismissed his concerns but eventually relented and sought the advice of Felix Semon, a laryngologist whom Augustus Harris employed to take care of his singers. Semon discovered a nodule on her larynx and ordered her to rest in the hope it would shrink. Nellie had little choice and on 28 July she pulled out of the last concert of the season, a production of *Carmen* for which she had rehearsed the role of Michaela against advice.

It was a disappointing end to an otherwise spectacular season as she farewelled Philippe and headed to Switzerland to recuperate in the village of Les Avants, high above Lake Geneva and known for its private health retreats, while he made a family visit with his mother and finalised plans to travel to America in September with his father.

The lovers would only be apart for a few weeks. In late September, after getting the health all-clear, Nellie joined Philippe at the Hotel Beau-Rivage where they spent three days before he returned to London and joined his father for their US visit.

On the surface the Hotel Beau-Rivage seemed a strange place to continue an adulterous affair given that she, Charlie and George had stayed there the previous year. Then again it was here, after the candlestick argument, that she had decided the marriage with Charlie was finally over. Three nights with her royal lover, who had booked in under the name Monsieur Revelle, seemed a poetic and fitting revenge.

## 17

# TO RUSSIA WITH LUST

The activities of the Duc d'Orleans had become something of a media sport in the first days of 1891. There were newspaper reports that he had applied to join the Russian Army but had been rejected, one even claiming that Tsar Alexander III had personally intervened, scoffing that 'our magnificent armies are not an asylum for an exiled prince'.

There were also reports that he had sailed to Lisbon to stay with his brother-in-law, King Carlos of Portugal, and had refused to attend a family wedding in Germany. He was also supposed to be planning an 'equestrian journey' across the wild frontiers of Asia to Afghanistan, and made another to the northern foothills of the Caucasus where he hunted bears, getting as far as Tbilisi, the capital of Georgia.

In fact, Philippe was in St Petersburg, having travelled to Russia under the pseudonym Comte de Nevers, and he hoped to reconnect with Nellie who was due to sing before the tsar. The impetuous young man's arrival had been unannounced but was eventually smoothed over diplomatically as he checked into the Hotel de France and lunched at the Winter Palace before joining a wolf hunt on horseback with Grand Duke Vladimir, the tsar's younger brother.

Philippe had left home after a blazing argument with his father. His marriage to Princess Marguerite was off, and he was now insisting that he should be able to choose his own wife rather than have a political arrangement foisted onto him. He hoped to find a wife among the princesses of the European courts but if there was none to his liking then he 'felt at liberty to choose a girl of good lineage who is already a Roman Catholic or willing to espouse her husband's religion', as the confrontation, leaked to several newspapers, was reported.

The Paris correspondent for the *London Times* observed: 'The young duke has decided to play a very original part in the social history of European Royal families. His moral sense is very high, and he has a decided will of his own.' The report added there were rumours of a 'deep attachment' to a young lady from one of England's best families who, alas, had no fortune and was not interested in her admirer.

Some newspapers were starting to get to the heart of the matter, including the *Manchester Evening News* which reported that 'the son of the Comte de Paris has fallen madly in love with a well-known operatic star, who is mysteriously described as Madame M. He met and became infatuated with the singer in London and is now accompanying her to St Petersburg.'

For the moment, at least, the tryst with Nellie was still a secret but for how long?

Nellie, having recovered fully from the throat scare, had enjoyed a sell-out autumn season at the Palais Garnier and her career, in her own words, was like a runaway snowball careering down a hill as she fended off requests to sing all over the world. As much as she would have liked to refuse them all, it made no sense because her reputation could melt away as easily as it was formed.

She felt comfortable living in Paris where she and George were now settled in a sprawling apartment on the Champs-Élysées and enjoyed a social life brimming with the arts. There was still no word from Charlie about when he would return to Europe so she was not concerned about being seen with Philippe again.

Nellie travelled by train to Russia with the de Reszke brothers who would accompany her in the three chosen operas—*Romeo et Juliette*, *Faust* and *Lohengrin*. The two-day journey was without incident until the train reached the Russian border where guards, unaware that they were guests of the tsar, decided to search their luggage. Or rather, ransack it. Nellie had been asleep but was woken by the shouting and looked outside to see that a cloak made for her to wear in the *Lohengrin* performance had been tossed into the snow. She tried to appeal to the Customs officers but it was only the intervention of a Russian passenger that saved the costume.

St Petersburg was a city of unspeakable sadness. A silence hung over its main square as she arrived to check into the Hotel de France in the half light of dusk. The quiet was broken only by a sleigh bell as she watched a homeless man vigorously rubbing his ear with snow to ward off frostbite. It made her feel melancholy, far from her family and friends; a loneliness she rarely felt in the adrenaline-packed world of performance.

But she was soon swept along by the 'glittering barbarous hospitality' of her Russian hosts who ate from gold plates and showered her with gifts—diamonds and sapphires and rubies and gold—that only emphasised the poverty she had witnessed outside. She met the ageing maestro Anton Rubinstein, who despite being almost blind managed to accompany her on the piano, and she marvelled at the 'fiery' Russian ballet.

The crowds warmed slowly to her performances of Juliet and Marguerite, but the response to Elsa on the third night was so overwhelming that a chair had to be brought backstage so she could sit and rest between countless recalls. One critic counted thirty-three of them.

As Nellie left the theatre that night crowds swarmed about her in the snow, waving programs to be autographed. It was a surreal scene, dreamlike in its beauty as she borrowed a pencil from a young man while others laid their coats on the ground like a carpet for her to walk across. Despite the frenetic desire no one touched her as she signed programs and made her way along the line of coats to the carriage which, she realised, had been filled with orchids.

She turned before climbing aboard, searching for the man who had given her the pencil. Somehow he had kept pace with her, hoping his prize would be returned to him. He reached out and took it, then snapped it several times between his teeth. As she rode away she watched as he handed out the broken pieces to his friends as if it were a religious relic.

Although Philippe was staying at the same hotel, he would not have accompanied her to the royal palaces. But he made his presence felt for the wrong reasons on the first night of the opera when, after her performance as Juliet, he leaped to his feet and began cheering. In his wild enthusiasm, Philippe seemed to have forgotten that members of a royal family led the applause if they were in attendance.

The tsar was furious. Theatre staff asked Philippe to leave but he refused, insisting that he explain his mistake personally to the tsar. But when he attempted to enter the royal box the grand duchess blocked his entry and advised him to leave quietly. News of the diplomatic incident reached Paris a few days later, several reports saying that Philippe had also been asked to leave the city.

❈

Discovery of their affair was inevitable, particularly in light of Philippe's ill-advised public display of enthusiasm for his lover. The society code of discretion had been smashed and they would pay the price of media pursuit as they left St Petersburg, bound for Vienna where Philippe had secretly booked two rooms at the Hotel Sacher, home of the famed Viennese cake, the Sacher-torte.

Yet again, discretion could have ensured secrecy but they could not help themselves, horseriding in the Vienna Woods, promenading at the Prater amusement park and dancing to Johann Strauss in the coffee houses of the Volksgarten Park. Being seen as a couple was playing with fire, even in a city where neither was well known.

It all came unstuck when they attended the Austrian opera, the Wiener Staatsoper, one night to see a performance of *Lohengrin*. They might have gone unnoticed except that Nellie was dying to try out her new jewellery acquisitions, including a spectacular bracelet given to her by the tsar which had her name engraved in diamond cubes, spaced apart by pearls strung together with a chain of platinum and gold.

It was a mistake. Austrians tended to go to a performance in the early evening before going on to dinner, which required practical evening clothes rather than the finery worn to attend an opera performance in Paris, Milan or London. Nellie in a low neckline—a *largement décolleté* as it would be described—stood out among the Viennese women in high-necked dresses, as did Philippe in white tie, swallow tails and a nosegay.

The Belgian tenor Ernest van Dyck, who was singing the lead that night, had a habit of surveying the house from behind the curtain before a performance. Looking out through a peephole, he recognised Nellie sitting in one of the boxes with a young gentleman. Intrigued, he told a journalist he knew from the local paper, the *Vienna Tageblatt*, who decided that the appearance of the famed singer and her guest, quickly identified as the young Duc d'Orleans, was worth adding to his article to be published the next day.

Before doing so, he decided to check with Blanche Marchesi, who was living in Vienna at the time and also singing with the opera. Yes, she confirmed, it was Nellie Melba. Despite having misgivings about her mother's favourite, Blanche tried to dissuade the reporter from writing the story. She failed.

The next morning Blanche sought out Nellie at the Hotel Sacher and showed her a copy of the article. It read, in part:

> Viennese society was very surprised in the course of the performance to see in one box a conspicuous woman covered in diamonds and very décolleté, truly a gala toilette, accompanied by a young, fair-haired man correctly dressed . . . The court party itself was upset and it was discreetly made known to the duke that his conduct was the cause of unfavourable royal comment.

Their cover was blown.

❧

Charlie Armstrong was in Paris; lean, tanned and impatient for his wife's return from Russia. He had arrived in London several weeks before and spent time in Rustington grieving for his mother who had died the previous year, her demise sudden enough to ensure that travel from northern Queensland in time to see her before she passed away was impossible.

It was not the only reason for Charlie's journey. He wanted to see his son, of course, but it was Nellie, or his pride in their marriage, that had brought him back. The horse stud was finished and it was time to make a final plea to his wife, perhaps negotiate a compromise that meant she would agree to come back to Australia for a period each year.

As he stood at the windows of the apartment, wondering why she was delayed, he must have watched the pampered crowds strolling the Champs-Élysées below. These were not his kind of people and neither should his son be exposed to their twaddle and bohemian ways. George, now aged seven, was old enough to be in England at a decent boarding school, like Charlie's old school at Worthing.

Charlie was not aware of the hushed whispers about his wife and the duc, and not fluent enough in French to read the snippets that had begun to appear in the Paris newspapers. And no one was going to raise the rumours with him personally.

He now knew that his mother had been wrong to keep reassuring him that all would be well, and that he was never going to persuade Nellie to come home and be the wife he wanted and expected. Her damn career had killed whatever relationship they had, and if he couldn't have her then he was going to make sure he got what he believed was his fair share of her earnings.

Their eventual reunion in Paris was unpleasant, and it was not long before his resentment over her independent and flamboyant lifestyle spilled over into open hostility. When Nellie objected to Charlie's demand that George be sent to an English boarding school, he thrust his fist in her face: 'I'd kill you except I would hang if I did.'

George had now become a weapon in the war between his parents as Charlie convinced the boy to take sides—'if your mother hits you then I will hit her'—and threatened Nellie that he would take their son back to Queensland, because it was his right as the father. Fearful that she was powerless to stop him, Nellie yielded to his demand that George be sent to boarding school and handed over £800, enough for Charlie to buy several dozen horses for his property. It seemed a small price to pay as he made plans to leave.

On the morning of 19 March Nellie accompanied Charlie to Gare du Nord so he could take the overnight train to London and then board a steamer for the six-week voyage back to Sydney. They were accompanied by a valet who carried Charlie's luggage from their carriage and set it down on the platform outside the Customs office.

What followed was farcical. After stilted goodbyes Nellie returned to her carriage with the valet, followed by two policemen who had been informed quietly by Customs officers that the man pretending to be a valet was, in reality, the Duc d'Orleans, who was sneaking back into the country disguised as a manservant for his lover. Their suspicions were raised because the man's bearings were 'much loftier than his station'. The police followed Nellie's carriage at a distance and then watched the apartment for two days before deciding that the duc had probably left the city.

The story was leaked a week later, sparking an outrage among Republican papers which were angry that the exiled prince would be audacious enough to come back into the city so soon after his imprisonment while the royalist papers were angry that Philippe had stooped to dressing as a servant just to be with a woman, and a commoner at that. The Minister for the Interior, Jean Constans, added weight to the story by demanding that the duc leave the city immediately or face arrest. The next day Philippe was said to have fled to Brussels.

In all the hubbub, no one seemed terribly concerned about the affair itself.

The growing scandal reached London a few days later when the *Pall Mall Gazette* reported that the duc had been smuggled into the city by Nellie, but the report was contradicted a few days later by the *St James's Gazette*, which insisted that there had been a mix-up, and that the man they assumed to be the duc was, in fact, Nellie's husband. The two men, both tall and athletic, could be easily confused for one another.

Normally not far from the headlines, Philippe had 'disappeared' and nothing had been heard from him since he had left St Petersburg. In the last days of March he reappeared, issuing a statement through the royalist paper, the *Paris Gazette*, denying that he had been in Paris and claiming to be almost 5000 kilometres away, in Tbilisi, on a hunting trip. He also denied the affair, blaming it on what he called French political partisans wanting to injure the Orleanist cause: 'He admits he has the highest admiration for Madame Melba's brilliant talents and that he has visited her in a box at the opera but he denies he lived at the same hotel.'

Nellie had remained silent when the story broke but finally responded by revealing that she had instructed her lawyers to 'detect and bring to justice' the person who had concocted the canard. And the shadow of suspicion fell on operatic colleagues:

'Madame Melba has been too successful to escape having numerous enemies,' the Paris correspondent for the *London Weekly* wrote. 'It is a great triumph to hold the first place at the Grand Opera in Paris and many of her less successful rivals cannot forgive her.'

Nellie had her own theory, as she told Robert Sherard one day while showing him a series of stories—'offensive paragraphs'—being published back in Australia. Emma Eames was behind it, she believed. Sherard, who by chance had been a school friend of Philippe, told her not to feed the frenzy by responding. Her career would ensure that she would rise above the scandal, he insisted.

Nellie's concern was not helped by news from London that Eames had been hired to sing at Covent Garden. A columnist for the theatre magazine *London and Provincial Etr'acte* observed:

I have a feeling that the engagement of Miss Eames will not exactly please Madame Melba. But as the latter does not appear on the scene for a month or two, the American newcomer will be able to do her spiriting before the arrival of the Australian diva.

Nellie was wrong about Emma Eames. It was true that there were enemies at work here but they were Philippe's foes, not hers. And if anyone was to blame ultimately then it was the young couple themselves. Both knew the social dangers their relationship presented and it seems naive, to say the least, if they expected to be able to flaunt their love in public around the hotels and theatres of Europe without being recognised and outed.

Then again, perhaps they didn't care. They soon would.

While newspapers in London, Paris and now Sydney and Melbourne openly discussed Nellie's failed marriage and indiscretion there was one person who was still in the dark—Charlie Armstrong, whose ship had just navigated the Suez Canal.

## 18

# MELBA NIGHTS

In the early hours of 12 April 1891 a fire broke out at 97 Avenue des Champs-Élysées. It spread quickly, the swirling flames and smoke blocking exit stairs for residents, many of whom ended up crawling out of windows and clambering across shop awnings to reach the safety of the pavement.

A crowd gathered outside and ladders were brought to rescue those trapped in the upper floors. There was shouting and excitement but no sign of panic. Everyone seemed accounted for as they waited for the horse-drawn fire brigade to arrive and douse the blaze.

All of a sudden the mood changed when someone realised that the building's most famous resident, the diva Madame Melba, was still inside. Smoke was beginning to fill her windows on the top floor as one brave soul repositioned a ladder and climbed up to her bedroom window, past the flames now licking at the frame, and smashed the pane with his clenched fist.

The man climbed inside to find the singer collapsed on the floor overcome by smoke. 'Apologies, Madame, but my business is pressing,' she would recall him saying as he roused and then guided her through the darkened room to the window before helping her descend the ladder to the street; the social shame of being seen in her nightdress and slippers forgotten in the emergency. The only thing Nellie brought was her jewellery box as she was whisked away in a cab to Mathilde Marchesi's house in nearby Jouffroy Street.

It was only the beginning of the drama. The city woke the next morning to news of the fire and the disappearance of the singer. Rumours that she had died quickly took hold, as the *Australian Star* in Sydney would report in dramatic fashion two days later.

For some time there were no definite particulars of the fire and its possible terrible import to the world of melody. Vague rumours were waved through the capital of the French to the effect that the great singer had been a victim to the remorseless conflagration and that she had been cremated alive, and that her wondrous voice had pealed forth for the final time in a shriek of death amid the flames of the doomed hotel. Not alone was Paris thrown into a fever of consternation, but the rumour was quickly and as indefinitely telephoned to London by recently completed batteries and telegraphed all over the Continent.

When she learned of the growing public concern, Nellie emerged to reassure people that she was safe and to tell the story about escaping a fire that had destroyed most of her possessions. She was alive but the experience had brought on a severe cold and she had to abandon her performance schedule for the time being.

But speaking publicly meant it was now impossible to avoid questions about her relationship with Philippe and whether she had smuggled him into Paris. Another crazy story had emerged in recent weeks, that she had brought him across the German border dressed as the driver of her carriage. Nellie dismissed both accounts and scoffed at the idea that they were having an affair, conceding only that the duc had followed her across Europe like a puppy.

'He is a mere boy, and it is cruel to link his name to mine.'

There was, of course, an upside to the rash of stories about a servant prince, illicit love and a narrow escape from death. It was bruising, personally and socially, but it was also publicity that a performer couldn't buy, and the directors of the Palais Garnier pleaded with her to return and complete her season of *Romeo et Juliette*. The crowds were clamouring to see and hear her, now a celebrity sinner as much as a singer.

Two weeks later, as she looked over her charred apartment and water-logged Érard piano, she received an offer of £30,000 from English impresario Colònel James Mapleson to visit America. Nellie's world was expanding.

♩♫

Montague Armstrong first learned of his famous sister-in-law's adultery from a whispered conversation overheard in the lounge bar of his London club. Challenging the speaker to provide proof of his gossip-mongering, he was shown an article in the *Pall Mall Gazette* that convinced him the stories were true.

By the time Charlie had stepped ashore in Melbourne on 29 April he had not only digested an urgent telegram sent by one of his older brothers but he had penned an understandably angry letter to his estranged wife who had just arrived in London from Paris to prepare for the new season at Covent Garden.

Nellie had moved into an apartment at 19 Ashley Gardens in Westminster; recently built and perfectly positioned for the season and its social whirl. The apartment was modern and luxurious for its time, with hot and cold running water and electric lights—the epitome of what George Bernard Shaw would later call 'The New'.

Shaw was well acquainted with Nellie and, in his role as a theatre critic for *The World*, had expressed reservations about her singing talents. Coincidentally perhaps, he would set his 1893 play *The Philanderer* at Ashley Gardens. The opening line reads: 'A lady and gentleman are making love to one another in the drawing room of a flat in Ashley Gardens.' He might as well have been writing about Melba and the duc.

Charlie's angry and threat-laden missive arrived as Nellie settled into the apartment and prepared for the opening night of *Romeo et Juliette* on 2 June. Given all the publicity of the past two months, she must have been expecting the day would come when Charlie found out about Philippe. Neither could she claim to be surprised by what she would later describe as her angry husband's 'violent and insulting' words. After all, fury and force had always been his modus operandi.

The written threats must have seemed empty given that he was on the other side of the world, although she still worried that he might try to take away her son. George was now attending boarding school, as she had promised. He was a shy boy, undoubtedly traumatised by his parents' unhappy relationship. He spoke English with a slight accent, which had immediately earned him a nickname of 'Froggie' that only exacerbated his self-conscious and awkward nature.

Nellie dreaded sending him back to school after they had spent the summer holiday together. Her own boarding school experience had been distressing, cut off from her family, and she did not want George to suffer in the same way.

The publicity about the affair had died down and London society seemed to be more accepting than Paris of their relationship, or was at least turning a blind eye to it. But not everyone was as open-minded. One critic offered about the upcoming season: 'It is hoped that Madame Melba's presence will not burden us with the society of that human remnant of the Orleans establishment who has been "going it" in one or two Continental capitals.'

Others, like the correspondent for the *Adelaide Advertiser*, thought it unlikely that the duc would appear.

Everyone is really waiting to go mad about Melba, who brings with her not only a noble voice but the prestige of a truly royal scandal. I scarcely think the Duke of Orleans will carry his admiration of the fair Australian's voice so far as to follow her to England, but should he wish to there is, of course, nothing to prevent him. Mr Harris would wish for nothing better. The 'Melba furore' would be immense.

He was right on one score and wrong on another. The public expectation about her arrival at Covent Garden had helped boost ticket sales for the season to their highest level ever and Augustus Harris had welcomed Nellie with open arms. But he was wrong about Philippe who arrived in London not long after Nellie and had taken rooms at 94 Mount Street in Mayfair, suitably distant from Westminster although they would soon be openly visiting each other's houses.

Philippe was in the audience at Covent Garden on Nellie's opening night. It was a triumph: extra chairs were packed into the orchestra stalls, which normally accommodated four hundred and fifty patrons, and more chairs filled the crowded alleyways. Newspapers across Australia carried the same excited Reuters report which noted that the Prince and Princess of Wales had been in the royal box for Nellie's performance and there had been numerous encores. 'The critics agree in declaring that her voice has increased in strength and volume,' the report crowed.

As powerful as her voice was that night, it was her acting that most critics noticed, with words like graceful and emotional replacing former observations about being wooden and stilted.

It was as if she had thrown off the shackles of expectation and had truly grasped her place at the forefront of opera.

The appearance of royalty that night was significant, a public declaration of their friendship and respect for Nellie and a clear signal that her affair with Philippe had a royal nod of approval.

The Prince of Wales had been in court during the day as a witness in what was to become known as the 'royal baccarat scandal'. It involved a card game played between a group of rich friends in a Yorkshire manor the previous year when one of the guests, Sir William Gordon-Cumming, had been found cheating. Gordon-Cumming pledged to never play again and then relented, accusing his friends of slander and taking them to court. He would lose the case but not before he forced the Prince of Wales to give evidence from the witness box, becoming the first royal brought involuntarily to court in more than four hundred years.

It had been a humiliating experience, courtroom sketches showing a rotund, unhappy man trying to avoid stares in a crowded room. Despite this, Edward insisted on going to the opera that evening to hear the soprano, to congratulate her publicly and then let it be known that she was invited to a private lunch at Marlborough House three days later.

Occasionally, newspaper social columns would mention Nellie and Philippe in the same account of a party or event, and their names both appeared among the most desired of the summer's society photographs that could be bought from studios for two shillings a pop. But it was at the opera where their infatuation was displayed publicly because Philippe was in the family box every night she sang, the unabashed cheer-leader for what would become known as 'Melba nights'.

Melba herself, rather than the opera, had become fashionable, according to *Fifty Years of London society, 1870–1920* whose unnamed author wrote of 'the average society woman': 'They think it horrid not to see Melba at least half a dozen times a year.'

Not only did audience members notice Philippe, but they would also speculate about the jewellery Nellie wore and whether the sparkling diamonds were gifts from her young royal admirer. On the last night she performed in *Lohengrin*, Nellie wore a fabulous cloak during the second act which was later identified as an heirloom worn by members of the Orleans family at royal functions. 'Has the refining influence of one born in the purple had any effect on the manners and customs of the fair cantatrice?' one syndicated columnist wondered.

There were other reminders of the different worlds they inhabited and the difficulties it presented, like the night Philippe attended a banquet at which the host had recreated the famed Roman feast of Heliogabalus, complete with an avenue of potted oak trees, a velarium supported by gold-leafed pillars, birds and roses, and marble nymphs. As the guests sat down to a sumptuous meal they could hear a band playing from the cellar beneath and the voices of singers concealed behind curtains—paid performers for the aristocracy.

Nellie Melba was among the performers.

## 19

# 'I'LL WHIP HIM AND SEE WHAT HE'S WORTH'

Charlie Armstrong had been stewing about his wife's disloyalty since getting his brother's telegram. Of all the challenges he had faced in his thirty-three years, this must have been one of the most testing; a physical man who was physically helpless, unable to confront and pummel the fellow who dared to try to steal the woman who he believed was his to keep as he desired. Charlie Armstrong was a swordsman, a horseman and a pugilist who desperately wanted to taste the tang of his opponent's blood but he was too far away. At least for the time being.

But it would be wrong to dismiss him as a barbarian. For all his apparent shortcomings, Charlie regarded himself as a man of character; quiet and resolute, he threw his lot in with the struggles of the common man rather than his aristocratic background, as one early Queensland trade union leader named Julian Stuart would recount, acknowledging Charlie's support during a court case over the famous 1891 shearers' strike that spawned the Australian Labor Party. As he sat in the dock, Stuart recalled seeing Charlie in the crowded room: 'He shouted cheery greetings, unawed by the men in blue who tried to silence him.'

There was another reason that Charlie was delayed in returning to London. In late July his brother George, the Melbourne doctor, poisoned himself by swallowing carbolic acid. The death caused newspaper headlines in Australia, as much because of its mystery as his horrific choice of death.

George's sister-in-law, Ellen, told the coroner that George was a healthy but nervous man; a teetotaller who didn't sleep well. He had been 'in trouble of late', she offered in evidence without elaborating, but had said nothing to her that suggested he might self-harm. In fact, he had gone to bed around 11 pm in what she thought were good spirits. But the next morning she found him dead, face down on the rug in his downstairs consulting room.

An autopsy revealed that George Armstrong, aged just forty-nine, had a healthy heart and lungs but a corroded stomach lining which the acid had eaten away. The coroner ruled it a suicide but said the cause of his desperate state of mind would remain a mystery.

As his only next of kin in Australia, it fell to Charlie to oversee probate, a task made more complex because George had not left a will; another sign that he had taken his own life on a whim.

Although there were sixteen years between them, the brothers had clearly been close. Their similarities could be seen clearly in a rare photograph of George, Charlie and Montague, probably taken at Rustington around the time of young George's christening, where they posed casually; three brothers with the same masculine air of don't-mess-with-me confidence.

Charlie was still in Melbourne in early August, increasingly anxious to get back to London and confront Nellie, but it would be early October before he had settled the estate, buried his brother and made the sea journey back to Europe. By the time he arrived, Nellie had left the city and gone back to Paris, taking their son with her.

Even more infuriating was the fact that Nellie, aware that Charlie was on his way, had filed for a legal separation and to bring George under the protection of the Chancery Court with high-powered allies, Lord Alfred de Rothschild and Earl de Grey, appointed as trustees. It was a provocative move, her only recourse according to the lawyers to ensure that Charlie could not carry out his threat to leave the country with his son without approval from the court. But if she thought that Charlie would simply give up without a fight then she was mistaken.

Still homeless because of the fire, she had settled into the first floor at Jouffroy Street under the protection of Mathilde Marchesi, who helped her prepare for the autumn season at the Palais Garnier. Her only public performance would be a fleeting visit to Brussels to make a special appearance at the Theatre de la Monnaie.

On the morning of the concert she was at a nearby hotel when Charlie, unannounced, arrived downstairs and demanded to see her. Hoping to avoid a confrontation, Nellie packed quickly, left by the back stairs and took the next train back to Paris while Charlie, who had been told that she could see him, waited patiently in the hotel foyer. The theatre manager was left with the task of announcing that she wouldn't be singing after all.

But it was only a matter of time before she would have to face her husband. Journalists lay in wait outside the Marchesi house and crowds grew each day as word spread across the city. Nellie's friends came to visit but were turned away as she bunkered down. But Nellie was delaying the inevitable and, on Friday 30 October, she was called to the door where, 'a smart London solicitor' stood with a folder of documents which she had no choice but to accept.

Charlie had upped the stakes, not only filing for divorce on the grounds of adultery but naming the duc as a co-respondent and demanding £20,000 in compensation. The journalists had got what they wanted, many reporting the next day that Nellie had taken the news badly, among them *L'Evenement*: 'Madame Melba was extremely affected by it, so much so that for an hour she was prostrated with a violent attack of nerves, followed by a long session of crying.'

Nellie had been struck by the reality of her vulnerable situation and what was on the line; not only her career, for which she had struggled so hard, but the almost certain loss of her son if Charlie won. Nothing about her life was ever going to be private again.

Philippe had disappeared on a hunting trip again, this time to the forests of eastern Czechoslovakia with Baron Moritz von Hirsch, a German financier famed for his canny investment in railways and admired for his philanthropy, and in particular his aid to Jews being hounded out of their homes and businesses. In 1891, a few weeks after Nellie and Philippe had been to St Petersburg he had created a multimillion-pound fund to help Russian Jews escape persecution and emigrate to America. Its impact would be felt for generations to come.

The visit, once again, appeared to involve the hand of the Prince of Wales, not only because he was a close friend of the baron but because he had also stepped in on Philippe's behalf to retain the services of George Lewis, one of London's best-known criminal lawyers who had represented the prince during the great baccarat scandal.

Charlie's lawyers got wind of Philippe's visit to von Hirsch and tried to serve him with the divorce documents by sending a man to the city of Brno near where the baron owned a castle called Veveri. But the attempt failed, the man turned away at the gate. Now alerted, Philippe was smuggled out of the country on a late-night train, bound for Vienna, only to find that news had leaked that he had arranged an audience the next day with the Emperor Franz Joseph at the Schönbrunn Palace.

Philippe was clearly not expecting to be recognised because, as he stepped from a train the next morning, he was approached by two men in evening dress who bowed and asked if they could present him with a petition. When he held out his hand, they gave him a bouquet and a roll of papers tied neatly with a ribbon.

He handed the flowers to a servant and unrolled the papers, expecting to read a petition for a cause for which he might agree. Instead, he saw the word *divorce* and flung the papers onto the platform, angry that he had fallen for the trap and shouting after the men as they hurried off. But the damage had been done and the papers, now scattered across the platform as his attendants scurried to retrieve them, had been served, which meant he had been dragged into an unseemly affair.

The incident sparked a rash of newspaper reports, fed by Charlie who was making himself available for interview and happy to speak candidly about his desire not only for revenge but to seek satisfaction.

A reporter from Dalziel's News Agency in London found him at the Hotel Belgravia in Victoria Street, just a stone's throw from Nellie's apartment, which gave the impression that he had placed himself where he could keep an eye on her comings and goings, and to confront Philippe if he chose to slip back into the city.

Charlie was daunting to interview, a tall, large man with hands that gripped like a vice and blue eyes made more intense by a Queensland tan. Clearly wary of his reputation as 'the finest fencer, cleverest boxer and the most deadly pistol shot in Australia', the reporter was careful in the way he framed his questions in case he upset his subject.

When had he become aware of the duc and the pursuit of his wife?

Charlie didn't answer immediately as he considered the sequence of events since he'd first confronted Nellie. It had been the root cause of their argument when she returned to Paris in the last days of February, although he hadn't known at the time that she had been with Philippe in Vienna on her way back from St Petersburg:

'I had heard that he was following her everywhere,' he said eventually.

I alerted Madame Melba that if this occurred again I would know how to end it. My wife begged me not to add to the contents of the newspapers and she told me that Madame Emma Eames was doing everything possible to harm her through pure professional jealousy.

The reporter pressed a little harder. If he wanted to reconcile with his wife then why had he filed for divorce?

Charlie's eyes hardened. 'She has taken recourse to the law to attempt to stop me from seeing my son, so I have decided that I too will service myself of the law to punish her.'

But the law would not be enough, he added, revealing that he had recently spent several days in the Buckingham village of Stowe near where the Orleans family now lived, hoping to find his adversary who he believed was returning to London. When he was asked by villagers what he was doing, Charlie had replied: 'Hunting small game but I've had no luck.'

'I want to duel him. I'll whip him and see what he's worth,' he told the Dalziel reporter.

The reporter had left his most delicate question to last. Nellie had filed a counter-claim in which she laid bare the behind-the-scenes details of their marriage, including Charlie's threats and violence. The affidavit made ugly reading. Did he want to defend himself?

Charlie's denial was forceful although it read a little stilted when translated and published the next day in *Le Petit Parisien*, one of France's most prominent daily newspapers.

> These accusations are completely false. I have never, ever delivered any act of cruelty against Madame Melba; not in Australia, not in any other place. It is very easy for me to prove this by her own letters that all the accusations that she made are absolutely false.

On the evening of 6 November, less than a week after news broke about the divorce scandal, Nellie made a reappearance at the Paris Opera where she played Ophelia in front of the biggest audience of the year.

She responded with a performance that Charles Gounod later said would ensure that she would be at the forefront of the great sopranos. The critics agreed, as the *Pall Mall Gazette* reported: 'Such enthusiasm has not been witnessed for many a day, and the fair prima donna was recalled numberless times.'

The thunderous response was too much, the pent-up anguish released as she walked onstage for her eleventh encore, but it only made the audience clap louder, *huzzaing* as Nellie recovered her composure and blew kisses left and right, her eyes streaming. Two nights later it happened again, this time when she was performing as Marguerite in *Faust* to a full house, many of whom had cheerfully paid a premium just to say they had been there on the night.

Far from being shunned by the allegations that she was a scarlet woman embroiled in a titillating entanglement, the divorce had become a *cause célèbre*, with details of Nellie's marriage problems providing context to her affair with the prince. Friends like Lady de Grey and Lady Lytton, wife of the French ambassador, made it known that they were supporting a woman who had been a victim of domestic abuse, even hosting a musical evening for 'all the great ladies of the French capital' including Madame Carnot, wife of the French president.

Nellie's affidavit, written in neat cursive script, provided graphic details of the repeated stormy confrontations between her and Charlie over the past eight years. Individually the incidents looked bad enough but collectively, it was shocking and left no doubt that the marriage had been a mistake long before Philippe arrived on the scene.

Nellie had been punched so hard in the face that she'd lost her hearing for several days, kicked in the legs until they bruised and struck in the back with a brass candlestick hurled across a room as she fled in fear. Charlie had chased her around a hotel room with a razor and even held a sword to her throat. There was extortion, bullying and threats but most shocking was the assault with the buggy whip back in Mackay just two months after the birth of George, who would witness much of the unhappiness between his warring parents.

Charlie's denials did not ring true. Instead of expressing some regret about their relationship, it was clear that he believed the incidents were minor and did not amount to violence or cruelty. He told newspaper reporters who sought him out that he had letters from Nellie which proved him right, but produced none of them.

Back in Melbourne, David Mitchell also played down the seriousness of the allegations, telling a friend: 'My girl Nellie had a bad temper and Charlie Armstrong had a bad temper. They lost their tempers on the same day.'

But many in the media felt differently. An editorial in the *Sheffield Evening Telegraph* was typical of the response:

Madame Melba is not going to sit down complacently under her husband's accusation . . . she has filed a counter-suit against her husband on the grounds of cruelty. Divorce proceedings in which so famous a songstress as Madame Melba was concerned must have made a sensation under any circumstances; but the appearance of a young prince as a co-respondent adds a thousand-fold to the piquancy of the affair.

Some took it less seriously, as the Paris correspondent for *The Globe* newspaper reported:

The divorce case in which the Duc d'Orleans and Madame Melba are concerned has occurred just in the nick of time for the gossips on the banks of the Seine who were beginning to despair of having something scandalous enough to expiate this season. That they are delighted is easy to understand, for it is not often that they have a prince of royal blood and heir presumptive to the throne of France to chatter about, and particularly when a charming and popular songstress is a character in the same story. Rightly or wrongly, society in Paris is not severe on them; on the contrary, there is an air of romance about them which goes to the heart of the French, who are nothing if not sentimental.

Nellie Melba was now being besieged by the curious and the sympathetic.

> She is tall and graceful, and her beauty is somewhat of the Southern type, with soft, large eyes and an abundance of flowing locks. On first sight she seems cold, but, as she warms up to her part, her classic features become animated, and it is then that her charms assume an irresistible sway over the audience.

If she wasn't already the most famous singer in the world then the divorce had given her the crown as the most marketable.

Offers poured in for the 'injured lady'. Augustus Harris found himself having to negotiate a new contract with his star, forced to compete with other London theatre owners who wanted to take her away from Covent Garden and present 'a season of Melba'.

Not only would he double her nightly fee but she also had a list of demands, beginning with only singing on two 'fashionable' nights a week and that she be allowed to select her own cast members. She demanded 'proper rehearsals', that her appearances would be advertised six nights in advance and that Harris was not allowed to heavily discount ticket prices. He agreed to them all, although Nellie was still hesitant about signing and delayed any decision.

The new manager of the Palais Garnier, Eugene Bertrand, conceded he would also have to pay her more, declaring that she could now command the same fee as Adelina Patti. Nellie also accepted a 4000-franc offer to sing at the opening of an international exhibition in Palermo and was renegotiating a tour that would include Australia and America, paying her an astonishing £600 a night.

But among the accolades, there were always reminders about a woman's role in nineteenth-century society. In September she agreed to perform at a grand society wedding ceremony at Notre Dame Cathedral. The prospect of one of the world's great voices soaring in such acoustic splendour should have brought tingles to the spine; instead it brought the wrath of the ageing Archbishop of Paris, Cardinal Richard, who didn't want a woman's voice to be heard inside the cathedral.

Rather than abandoning the idea, the mother of the bride persuaded Nellie to hide behind the organ where she sang while a choirboy stood in front of the audience and mouthed the words as if it were his voice. The 'ruse was an immense success' according to a report in the *L'Écho de Paris*.

Nellie also had to deal with the prejudice against the virtue of women who went onstage, as the correspondent for the *South Australian Register* wrote:

No one in France expects morality of a high order from any woman who goes onstage; the jealousy of an artiste's husband is to Parisians incomprehensible. If he really is jealous why does he let his wife expose her beauty, her charms, her talents to be gloated over night after night by hundreds of lascivious eyes, they ask.

**Nellie remained silent.**

## 20

# CROSSING BOUNDARIES

Philippe had managed to evade both the media and Charlie Armstrong but he couldn't outrun his own family who descended on Stowe House in London to confront their tear-away son, nephew and cousin. His taciturn uncle, the Duc d'Aumale, led the *interdiction judiciaire* along with leading political royalist Gabriel Paul d'Haussonville and a Monsieur Bocher who managed the duc's finances, prompting speculation that he was in debt and borrowing heavily.

The Orleanists didn't care about Philippe's sexual adventures, and even less about whether he was actually in love with this singer. The Comte de Paris and his closest advisors had turned a blind eye to Philippe's initial dalliance with Nellie, dismissed the clandestine meetings in Switzerland and Vienna as inconsequential, and they had smoothed over the diplomatic blunder in St Petersburg.

But the arrival of Charlie Armstrong had changed matters. The young prince's pursuit of a famous singer might have been viewed as a frivolous delight by many but it had become serious business when Charlie sued for divorce, and even more so when he issued a public challenge to a duel in order to defend his honour.

The comte had rejected the idea out of hand, not because he feared for his son's life but because he was of royal blood and Charlie was a commoner, the son of a minor aristocrat.

But there were those who felt the action cowardly, as one *Figaro* columnist had expressed:

If the Duc wished to stand well in French eyes he would not shirk a challenge from the lady's husband. That, rather than a cheque, might settle the point of honour. If he were mortally pinked France would have one medicine-man pretender less, but she lacks no saviours of society.

Philippe was ordered to lay low and banned from seeing Nellie. Instead, he went to Portugal and stayed with King Carlos for a few months. Could the lovers stay away from one another? The answer would be no.

Charlie, still in London, had also copped a varied public response to his legal challenge. Some saw him as a fearless avenger with every right to bring his errant wife to heel while others, shocked by the cruelty allegations, had decided he was an idle bully who lived off the success of his wife.

None of this bothered him much, of course, confident that

the law was on his side simply because he was the husband and father. If his wife wanted to pursue the matter then it would be decided by a 'special jury' made up entirely of men, and no one was in any doubt about which side the decision would fall. Certainly, the betting men of London who wagered on anything, including raindrops racing down a window pane, believed that a wronged man would always win over his wife.

Charlie shrugged off attempts by the duc's lawyers to settle matters, even when Nellie and Philippe agreed to sign a document that admitted there 'may have been an indiscretion'. Instead, he applied to the court to formally interview witnesses in Lausanne and Vienna who could confirm the incidents of adultery.

A waiter at the Hotel Beau-Rivage had come forward to say that he had recognised Philippe. The waiter's interest was piqued because of the obvious tete-a-tete between the prince and Nellie as they dined together each night. 'They acted like a couple,' he was reported to have said.

Charlie's investigators had also been to Vienna where they confronted the manager at the Hotel Sacher who confirmed, reluctantly, that Nellie had stayed at the hotel in late February. But the manager's demeanour changed when asked if the duc had also been a guest under the name of Monsieur Villiers, and if it was true that they had checked into adjoining rooms, numbers 34 and 35, which were connected by an internal door. Although the manager refused to breach the privacy of his guests, a chambermaid and two waiters were said to know more and might be willing to talk.

As 1892 beckoned, Charlie's lawyers petitioned the court in London to allow them to establish an independent commission in Vienna so they could interview hotel staff who, they believed, would corroborate the story. An Austrian court had already agreed to the idea, backed by the Emperor Franz Joseph who, still peeved at Philippe's behaviour in the Vienna opera house, had made it clear that he would not tolerate *Le Petit Duc* being given preferential treatment.

❦

The case had highlighted the complex lives of two people who were determined to be together despite efforts to stop them— 'The best years of my youth', Philippe would describe his love affair with Nellie many years later.

These were not the words to describe a romantic fling of no consequence, which continued to be the prevailing public reaction to their affair. No one seemed to take it seriously, partly because of their age difference but more so because of the practicalities of a member of the House of Bourbon kings marrying a commoner.

On legal advice, Philippe and Nellie publicly continued to deny the affair but, behind the scenes, and in spite of warnings from those same lawyers, they continued to find ways of seeing each other, if only briefly and in secret. After her performance in Palermo in January 1892, Nellie had travelled to Marseille where she had been booked for three performances before continuing along the coast to Nice, on the Riviera, for several more appearances.

In her 1925 autobiography, Nellie would claim that the visit was impromptu, caused because she only had £200 left in her bank account.

> I had no prospect of an immediate engagement, nothing. So I said to myself: 'I'll gammon. Nobody shall know I'm hard-up.' I went to Nice. I went with two maids instead of one, and took the best possible rooms in the best possible hotel. What would have happened if not for a stroke of luck, I do not know. Probably I should have languished in the debtor's prison. But it happened that Mr [impresario Maurice] Grau was at Nice for a holiday and said to me: 'Would you like to sing here this season?' With assumed indifference, I replied that I should not mind, but that I imagined all artists would have been engaged. 'Oh, I'm sure they'll be delighted,' he said, 'and I can get you four thousand francs a night.' I waved him away. 'I wouldn't dream of singing for anything less than five thousand francs,' I said. Well, I was given my five thousand francs.

It is clearly a fanciful tale, particularly as her appearance had been announced the previous November. The tale is made sadder by the fact that, almost thirty years after the event, she still could not bring herself to tell the truth about the love of her life. The hidden purpose of her trip to Nice—other than to refill her depleted coffers—was to meet Philippe who had arranged for a yacht to be moored outside Nice harbour, which served the dual purpose of ensuring that he did not step onto French soil and face arrest as well as hopefully enable them to be safe from prying eyes.

It seemed an especially romantic gesture, particularly as the city was in the midst of its annual carnival, which included a flower parade, the *Bataille de Fleurs*, during which dancing crowds shower each other with rose and carnation petals. Nellie was in the thick of it, in a parade float decorated with papier-mâché swans in deference to Lohengrin, the heroic knight of the opera who arrived in a boat drawn by a swan. The float won first prize.

Although Philippe had succeeded in not breaching his exile, at least technically, it seemed inevitable that Nellie would be spotted, particularly when she didn't return to her accommodation at the Hotel Westminster overlooking the Bay of Angels on the nights that she wasn't performing.

There were reports that she was being driven secretly north, across the border to the Italian city of Sanremo, to meet up with Philippe who had abandoned the yacht for a room at the Grand Hotel des Anglais where he had checked in under the name Crawshay. They were seen going on drives along the coast and through the countryside, and dining at the hotel, seemingly oblivious of a man named Tabourdin who had been hired by Charlie's lawyers to track Nellie's moves.

Tabourdin followed as Nellie was driven back to Nice—about an hour's journey—on the morning of each performance for rehearsal, before returning after that night's performance to her lover. Her bed at the Westminster remained untouched.

The cat-and-mouse game continued for a fortnight, even after newspapers were given titbits to publish in an overt bid by Charlie's lawyers to increase pressure in the courtroom back in London.

On 10 February 1892, the morning after her final concert, Nellie checked out of the hotel announcing that she was travelling to Marseille, only to be seen boarding a train for the city of Ventimiglia, on the Italian border, where she joined Philippe to catch another train bound for Genoa.

When confronted by newspaper reporters, Nellie ignored the questions about Philippe by insisting that she was not at liberty to discuss the divorce proceedings. Later, when she returned to Paris, she laughed off the stories as absurd. 'I did not see the Duc down there at all. As you know, he has been staying at the Portuguese Court with his father.'

Many years later, biographer Joseph Wechsberg revealed he had spoken to some of Nellie's friends about her relationships with men. One unnamed friend said she'd been in Nice at the time and had a 'terrible row' with Nellie. 'She had been seen constantly with a man there,' the friend told Wechsberg. 'People talked and I opened my mouth. I told her she was still married though she certainly had no husband. Nellie got mad and gave me a piece of her mind, and she gave it to me straight. Afterwards I never said anything again.'

Another friend admitted:

Of course, all of us knew about the Duc d'Orleans and none of us talked about him. He was the only man in her life who was really important. It was *La Traviata* all over again—the beautiful woman who loses the man she loves because his family steps in. A corny story, and one of her most famous parts—on and off stage.

Few believed Nellie's denials about meeting Philippe during the Nice concerts, including a furious Comte de Paris who announced that his son would embark on a cultural tour of Asia Minor. The press response was suitably cynical: 'His object is to place a substantial distance between Melba and the young man,' was typical of the reportage. In the end, the duc did not go.

❦

Despite her outward calm, Nellie was becoming distraught at the never-ending attention, which was beginning to affect her performances, most noticeably in Rome where she had travelled after farewelling Philippe in Genoa to sing at the Teatro Argentina, the city's main opera house. She would later reveal that anxiety had drained her voice of colour, something the audience sensed, according to the Dalziel's News Agency report, published back in London a few days later:

> The critics do not seem very favourable to Madame Melba. They consider that her performance was inferior to what her reputation had led them to expect. She has, they say, a limpid, agreeable voice, but that her intonation is rather monotonous.

But the audience also seemed aware that the controversy over the divorce probably contributed to the lacklustre appearance. 'It is generally thought that the extreme "putting" [pressures], which the prima donna received immediately before her appearance, accounts in some measure for the want of success attending the performance.' It was a rare critical setback as she headed back to the sanctuary of Paris.

American newspapers were now taking an interest in the divorce case. The *Chicago Daily Tribune* sent its correspondent to interview Nellie at her new apartment at 9 Rue de Prony, a fashionable address in the 17th arrondissement and a stone's throw from a large park where George would have space to play.

The correspondent found a fragile figure posing in a 'charmingly furnished' sitting room surrounded by bouquets presented to her the previous evening after a performance of *Hamlet*. The audiences in the French capital were kind, Nellie said, adding that she intended making the city her home when she wasn't touring. But her face fell when the journalist ventured on to the subject of Philippe and the divorce proceedings: 'The subject is the one which of all others is most unpleasant to me. I would rather not talk on that.' The conversation ended there.

Nellie was a singer, an artiste who set herself up for public scrutiny and judgement every time she walked onto the stage. She lived for the plaudits and bouquets and had smarted at slights, real or perceived. She took pride in her voice but knew that, as an actor, she was wooden, fighting to break free from the stoic, Presbyterian roots that welded her feet to the floor.

But these media judgements about her private life crossed the line. Where the French were liberal and the English were discreet, the Australian media seemed to take delight in ridicule. And some of the harshest words were made by women, such as Emily Crawford, a respected Paris correspondent for several newspapers, who insisted in a report published in Australia that Nellie had enslaved the young duc, and issued a cutting appraisal of her character and intellect.

'She is a lady of off-handed manners, rather playful than grave, with a will of her own but does not strike one as masterful,' Mrs Crawford had written.

> Her flow of animal spirits makes her agreeable socially. She has a deal to say about herself. All that she says arises out of the impressions of the moment or from the talk that is going on about her. There is not much in it for an interviewer to dress up into point. Yet it is pointed, and, if not exactly original, is not commonplace.

In her desperation Nellie wrote to her father, imploring him to ask the Melbourne newspapers to stop publishing stories. David Mitchell agreed to do so but this only seemed to add fuel to the fire as reporters not only revealed the request but threatened to publish Nellie's letter if they could lay their hands on it.

*Left to right:* Nellie (Helen) Mitchell and her sisters Belle (Isabella) and Annie (Ann).

Charlie Armstrong (right) with brothers George and Montague.

Nellie in her wedding dress, 1882.

Nellie and Charlie's Mackay homestead.

Nellie and George in Paris circa 1887.

Nellie pictured for her Brussels debut.

Nellie and her teacher
Mathilde Marchesi.

The 19th-century interior of Covent Garden
Opera House, where Nellie was a star.

Nellie's patron Gladys De Grey incorporated a 'slave' as part of her
fancy dress costume, which cost a rumoured £5000.

A fresh-faced Nellie as Ophelia in 1890, the year she met Philippe d'Orleans.

Nellie in her Paris apartment
in 1891.

Philippe became a
celebrity after being
imprisoned in 1890.

Philippe dressed to join the French Army in 1888. He would be called 'Prince Gamelle'.

LE DUC D'ORLÉANS DANS L'INDE

An artist's impression of Philippe in India, fighting off a tiger which had leaped onto his elephant.

An artist's impression of Nellie as Elaine in Bemberg's opera of the same name.

Nellie as Rosina in Rossini's *The Barber of Seville*.

Nellie as Marguerite from Gounod's *Faust*.

Nellie with her father David Mitchell in 1902.

The Duc, a sea captain, exploring the
Arctic Circle, circa 1909.

In 1904 Nellie was reunited with son George after more than a decade.

Philippe's polar bear exhibit in the Musée d'Orsay in Paris.

Nellie on her way to London in 1919 to reopen Covent Garden Opera House, where she would be reunited with Philippe.

In July 1920, Nellie became the first singer to record a radio program, with a rendition of 'Home Sweet Home'.

Nellie's funeral procession through Melbourne in 1931.

## 21

# *ARMSTRONG V ARMSTRONG*

George Lewis had a reputation for being a lawyer with a talent for managing to keep celebrity skeletons firmly locked away in the closet, so much so that he would earn a mention by Arthur Conan Doyle in the 1924 Sherlock Holmes novel *The Adventure of the Illustrious Client* for 'arranging that delicate matters be kept out of the papers'.

He was also proving his worth representing the Duc d'Orleans, co-respondent in *Armstrong v Armstrong*, by challenging Charlie's aggressive move to seek approval to conduct ex-parte interviews with staff at the Hotel Sacher in Vienna and lodge signed affidavits as part of his evidence back in London.

In the same week that Nellie and Philippe were dodging reporters and agents on the Italian Riviera, Lewis, a lanky and considered figure who sported a handlebar moustache and monocle, was telling High Court judge Sir Francis Jeune that

201

he should be concerned about the potential interference in the British justice system.

It was one thing to leak salacious stories about adultery to the newspapers and entirely another to present credible proof to a court of law. Evidence shouldn't be collected in such a fashion and admitted in court without the ability of other parties to cross-examine the witness.

His prodding worked as Justice Jeune took the bait and issued a restraining order blocking the planned interviews in Vienna which, mimicking the words of Lewis, would be 'vexatious, useless and an interference to the proper course of justice'. Charlie's lawyers appealed on the basis that the hotel staff were not able to travel to London to give evidence in person and were already beginning to fall by the wayside. The argument fell on deaf ears.

Lewis voiced another concern, this time about jurisdiction. Charlie had been born in Ireland and grown up in England but he had left for Australia in 1877 at the age of nineteen and had clearly established a life in the colonies with no intention of ever returning to England to live. So where was he actually domiciled and was he entitled to even raise a divorce case in London?

Nellie was an Australian living mainly in Paris and the duc seemed to flit from one European kingdom to another on a whim and an invitation to go hunting. To top it off, Charlie and Nellie had been married in Brisbane. Surely the case should be heard in Australia.

To back up their case, Lewis lodged a petition which must have cut Charlie to the quick. He was only five when his father,

Sir Andrew Armstrong, died but he'd been taught to be proud of his father's legacy, in particular a speech he made in Parliament in 1846 for laws restricting commerce in Ireland to be loosened to help almost three million people living in a state of destitution. In a passionate address, Hansard would record him declaring: 'I never can be satisfied that my country should be bound in calf-skin while that of England is bound in gold and morocco.'

And yet the Lewis petition claimed that Sir Andrew had 'quit' Ireland soon after Charlie's birth and, despite raising a large family, had never established a permanent home in England, instead living in 'furnished homes and hotels'. Likewise, his widow had continued to move from place to place, even across Europe, without establishing a home.

Justice Jeune agreed. Charlie had to prove he was not just a resident but domiciled in England before the case could continue. But happenchance had given Charlie the opportunity to do just that. He had been approached by a man named Henry Bentinck Budd who owned a horse stud at East Grinstead in Sussex, south of London. Budd had read the newspaper stories about the divorce and wondered if Charlie was the same man who had tamed the bronco Misery at Buffalo Bill's Wild West Show five years before. Budd had been there that day and watched in admiration as Kangaroo Charlie had tamed the wild horse. Now he needed an expert horseman to turn some horses he'd bought off a boat in Liverpool into saleable and useful animals. There were fifty of them of varying sizes, untamed South American broncos that Budd thought would make good hunters and polo ponies.

Charlie seemed the perfect man for the job and he grabbed the chance with both hands. He had struggled living in a London hotel with nothing to do but fume, and now he could save some money to pay the legal bill and get back to doing what he loved.

The *New York Herald* found him at the property in March, a few weeks after Justice Jeune had delivered his edict. The paper was doing a story about horses and not interested in the Nellie Melba drama. The reporter found a man who exuded a calm firmness rather than the smouldering anger exhibited during the Dalziel interview.

Nellie wasn't even mentioned in the lengthy feature published a few days later, rather the reporter had watched in admiration as Charlie kept a group of potential buyers spellbound while he quietened a newly arrived horse. 'In fifteen minutes it was all over, and the bronco trotted to his new home with his new and probably first master as if he had made up his mind to turn over a new leaf and put his foot on it.'

If only Charlie could tame Justice Jeune.

❧

If Nellie had been able to see her estranged husband in his natural element she may have been less anguished about the road ahead. She might have thought that, for all his short-comings, it was possible for Charlie Armstrong to be content with his lot and a good father. Both of them knew that they didn't belong together, not just because they were both head-strong and bad-tempered but because they wanted different things in life, but there was an opportunity to forge a common path for their son, who was about to turn nine years old.

George Lewis had won Nellie a reprieve, at least for the moment, as she contemplated the London opera season. Despite her success at Covent Garden the previous two years she had delayed her answer to Augustus Harris, concerned that the divorce case might impact on audience numbers. She also had her eyes firmly set on conquering La Scala in Milan and heading across the Atlantic to New York.

Harris had no doubt that his star singer was a drawcard and Lady de Grey implored her to return to Covent Garden, assuring her that she had public support in Britain, but it was a little-known composer named Herman Bemberg who made the difference.

Nellie had met Bemberg, the son of a French banker, the previous year and immediately liked his clown-like sense of humour, shuffling towards her on his knees while offering her flowers. It played to her own sense of fun, a reminder of childhood pranks like the day she used a fireside bellows to blow air up the trouser leg of her father as he played the harmonium, or when she dressed as a nun and canvassed to raise money for charity.

'It appealed to my democratic Australian character,' she would later write. 'He treated life as an immense fantastic joke. He was like some faun dancing mischievously down the Champs-Élysées.'

In May 1892, as she contemplated her summer plans, Bemberg came to her with a new opera called *Elaine*, based on the Arthurian poem by Lord Alfred Tennyson about Elaine, the 'lily maid of Astolat', who died of a broken heart after being rejected in love by Lancelot, knight of the Round Table.

The storyline and the music were appealing but, most importantly, Bemberg's opera was written and dedicated to Nellie and he wanted her to play the lead role, with Jean de Reszke as Sir Lancelot. When he revealed that Harris had agreed to add it to the summer program, Nellie couldn't refuse.

*Elaine* would be produced five times that year but be regarded as only a modest success in a season that otherwise confirmed Nellie's stardom and her ability to switch easily between roles, from Elsa to Marguerite and Juliet to Michaela in a matter of days. There were a number of private appearances and a state concert at Buckingham Palace where, dressed in pale yellow satin, she won the murmured approval of Queen Victoria, read by those watching as being as much forgiveness for her affair with the duc as it was approval of her performance.

Even her acting had improved, although it was the quality of Nellie's voice that continued to enthral, as the critic for the *Pall Mall Gazette* concluded: 'Madame Melba's voice is so perfectly beautiful that it produces a new impression each time it is heard.'

Most striking though was the response of George Bernard Shaw who, although generally unmoved by the opera, found it a revelation in another sense, as he wrote for *The World*.

I am obliged to *Elaine* for one thing; it reconciled me to Madame Melba, who is to all intents and purposes a new artist this year. I do not mind confessing now that I used not to like her. Whilst recognising the perfection of her merely musical faculty, I thought her hard, shallow, self-sufficient and altogether unsympathetic ... I find Madame Melba transfigured, awakened, no longer to be identified by the old descriptions—in sum, with her heart, which before acted only on her circulation, now acting on her singing and giving it a charm which it never had before. The change has completely altered her position; from being merely a brilliant singer, she has become a dramatic soprano of whom the best class of work can be expected.

## 22

# A JUST DESSERT

Philippe had stayed away from London for most of the summer, corralled and guarded on the continent by his mother and father who accompanied him as far as Folkestone when they returned to the UK in mid-July. But that's where the oversight ended as their son moved back into central London with every intention of seeing Nellie.

Friends like Alfred de Rothschild would give the couple places to circulate freely in society, as an actor and card magician named Burr McIntosh would recall some years later during an interview with the Chicago *Inter-Ocean* newspaper. McIntosh was hired one weekend to entertain guests at the Rothschild mansion near Hyde Park. It was an informal setting as he wandered through the vast rooms where people stood or sat in small groups.

He made a beeline for two women and a man talking quietly in a corner at the far end of the room, the women side

by side on a couch and the man in a high-backed chair opposite them. McIntosh stood beside the chair, waiting patiently
for an opening to introduce himself. Eventually, one of the
women looked up. He recognised her as Nellie Melba: 'Would
you care to see a card trick, Madame?' he asked, bowing
slightly to both women, the other he knew as the American-
born Duchess of Manchester. The gentleman, who'd had his
back to the magician, now turned. It was the Duc d'Orleans.
McIntosh was taken aback given the publicity about the
divorce, and tried not to reveal his surprise as he showed the
trio some tricks.

Philippe still had his house in Mayfair but had checked into
the Savoy Hotel where Nellie was also staying. His absence
was noted one morning when the Duke of York stopped by
the duc's empty house where he knocked several times before
a 'fiery young maid' finally came to the door. She grew angry
with the duke who asked if Philippe was at home: 'No, he ain't,
and you're being a puffick nuisance,' she told the shocked royal,
later to become King George V, before slamming the door in
his face.

One of the attractions of the Savoy was its chef. Auguste
Escoffier was revolutionising French cooking and kitchen craft.
The 'King of Chefs and Chef to Kings', as he would become
known, was seducing London with his sumptuous dishes,
velvet sauces and revolutionary concept of à la carte dining.
The hotel restaurant was overflowing each night with the city's
social elite whose attendant footmen formed lines on the pavement outside as they waited.

Thursday 28 July would be a particularly memorable day. It was Nellie's last performance for the season, or at least the summer because she would return in the autumn for another series of concerts. She was playing Elsa in *Lohengrin*, a role she had sung five times since June among eighteen performances in five different operatic roles for the season.

After it was over, the encores complete and the bouquets collected, she went back to the Savoy where Philippe had organised a celebration. A few nights earlier Nellie had given Escoffier a ticket to a performance of *Lohengrin* in appreciation of his cooking. Clearly delighted with the gesture, Escoffier had decided to return the compliment.

When the main meal was finished, the great chef emerged from his kitchen with members of his staff carrying a swan carved out of ice, in homage to the opera he had seen. At its centre was a silver tray in which sat a dessert he had created in the singer's honour: hand-churned vanilla ice-cream topped with peaches, peeled and poached in vanilla syrup and drizzled with spun sugar. He called it *Pêche au Cygne*, or peach with a swan, but a few years later, after he had moved to the Ritz Carlton Hotel, he would finesse the recipe and smother the peaches in pureed raspberries. *Pêche Melba* was born.

(Escoffier would also create a dessert named after Philippe. *Pêche Petit-Duc* would feature peaches on vanilla ice-cream, covered with slices of pineapple macerated in maraschino and kirsch and dotted with red currant jelly. Both recipes appeared together in his 1907 cookbook *A Guide to Modern Cookery*.)

Nellie's version of the Peach Melba story was invented, presumably to hide Philippe's role. In her autobiography account, Nellie was lunching alone in her room on a glorious spring day: 'I was particularly hungry. Toward the end of it there arrived a little silver dish which was uncovered before me with a message that Mr Escoffier had prepared it especially for me. As much as Eve tasted the first apple, I tasted the first Peach Melba.'

❧

Behind the scenes, the divorce case had been dawdling but things changed suddenly in mid-July when Nellie's lawyers revealed they had commenced proceedings in Australia to have Charlie's property—almost 1300 acres (525 hectares) of land—vested in her name.

The move was launched under a new Queensland *Married Women's Property Act* that gave women the right to hold assets under their own name within a marriage. If Charlie was going to insist on a divorce and financial settlement, then Nellie was determined to ensure that she got a share of the assets that her income from singing had helped to create.

The tactic appeared to have an impact; the threat of having to hand over his property, or at least part of it, to Nellie was enough to cause Charlie to rethink the divorce. It was also evident that he and his lawyers were struggling to establish his domicile in either England or Ireland, as the court had said he must before the case could proceed. Things were falling apart.

On 6 August, *Armstrong v Armstrong* was quietly removed from the court list, the registrar recording simply: 'Upon hearing the solicitors of the petitioner and by consent of all parties, I order that the contentious proceedings herein be discontinued and the petition dismissed without costs on either side.'

Of her marriage, Nellie would never be drawn beyond this simple statement: 'I was married to Mr Charles Armstrong when I was young. My husband was not musical and I soon found that domestic life did not fill the entire range of my girlish fancies.'

And that was that. Although their friends and families heaved a sigh of relief, journalists were disappointed that such a promising courtroom confrontation had fizzled and died. With little else to write, they began to speculate about the contents of a rumoured private settlement in which, it was claimed, Nellie had agreed to pay her estranged husband £1000 a year.

If that was the price of marital freedom—the equivalent of five performance nights—then Nellie was prepared to pay it. She had avoided an unseemly court case and a divorce that would, in all likelihood given the norms of the day, have granted custody of George to his father. Instead they remained married, at least technically, and shared time with a son they both loved.

'I'm so happy,' she told Mathilde Marchesi in a letter.

The end of the court case would also herald an end to the love affair with Philippe, the unveiling of Peach Melba was one of their last nights together. It was a moment of delight and triumph but one of realisation that the relationship could never work, the pressure of the d'Orleans family for Philippe to move on and find someone of his own kind had proved too great.

By mid-August Nellie was back in Europe, with George in tow, at the French spa retreat town of Aix-les-Bains to recuperate, as had become her habit, before preparing for a trip to America where she had been booked to make her debut.

But her hopes were dashed when she arrived back in Paris to be told that the Metropolitan Opera House in New York had been gutted by fire and the opera season had been cancelled. The directors, Maurice Grau and Henry Abbey, were on their way to Paris to discuss her fees, to which she was still entitled. Nellie needed the money but in the end she waived her fee, the conscience of her Presbyterian upbringing outweighing any financial consideration.

Philippe too had found a distraction, announcing that he was going to explore the African continent. At the end of October he set out from London with three servants, bound for the port city of Berbera in Somaliland, from where he planned to explore the continent through Kenya to Lake Victoria. The 1500-kilometre journey would take six months, he estimated, after which he would return to London to write about his adventures. It was a far cry from chasing Nellie Melba around the opera houses of Europe and an experience which would be a telling point in his life.

Charlie was not as fortunate in the months after the case ended, breaking his hand and arm in a boxing match when his right fist crashed into the elbow of an opponent trying to defend himself against Charlie's onslaught. Friends wondered why he no longer went to the London clubs he once frequented. Instead, he withdrew to East Grinstead and laid low.

# 23

# FACING THE MUSIC

Jack Moore had a favourite story about the young, ambitious woman he met as Mrs Nellie Armstrong at a party in Sydney in 1885 which, he believed, went to the heart of her character. It had happened far from the lights and glamour of Covent Garden or the Palais Garnier, even the warm enthusiasm of a full house at the Melbourne Town Hall or Sydney's Theatre Royal.

The night that typified Nellie in his eyes happened in 1885 when she returned to Sydney after her concert series with Johann Kruse. Moore accompanied her and a small troupe as they travelled 200 kilometres inland from Sydney to play several concerts in Bathurst, the town where Australia's gold boom had begun. It was hoped to introduce some 'high-class music' to a community that, in the words of a local journalist, preferred 'burnt cork minstrelsy and circus buffoonery'.

It began badly when the priest at the local cathedral objected to one of the concerts being held at the School of Arts' hall on a Sunday. His angry sermon prompted an emergency meeting of the school board which bowed to the pressure and shut down the concert on the basis that it was an attempt to secularise the Sabbath. David Mitchell would have approved.

The controversy seemed to have an impact on overall attendance, the hall barely half full for the Friday night performance, although Nellie was encored and one local reviewer described her voice as 'a high soprano of exceptional power, sweetness and flexibility'. The second night was worse with just a handful of people turning up as the performers debated whether to continue. Finally, the concert organiser agreed to allow a couple of instrumental performances before ending the show and refunding the tickets.

But the night was far from over. As the knots of disappointed audience members left, two older ladies remained in their front-row seats and clamoured for Nellie, whom they had travelled some distance to hear. 'Just one song,' they cried. Backstage, Nellie couldn't believe her ears, her disappointment replaced by the thrill of her voice being recognised and desired. She told Jack to close the doors after the others had left before giving the two women a full concert to themselves. 'The queen of song had arrived,' Jack said proudly.

It would be seven years before Jack crossed paths again with Nellie. In the autumn of 1892 he travelled to London on business and took a few days to cross the Channel and visit Paris with a friend. He arrived to find Nellie in the news as her divorce case was settled, and he told his travelling companion of their friendship when she was simply Mrs Nellie Armstrong, a young singer finding her way. But now she was Madame Melba, just as she had predicted the night they walked back to her hotel from the Theatre Royal. It was unlikely that she would remember him, as he would write years later. 'It seemed impossible that even a fellow Australian could call upon Melba and ask her to allow the threads of acquaintance in Sydney to be picked up on the other side of the world where she was the shining star of the first magnitude.'

The Englishman thought otherwise. Jack should leave his details at the theatre where she was performing, he suggested. She might respond but, if not, there was no harm done given that his expectations were so low. Jack agreed, the card was presented to the front desk of the Palais Garnier and the two men spent the rest of the day sightseeing around the capital before packing for their return that evening to London.

While settling his hotel bill, Jack was told there was a letter waiting for him. It was from Nellie, and she wanted to see him. Then, as he read the letter, a carriage pulled up outside the hotel. It was Nellie who insisted that he delay his departure, leave the hotel, and instead stay at her apartment so she could show him the best of Paris.

He relented and spent the next fortnight at Nellie's apartment, driven around the city, introduced to her friends and invited as a guest backstage at the opera. 'She gave me her time and company as if our friendship in Sydney were warrant enough for the best she could provide,' he recalled fondly. 'She was the same cordial, warm-hearted woman that I had first met. Melba was no different from the Mrs Armstrong who had come to Sydney to try her voice upon music lovers.'

❧❧❧

As much as Jack Moore was extolling Nellie as someone who had not forgotten her roots and those who helped her, it was also true that his arrival in Paris was fortuitous for her. She may have prevailed in divorce court, and stopped Charlie from ruining her career and taking their son, but she had lost Philippe, their love exhausted by the scrutiny. Jack was a reminder of home and a friend, rather than a lover, at a time that she was alone.

This was also a time of change. Instead of the excitement of New York, she would hitch her wagon to a provincial English tour, an uncertain step given the hit and miss nature of such tours. She was stepping from the rose-strewn stage of Covent Garden to the boardwalk of the local town hall in rural England. It was also an experiment in entrepreneurship, a self-funded venture that included a troupe of eight singers and musicians. They played in a dozen cities in England, Scotland and Ireland, where she would be feted but left feeling deflated by the half-hearted public response. She would also be left with a 300-guinea debt to pay.

First though, there was the autumn commitment at Covent Garden where Augustus Harris wanted her to sing a new opera, Giuseppe Verdi's *Aida*, about an enslaved Egyptian princess. It was a risk though because it was a role that demanded a voice powerful enough to compete against heavy orchestral music.

It also required more dramatic acting, and questions still remained about her acting ability. One wag had even quipped that when Melba wanted to show emotion she raised one arm, and two arms to signal intense emotion.

Madame Marchesi was against the gamble, so Nellie turned to composer Paolo Tosti to help her prepare. The risk would be worth the effort.

Although nervous on the opening night, her performance was hailed a great success, made even more memorable when she became embroiled in a scrap with her co-star, the mezzo Guilia Ravogli, over ownership of a gigantic basket of flowers presented onstage during the encores. Melba won out, the newspapers conjecturing whether the bouquet was a gift from the Duc d'Orleans, hence her determination to claim ownership.

Nellie had won over the critics, *Sporting Life* summing up the response by describing it as an event of supreme importance in the history of lyrical stage: 'She acquitted herself, after the first, somewhat nervous plunge with great distinction ... The Australian remains the brightest particular star of the Covent Garden firmament.'

As for her acting, the critic for *The Graphic* concluded:

> The performance in *Aida* was a remarkably fine one, and Madame Melba, apart from singing the music like a thorough artist, showed how greatly she is improving as an actress, the coldness which formerly marked her impersonations having almost disappeared.

Nellie had conquered Covent Garden and the Paris Garnier but there was another peak which had to be scaled if she was to be considered the best—La Scala in Milan.

※

Nellie's relationship with Mathilde Marchesi had been tested by her decision to sing the part of Aida and use Paolo Tosti as a tutor. For all the comfort she found in the mother–daughter relationship, it could also be smothering, particularly as both women were so fiercely opinionated and independent. But the opportunity to sing at La Scala in March 1893 would smooth over any differences and return them to a common cause, in which both would triumph.

It was one of the few times in her life Nellie's self-confidence was challenged, so she broke the ice and wrote to Madame, asking for advice and help. The answer, signed as *Mother Mathilde*, came quickly:

> My dear, dear Nellie, I was mad with joy to receive your letter. It's been an age since you gave me any sign of life. Fear nothing of the people of Milan. With your beautiful voice and some added emotion (that's what the Italians demand) you will have boundless success.

But even Madame Marchesi was not prepared for the reception Nellie would receive in Milan, which began even before she had stepped onto the stage. When she arrived at her hotel she was given letters, sent anonymously in a 'spidery hand', warning her to leave the city otherwise her life was in danger. More letters arrived the following day and musical colleagues, who would normally welcome a new performer, stayed away.

The animosity was driven, it was said, by rumours that she was not worthy of singing at La Scala and would fail, particularly as Adelina Patti had recently triumphed there. She received threats that the hotel elevator would be tampered with, causing it to plunge if she attempted to use it. There were other threats that assailants would be waiting in the dark streets outside to stab her, or, if she made it to the theatre, then hidden trapdoors on the stage would open and swallow her before she could sing.

As ridiculous as it all sounded, she could not ignore the intimidation, particularly when one letter-writer threatened to poison her food. Nellie felt trapped. 'Every mouthful of food I took seemed likely to poison me and I would not even go downstairs, let alone out of the doors,' she would later write.

She contemplated fleeing the city before being persuaded by her secretary, Louie Mason, to stay and defy the bullies. 'You can't go,' she said putting her hands in Nellie's and pleading to her face. 'It would not be you. You have to stay and face the music.'

Nellie knew that her secretary was right; to leave in the face of threats would be cowardly. 'I honestly believe that had it not been for Louie Mason I should never have sung at La Scala . . . and missed one of the greatest triumphs of my life.'

Her first-night jitters were, naturally enough, more acute than usual, not helped by the fact that she had travelled to the theatre under police escort and then had to wait for twenty minutes before making her entrance as Lucia to sing her solo. As she did so, Nellie could not help but glance at the audience, anxious to their reaction. The sight shocked her; it seemed that most had their backs to her, as if in protest. The sight almost caused her to forget her phrasing but she pressed ahead, trying to put the audience out of her mind as she let the music carry her away.

It was only when the roars of 'Brava Brava' began that she looked again, and realised the trick of La Scala was the arrangement of the seats in many of the boxes were turned away from the stage. As the audience became enthralled, they all turned and, by the end of her aria, they were all on their feet. The disaster had been a triumph, just as Madame had predicted.

Of all the reviews the next day, the flourishing words of Aldo Noseda, critic for *Corriere della Sera*, summed up her performance as 'a true and genuine success'. Many stars had fallen on the La Scala stage, he wrote. Nellie had won a great battle.

# 24

# MURPHY'S LAW

One morning in the late spring or early summer of 1893—nobody would ever be sure of the exact date—Charlie Armstrong turned up at the Worthing boarding school at Littlehampton to see his nine-year-old son.

A parental visit was not unusual in itself. Charlie had been to the school several times in the previous six months, sometimes taking George out for the day. They made one memorable trip to the nearby Goodwood Racecourse which the boy would always remember for the thunder of hooves and blaze of colourful jockey silks.

But Charlie's arrival on this day was unusual in that he was accompanied by his older brother, Montague, and they were taking the boy for good. George was told to pack his belongings because he was going on a long journey. School officials were forced to stand by and watch because George's mother had been at the school the previous day and given the decision her blessing.

Nellie was, in fact, a reluctant participant, pressured by Charlie to allow him to take the boy to America and join other Armstrong family members—cousins named Robinson—who had bought into a share of a plantation somewhere in the 'southern states' where Charlie's management experience from Mackay would be appreciated.

Charlie was still burned by his wife's affair and, even though she was no longer seeing Philippe, he couldn't escape the shame while in England. He needed a new start and George would be his hostage; he'd argued that the fresh air in America would be good for his son's apparently fragile health. It would also free Nellie to pursue her career without the worry of parenting responsibilities.

He promised to return in one year with the boy.

Fearing the worst if she refused Charlie, Nellie consented and went to George's school to tell him he had to go with his father. The boy had objected strongly to the idea because, after a rocky beginning, he had settled into the school environment and was reluctant to leave his friends. And he did not want to be without his mother. Nellie left quickly, her eyes filled with tears.

George loved the times when his mother was singing at Covent Garden because he would visit at weekends and stay with her at the Savoy where he was allowed to ride the lifts and help take the top hats from gentlemen as they arrived at the hotel. He felt a part of her world, spending much of his childhood backstage in theatres, watching his mother rehearse and mixing with the stagehands and musicians. He also felt comfortable in Paris, the city in which he had spent many of his formative years and where he had not been judged as being different.

But now he was going to America to start again, this time without the woman who had been alongside him his entire life. George walked out of the school between his father and uncle, carrying a cricket bat he would never get to use again. It was useless in a country where they didn't play the game. He and Charlie took a train to Liverpool and left the next morning on a steamer before anyone could change their mind.

George was seasick all the way across the Atlantic and would remember arriving, tired and bewildered, several days later in a small town where they stayed at a hotel until the cousin arrived to take them to the plantation. On the first night shots rang out from the bar below their room. A drunken brawl had broken out and George watched, horrified, from a window as the fight spilled out onto the street, men shooting at each other.

The name of the town was Murphy, built in what was once the heartlands of the Cherokee people until they were rounded up and sent across the Appalachian Mountains to a Tennessee reservation so white settlers could plant crops. When Charlie and George arrived, Murphy was a town in the middle of nowhere, only recently connected by rail and in many ways still recovering from the horrors of the American Civil War.

George had been taken from the centre of the industrial and cultural world of Europe to its very fringes in rural America, with no familial support apart from a father who had been absent for much of his life and whose only desire was to punish a woman who refused to obey him, and had the audacity to be independent and successful.

There was no school here for a young boy beyond the school of experience, living on the crumbling remains of a once vibrant rice plantation. If there was a place more remote than Mackay, then Murphy was it.

True to form, they would not last there long. Charlie did not see eye to eye with the management style of his relatives and, within a year, had decided to strike out on his own and seek a new fortune in the wilds of America. It was a lifestyle he knew only too well and one in which he had thrived in Australia but this time it was different because he had a young boy along for the ride.

And he was not taking him back, as promised.

⚌

New York. The name alone conjured up so many images for Nellie as she arrived in late November 1893 aboard the steamship *La Bretagne*, sliding past the Statue of Liberty on Bedloe's Island, so freshly raised that her copper skin was still turning green.

It was the streets of the city that she would remember most, the annoying shudder of iron-rimmed carriage wheels on rough cobblestones was in sharp contrast to the speedy hansom cabs on the 'smoother', well-worn roads of London. It echoed the difference between the old world and the new, as did the steam-driven heaters at the Waldorf Hotel that seemed to suffocate rather than warm her room as she rushed to open the windows in 'healthy English fashion'.

The Atlantic crossing had been terrible, the blizzard conditions and high seas making the voyage an endurance test. She was confined mostly to the cabin where her thoughts must have drifted frequently to 'Georgie'. It had been five months since Charlie had taken him and there had been no word of where they were and when they would return.

Nellie may have harboured hopes that, once in America, she would have an opportunity to find them, but the sheer size and disparity of the continent made her realise how impossible the task was. She had written several times but her letters, sent to a post office in Murphy, had gone unanswered. Was she being ignored, did George even know that his mother cared, or had they moved on and, if so, where had they gone?

She kept the anguish to herself, dark thoughts hidden behind the combined stoicism of her steely religious upbringing and the confidence shield of a performance artist. But there was no escape from the private heartache caused not only by the absence of her only child but, perhaps more so, the wrench of not knowing if he was safe and happy, or if she would ever see him again.

She was nervous about her American debut, and with good reason because New York audiences preferred the heavy drama of German opera to the delicate sounds of Italian arias, which were Nellie's bread and butter. Her appearance in Milan six months earlier had been a triumph against prejudice; but this time she would have to overcome preference.

As one critic observed, the American audiences 'care little or nothing for heroines who go out of their minds and give evidence of their madness in a series of shakes, trills, roulades and cadenzas of the most elaborate and inappropriate description'.

Despite her European success, Nellie was not regarded as a star here, particularly in an opera season that included appearances by two American sopranos—Lillian Nordica and her old rival Emma Eames—as well as Emma Calvé, the Frenchwoman who had made a spectacular debut in *Carmen* the previous week to become an immediate favourite among New York audiences.

Nellie was, in effect, a second-ranking performer and her stocks fell further when critics began questioning her decision to sing *Lucia di Lammermoor*, which was seen as an Adelina Patti opera and risked comparison against an icon. To add to her woes, one of the male singers fell ill the day before the performance and his replacement, a baritone named Victor De Gromzeski, was drafted literally as he was walking down the street past the theatre, and then sang off-key in the first act. Disaster loomed until Nellie's voice soared through the freshly painted auditorium. The audience rose with her and by the end of the mad scene they were on their feet.

'Madame Melba is at the zenith of her powers,' wrote Henry Krehbiel from the *New-York Tribune* the next day. He went on to say the audience 'gave Madame Melba such enthusiastic tokens of approbation as to convince her that she was permanently established in the good will of our public. It was a superb greeting, superbly deserved.'

The critic from *The World* described her as a virtuoso rather than a singer: 'Her command over her vocal resources, which in themselves are unusual, as the quality and range of her voice are exquisite, is little short of extraordinary. Even Patti can hardly be said to have surpassed her.'

It was one thing to wow critics for a single performance and another to convince the management, hungry for profits, to elevate her to the first order, alongside her rivals and competing for prime performance schedules.

It felt like her debut at Covent Garden in 1888, when she played to half-empty houses in the matinee and struggled to be acknowledged, but she was five years older and determined to succeed rather than flee in a cloud of petulance. 'If it's been Madame Eames and Madame Calvé at the start [of the season] then it will be Madame Melba at the end,' she told friends.

Roles as Ophelia, Gilda and Juliet followed to critical acclaim but the houses remained small by comparison to the audiences clamouring to hear Calvé in *Carmen* and Eames in *Faust*, and she still needed to show New Yorkers that she could sing more than Italian librettos.

Determined to take the challenge, she appeared as Elsa in *Lohengrin* which the *New York Herald* described as 'incomparably the most attractive thing she has done'. But it was her performance as Elisabeth in the Wagner opera *Tannhauser*, a role she learned in just three days, that helped stamp her authority on the season. *The Sun*'s WJ Henson said her performance 'amazed the soprano's friends, and put her enemies, if she had any, to confusion'.

New York had been convinced and the city was now talking about the exotic Australian enigma, particularly when she stood in for Emma Eames, who was ill, and sang Marguerite in *Faust* in front of an audience described by *The Sun* as 'scarcely ever equalled in size or surpassed in enthusiasm. Flowers were thrown upon the stage in profusion, mostly at the feet of Melba.'

Suddenly, Nellie was the talk of the town. Newspapers sent reporters to Nellie's suite at the Savoy (she had given up on the Waldorf's heaters) where she regaled them with stories about her colonial upbringing and unusual music education.

She came across as warm, engaging and down-to-earth, confident in the limitations of her voice as much as her potential. She was tall and graceful and yet plump and chestnut-haired. Photographs did not do her justice, according to the *New-York Tribune*:

> She usually looks heavy in face and figure, with a stolid, matronly expression, a dull eye and spiritless pose. She is, in reality, tall, alert and pliant, with a charming figure, round and supple; regular features in an oval face, always a bright and happy expression, and altogether an air of pretty dash and chic never hinted at in her photograph.

But it was a profile in the *Buffalo Evening News* that captured the nuance of her character:

> Mme Melba is a simple, natural woman, devoted to her art and fond of society and its diversion. Her favourite recreation

is dancing. With her fortune in her throat, she does not hesitate to go to the ball. Next to dancing she enjoys walking, riding, driving—anything to get into the sunshine. She is a capital talker and her salons in Paris are sought by musical and literary celebrities whose signatures make up a unique collection of autographs. The Australian diva is tall and slender, with a face rather dark and an expression distinctly sad, a woman whose whole appearance indicates dignity of character and an experience of bitterness and suffering. There is in Mme Melba a vast deal more than what shows upon the surface.

Such was the fascination that there was even a public debate about whether she should be invited to 'ornament the drawing rooms of The Four Hundred', a reference to the infamous list of the most powerful social elite of the city.

The publicity was pleasing to Nellie but the treatment of singers as social ornaments annoyed her, as she would later reflect:

In London, if an artist made a great success, he or she was received on the footing of absolute equality with the most 'exalted' people in the Capital. Not so in New York. An artist is an artist, and although she might be the subject of amazing hospitality . . . there was always a subtle difference between her and the rest of society.

The season was longer than any in Europe, the troupe travelling together for more than four months, including a tour through the Midwest. Among the large cities they visited were Philadelphia, Boston, St Louis and Chicago, where they played at the World's Fair. As Nellie got off the train in the Windy City, she saw a boy dressed in ragged clothes selling newspapers on the platform. It could have been George.

'How long do you have to stand there?' she asked the shivering boy.

'Until I sell all these papers,' he replied.

'How many have you got?'

'Fifty.'

'I'll buy them all.'

The Chicago visit was almost ruined when the *Sun-Times* claimed that Nellie, Lillian Nordica and Emma Calvé had been receiving 'conspicuous attentions of a fast set of young men', one of whom had spent $2000 on roses, wine and dinner. The tattle began when a businessman named Allison Armour, later to become famous for archaeology and plant research, invited the three singers to his box 'in full view of the watchful public', according to the paper. Armour and his friend, a Mr Chatfield-Taylor, were then said to have taken Nellie and Emma Calvé to dinner.

Nellie suspected it was the work of Emma Eames. Once again, she had found herself fighting prejudice and perceptions, this time that openly accepting hospitality from a well-wisher meant she was a woman of loose morals. She could almost see her father's disapproving scowl, all her accomplishments blotted by unbecoming behaviour.

Nellie responded by threatening to sue the paper for

$100,000 and demanding a retraction, as did the other two singers: 'As a stranger in a strange land, as a visitor to America for the first time, I ask for your consideration due to a foreigner and a woman,' she wrote in a letter to the editor. 'I find in your valuable paper an article which serves no purpose beyond maligning defenceless women,' she wrote.

> I find my name coupled with a man I do not even know, cred-
> ited with an offence to my womanhood and my art, both
> of which I prize as every honest woman should. As I do not
> even know either of the men with whose acquaintance you so
> freely credit me, as the article in question is based upon this
> acquaintance, and as its entire purpose is calumnious, permit
> me to ask you that a full and proper retraction be made in your
> columns.

The paper apologised unreservedly the next day.

Back in New York there was a supplementary season. On the last night she again sang the part of Lucia but this time the theatre was packed, people buying last-minute tickets to stand in the aisles to hear her. They chanted 'Melba' at its end and continued through the encores even after she had removed her costume, forcing her to return to the stage in a dressing gown and sing the popular ballad *Home Sweet Home* next to a piano hastily pushed onto the stage.

There was a concert finale the following night featuring the entire troupe. Melba sang the mad scene from *Hamlet* after which theatre managers Maurice Grau and Henry Abbey led her back onstage, standing either side of her and bowing to the thunderous ovation. The program had been a financial success and Nellie Melba had done as she had promised. She was the star.

That night, members of the orchestra and several prominent patrons followed Nellie back to the Savoy where she was cheered as she stood on the lobby balcony. New York hadn't seen fanfare like it since Adelina Patti was in her prime and Nellie could not help but be moved, as she told the crowd: 'The future can have no pleasanter souvenirs for me than those I take away from America, and if I do not return, believe me it will be no fault of mine.'

But her reasons for wanting to return were more complex. When Nellie sailed out of New York harbour a few days later all she could think of was the boy she was leaving behind somewhere in the backblocks of America.

## 25

# A RESOLUTE INTENT

The year 1894 would be a period of dramatic change in the life of Philippe d'Orleans. His journey through Somalia had turned from exploration into a big game hunt and he returned to London with his catch—a lion, rhinoceros, leopard and buffalo among them—whose carcasses were promptly stuffed and put on display in York House, which he now called home. He was the very essence of a nineteenth-century aristocratic sportsman.

The pièce de résistance of his big game trophies was the head of an African bush elephant he'd shot in the country's north, which would later be revealed by prominent British naturalist Richard Lydekker as a new species, defined by its small, straight ears and named *Elephas africanus orleansi* after its killer. In an era when big game hunting was considered brave and hunters' kills as important contributions to science, the head would become a discussion piece for Philippe's guests during the season in London.

Philippe spent the European summer steering clear of Nellie Melba as best he could. He travelled across Europe, as was his wont, but when in London the task was more difficult, because the Prince of Wales was a common friend and it was difficult to ignore social invitations from the next King of England.

The press were ever watchful, particularly as Philippe insisted on attending the opera where he could sit in the family box and admire his lost lover.

Philippe's attendance did not pass unnoticed by the news-papers, especially one night when a giant bouquet was carried onto the stage and presented to Nellie after a performance. She must have glanced in his direction, even if inadvertently, because several newspaper gossips made mention of the flowers, and their rumoured purchaser, in their columns. The two passed each other at the Savoy but, otherwise, the prince and the song-stress mixed in different social circles, the affair clearly over, however regretfully.

Besides, Philippe had other issues on his mind. His father was desperately ill with an 'internal malady' that had laid him low at Stowe House. Doctors had attempted to remove a stomach tumour but the operation was not considered a success. As the summer deepened, his condition worsened and it soon became obvious that, although there were moments of respite, it was just a matter of time.

The cancer—a word that was not uttered—had taken hold and was spreading. It seemed the whole of Europe was watching and praying for the Comte de Paris, even inside France. Newspapers provided daily reports and there were well-wishers from Buckingham Palace, the Spanish Court, and the Pope in Rome among others. Catholic churches in Paris held special masses where packed congregations prayed for a heavenly miracle but waited for the inevitable human outcome.

Louis Philippe Albert d'Orleans, grandson of the last Bourbon king, died quietly on 8 September 1894 surrounded by his family. His body lay in state for two days while hundreds came to pay their respects to a man, considered modest and a liberal intellectual, who might have been king but instead lived more than half his fifty-six years in exile.

There were special editions of Paris newspapers and representatives of Europe's royal houses made their way to London for the funeral. In life, the comte was dismissed as the apostle of a ruined cause, but in death he was exalted as a man of quality who was never able to demonstrate his real ability.

His oldest son, the *enfant terrible* Philippe, was now next in line to the French throne. The Duc d'Aumale, the comte's younger brother, found his nephew one night in his apartment. The young man was pacing the floor, distraught and angry at his father's death.

'My poor father died in exile, and consequence of exile,' he shouted. 'It is exile which has killed him. Anything, anything rather than exile, inaction and inability to serve one's country. I will risk my head to return to France; I would risk my head rather than be forced out.'

Behind Philippe's anger there was a sense of guilt, that his affair with Nellie had somehow contributed to his father's demise. The comte had fallen ill just as the relationship was revealed publicly. At first, it was deemed to be gout—painful but treatable and not life-threatening—but as time went on, it became clear that the situation was more serious.

When Charlie Armstrong challenged Philippe to a duel, the comte was being told by specialists that he had a stomach tumour that could be fatal and had to be removed. And when the scandal of divorce was being played out before the High Court, he was recovering from the operation.

The comte didn't blame his son, imploring his counsel of advisors to ignore the young man's previous follies and unite around Philippe for the common cause—the return of the royal family to Paris. He believed that the Orleans could rule again, but in a modern context, as he expressed to Philippe who sat by his father's bedside in his final hours.

There were many who questioned whether *Le Petit Duc* was up to the task. He had shown pluck and a spirit of defiance when he attempted to sign up for the army, they said, but his 'love of opera', as one columnist quipped, might have stultified any remote chance his family had of returning to the City of Love.

Others overlooked the indiscretion of Nellie—hardly an unforgivable act for a Frenchman, they argued—but questioned the decision not to 'walk out' with Charlie Armstrong as an act of cowardice.

Of all the criticisms of Philippe, this was an unfair observation because he had not been afraid of the confrontation. For once, he had done what he was told. Charlie may have been a gifted boxer and horseman, even a fencer good enough to win a competition among members of an upmarket Brussels gym, but Philippe was a sportsman himself and the recipient of a royal education including the art of fencing. The reason Philippe didn't accept Charlie's challenge was his father's fear that, just when he had been told of his own imminent death, his son might also be killed. It was a risk not worth taking.

But what lay ahead? For a century, members of his family had been born or died on foreign soil, beginning with his great-grandfather, King Louis Philippe I. And now his father would be interred in a chapel at Weybridge in Surrey, banned even in death from returning to France. Could Philippe bring them home?

More than one thousand 'French Legitimists' travelled from London to attend the funeral. Afterwards Philippe addressed the gathered crowd outside the Roman Catholic Chapel of St Charles Borromeo. The misty rain that had fallen all day seemed appropriate.

Would he be content to follow his father's lead and simply wait, however hopelessly, for the chance that the family would be recalled to France? Or would he try to force the issue politically? His words were printed in full by several newspapers, scoured for a sense of how the young prince—the new Pretender—might act.

I know the rights which that heritage confers, and the duties towards France which it lays upon me. Guided by the splendid example which my father gave me during his life, and which he consecrated by his death—so courageously faced and accepted with such Christian resignation—fortified by your support and that of the absent friends who have already conveyed to me from all parts of France the expression of their devotion and appealing to all men of good feeling, I will fulfil, without faltering, the mission which devolves upon me. Though young still, I am conscious of my duties. With my great love for France, I shall devote all that is in me of strength and vigour to accomplish them, and by God's help I will accomplish them.

*The Globe*, like many papers, was unsure what might happen:

> Only time can show whether the Duc d'Orleans will follow the advice that the Monarchists should hold their doctrine as a pious opinion, but make no overt attempt to put it in practice. If he is as impulsive as some of those who know him believe, he will find it difficult to do so. But new responsibilities may work a change in his temper.

The speech was dismissed by mostly Republican papers in Paris as 'platonic' and that it would have little impact in France whose governing class was being filled with professional men—lawyers, professors, journalists and doctors among them who favoured the Republic over the return to a monarchy.

By contrast, royalist journals praised the prince's 'resolute intent', while clerical organs suspended their judgement. Philippe had already flagged that he was unlikely to live in England, preferring a smaller London residence to the vast rooms of Stowe House and wanting to spend more time visiting European courts and being in Brussels, where he was within touching distance of Paris. Perhaps that was the clue.

⧉

Philippe's chance to restore the throne, however slim, would come sooner than he might have hoped. The French government had been rocked in June 1894 by the assassination of President Marie Carnot, who had been stabbed by an Italian anarchist as he sat in his carriage outside a theatre in Lyon.

Carnot's death had sparked a new political crisis for a system of government that seemed to have been in constant turmoil, and the subsequent election of Jean Casimir-Perier to replace Carnot only added to the mayhem. Casimir-Perier had previously been Prime Minister but lasted only six months. Now he wanted to try high office again. But barely six months later, Casimir-Perier resigned, rocked by internal instability.

The National Assembly would once again have to find a leader who could unite the disparate Republic—the thirty-first ministry in the twenty-five years since the Third Republic was born and the Orleans family exiled. Was this the opportunity for which the royalists had been waiting?

On 16 January 1895, Philippe and his supporters gathered inside the Lord Warden Hotel near Dover's docks amid mounting speculation that a steamer would arrive from across the Channel to take him back to France. But a premature return to Paris was dangerous and could backfire politically. Instead, he chose to wait for the vote.

If the assembly remained divided and deadlocked then he could move within hours. Just before the vote, and despite attempts to block its distribution, he released a manifesto in which he declared confidently that the return of the monarchy was inevitable.

The Republic in France can never be more than a provisional regime—the events now passing prove this once again. The hour is near when the country will wish to revert to the form of government which was the glory of its past, which will be the guarantee of its future. Let our friends give us fresh proof of their abnegation and patriotism by joining with all good citizens in electing from among the candidates the man who will be best able to preserve order and social tranquillity at home, while ensuring respect and honour for the country abroad. Let us work today for the salvation of the country—tomorrow we will work for its greatness.

The drama would unfold the next day with an unexpected victor emerging. Felix Faure was the son of a furniture maker who had worked as a tanner before becoming a successful businessman.

In truth, the result mattered little to Philippe. The French President wielded little political power but the continued political instability was invaluable to his cause, and would ultimately determine if the monarchists would return to power.

Interviewed by the royalist paper *Matin* a few weeks later, Philippe would not be drawn on his plans: 'That is my secret and the secret of the future. I will continue the struggle until I succeed—until I conquer.'

## 26

# THE FIRST SINGER IN THE WORLD

As Philippe grieved for his father and launched an audacious attempt to win back his family's fortunes, Nellie sailed again for America. The London season had been its usual success and she had won over the testy audiences of La Scala for a second time, the highlight of which had been meeting and singing for the ageing maestro Giuseppe Verdi.

He had been in the audience for a performance of his opera *Rigoletto* and had come to her dressing room afterwards. 'He bowed sternly, almost stiffly,' she would recall in her memoir. 'It was like a tree trying to bend . . . of some gnarled, wonderful old tree. There was an impenetrable reserve about him, which made one's conversation with him slightly stilted. And yet, he had bright eyes, like a boy's, and eager restless hands.' A signed photograph would be among her most treasured possessions.

But for all that Europe had to offer in terms of cultural history, prestige and old masters, Nellie longed for a new challenge and America seemed to offer that opportunity, both critically and financially. Besides, it would give her another chance to find George.

She had left amid fresh announcements about her long-awaited trip back home. As usual, the Australian media coverage was emphatic—the tour would definitely happen and she had agreed to a huge fee, this time £350 per night for twenty concerts. She had even signed a contract with Melbourne promoters, or so it was said.

The stories seemed to be confirmed by Nellie in a letter she wrote to Belle, which found its way into *The Argus* newspaper: 'I am really going to arrive in Australia next May. Mr Henry Abbey is going to take me straight from America.'

But by the time the ship docked in New York a week later, the story had changed. The contract was not signed but had merely been sent to Nellie for her approval, the fee a sticking point because it included wages for other performers. The definite had become a maybe, and the May arrival more likely to be August. Australia would have to wait yet again.

Nellie tried to explain the situation in a letter to the newspaper. She would begin her American season with a twenty-concert tour, followed by seventeen performances at The Met in New York before returning to London for the Covent Garden season for which she was contracted to appear. 'I hope the public will not mind this little delay, and that they will have as much pleasure in seeing and hearing me as I shall have in seeing and singing to them.'

Her arrival in New York sparked a rash of newspaper stories. Just a year before she had to settle for second-string roles, but now she was the centre of attention, earning $1000 for each performance of her own choosing.

At first the questions centred on her relationship with Philippe, whose support among French royalists was said to be wavering because of the revival of the story about him appearing in Paris dressed 'in livery' as her servant. It was one thing for a prince to be caught in a love tryst and entirely another to be seen in menial uniform demeaning to his own standing.

Until now, Nellie had steadfastly refused to comment about the incident, as she told the reporter from *The World* who arrived at her hotel the morning after her arrival:

> For reasons of my own I have never before spoken to any newspaper representative on this subject. I say now that the Duc d'Orleans did not come to Paris as one of my servants, although the statement was widely published at the time. Monsieur Lose, the Prefect of Police, has since confessed to me that he had my house carefully watched and satisfied himself not only that the Duke was not only NOT with me but was not in Paris. In fact, he was at the time in Russia and my husband was with me.

But the papers wanted to delve more into Nellie's own story, intrigued by her humble beginnings in Australia and eager for details about her life as a diva. A journalist with the *Chicago Daily News* named Amy Leslie had called at her Paris apartment for a pre-tour interview, and written with grandiose flourish about La Melba's trappings of success, 'a maze of beauty, comfort and luxury' from the Le Trianon furniture, Dresden and Watteau plaques to the silk tapestries and embroidered screens, copies of the great wall hangings in the Palace of Versailles.

There were gilded chairs and inlaid divans in rooms lined with sculptures, and mahogany cabinets filled with Bohemian glassware and Royal Worcester china. Everywhere Leslie looked there were gifts from emperors and queens and Indian princes—autographed pictures, notes of friendship and adoration, jewelled knives, handfuls of roped pearls, amethysts, agate and cornelian lying in bowls, and scrolls of homage.

But for all her sumptuous descriptions, it was Leslie's powers of observation that stood out; noting the careful placement of the Duc d'Orleans' portrait on the mantlepiece and the absence of Charlie Armstrong's in the drawing room. Most poignant though was Nellie's bedroom where marble steps led to a golden bed in which Marie Antoinette once slept. In here the walls were almost bare, except for 'the solemn little face of her pretty boy George'.

'Tomorrow is my boy's birthday,' Nellie told the reporter as she stood looking at George's portrait. 'He is so far away, and I want everything about me to remind me of him all day long. He is like a growing flower to me.' She stopped, head bowed for a moment as if collecting herself. When she raised her head again, Leslie caught a fleeting touch of melancholy. 'He comes to me only in the summer, you know,' she lied, pointing to George's bedroom across the hall that had laid untouched for over a year.

It was not the first time Leslie had visited Nellie, nor the only time Nellie had talked about her son. A few months earlier, during the London season, Leslie had met Nellie in her hotel room late one night and found her rearranging flowers: ferns and long-stemmed roses, marguerites and wreaths of asparagus leaves stripped from bouquets thrown onto the stage a few hours before after a performance of *Carmen*. She was balanced at the top of a rickety ladder, sleeves rolled up almost to her shoulders and petticoats tucked to her waist, pricking her fingers and drawing blood as she twined the flowers around the chandeliers to decorate the room.

The reporter was astounded that a diva was doing housework and asked why no one was helping her. 'Well, you see, early in the morning my little boy will be here and I want the room to show that I thought of his coming and am ready to welcome him with all my heart,' Nellie replied from the top of a ladder. 'What would he care if anybody but his mamma decorated the room for his home-coming?'

It might have seemed strange to some people but Leslie understood. An opera singer herself, she knew the sense of late-night adrenaline that continued long after a performance, and the bouquets meant far more stripped and rearranged for George than as floral trophies perched on shelves and tables.

'It was the most sweet and seductive role in which I ever beheld a celebrated woman,' she would write. 'Melba, with the world at her feet, forgetting everything except that her only child was near and that the preparations for his welcome should be the work of her hand. It seemed to me as I watched her anxiously testing colours, winding fine greens in among the pink and crimson, her hair tumbling down about her neck, her face flushed and her arms full of prickly roses, that there was true poetry in this midnight labour.'

But George would not be arriving in the morning. Nellie, in her grief, was preparing the room for a son she had not seen for more than a year and would not see again for many more.

※

In London there were Melba nights at Covent Garden but in the 1894–95 season in New York there was the 'Melba rage', as the *New York Globe* would describe her ability to fill the theatre.

> The Melba rage which had possessed New York will always be remembered as one of the most extraordinary manifestations of enthusiasm for art. It is doubtful whether demonstrations of equal intensity have ever before been witnessed in the metropolis.

Nellie's change in fortune had been in contrast to her rival Emma Eames who was out of favour. The *New York Tribune* blamed Eames' fallen star on a spat she'd had with Emma Calvé the previous season; the French soprano was angry that she had been snubbed socially and believed Eames was behind the slight. Calvé refused to take applause onstage with Eames at the season finale and left vowing she would not return to the city and sing if Eames was in the same company. Maurice Grau and Henry Abbey had backed Eames, so Calvé had stayed away for the new season. In response, audiences blamed Eames and boycotted her performances, as the *Tribune* reported.

> Eames is evidently much distressed by the change in her fortunes ... It is hard for a prima donna to vacate the centre of the stage in favour of a soprano who hates her. Between Melba and Eames there has always been ill feeling. These great singers never have and probably never will speak to each other.

Nellie couldn't help but gloat privately. 'The other night Eames sang *Faust* and there were not five hundred people in the hall which holds nine hundred. It was a good lesson to her and she is in her own country here. HA! HA! God is punishing her.'

It wasn't just New York where Nellie shone, as Grau took his major stars on tour in a company that included the de Reszke brothers and Lillian Nordica among others. But it was Nellie who attracted most of the attention.

There were more than four thousand people crammed into a hall in Indianapolis to hear her, one quarter of whom had to stand. When she finished the crowd seemed stunned into silence, but only for a moment, as the local paper reported: 'The great audience convulsed with the wildest applause. Men shouted and women cheered.'

In Chicago she was crowned as the next Adelina Patti:

> The great Australian songstress demonstrated that the world need not be inconsolable for the loss of Patti. Like Patti, Melba draws the crowds; like Patti, she incites them to prolonged

outbursts of applause ... there is possibly no one on the operatic stage at the present time who can dispute Melba's supremacy.

In St Louis, she overshadowed other cast members: 'It is singular how the peculiar quality of her voice contrasted with those who preceded it, beautiful as they all were,' the critic for the *St Louis Globe-Democrat* reported.

It was like a high silver bell mingling with the deeper vibrations that could not conceal it, no matter how immense their volume. There is a good deal of poetry about Melba's singing and chaste impersonations, and it is best for the world to acknowledge without further delay that she will live in the annals of the lyric stage as one of the great queens of song.

When she appeared in Boston, people tried to sneak into the theatre using tickets bought for a different night. It didn't matter what she sang because Melba was 'purity itself', as the *Boston Globe* critic concluded:

Mme Melba is unquestionably the greatest vocalist of the day. It is useless to speculate upon her merits compared to those of Patti when the latter was in her prime. Melba is superior today. That is a fact proven by direct comparison. Melba is now La Diva, and the homage due to the first singer in the world belongs to her.

Nellie could sense a business opportunity. America's cities were crying out for arts and culture. Why not form her own opera company and take it on tour across America? It was an audacious plan of which David Mitchell would have been proud, and when she met a young man named Charles Ellis who managed the Boston Symphony Orchestra, Nellie decided that he was the man to help her make it happen.

Not everyone had her confidence, including William Henderson, the influential critic for the *New York Times*, who regarded her move as arrogant and predicted that she would fail.

> It is reported that Mme Melba's opinion of her own attractiveness has grown too great to be. She seems to be labouring under the fond delusion that she is the brightest particular star who draws all the money for her managers, and it is said that she hopes to come to America next year at the head of an organisation of her own. If she does endeavour to emulate the example of Mme Adelina Patti, her experience will be short and not sweet. She will lose a great deal of money—or someone else will—and she will go back to Europe a sadder, if not a wiser woman. There is no living singer who can carry the burden of an opera season in the United States unaided.

The challenge had been issued. In May, as Nellie returned to London for the Covent Garden season, Ellis confirmed the tour would go ahead, beginning with a concert in Montreal in October.

## 27

# A FALL FROM GRACE

In the last days of April 1895, as Nellie took the raucous applause and encores of the New York audience for her performance of Lucia and then boarded a steamer for London, Philippe was camping in a houseboat on the edge of marshland in Spain.

He had been hunting near the mouth of the Guadalquivir, a river that flows from the Cazorla mountain range through Cordoba and Seville before it flows into the Atlantic near the aptly named town of Bonanza. At its mouth is Las Marismas, marshy lowlands known for rice plantations and flocks of flamingo and bustards, which nested in the high grass and still waters.

There had been an enthusiastic response to his Indian and African collections, lent to the Imperial College under the sponsorship of his friend, the Prince of Wales, and now he wanted to expand and create displays of all creatures great and small.

His trips to Spain had been taking him further and further inland, following the river on horseback as he searched for different specimens. Returning to his campsite one evening, Philippe spied a flock of birds but, as he urged his horse forward, it slipped on the muddy ground and fell, rolling on top of its rider, bruising his ribs and breaking his leg in three places.

It took two days for his companions, including Queen Victoria's son-in-law Prince Henry of Battenberg, to get Philippe to Seville on the back of a mule, by which time he had developed a high fever. Word reached London that he was seriously ill and could die, not of his injuries but from malaria, which was prevalent in the marshlands.

There would be daily newspaper updates but, a week later, when Philippe's improving condition coincided with Nellie's return to London and publicity about her upcoming appearances on the Covent Garden stage, the worry turned to amused speculation that he had not fallen from a horse but had been stabbed by an angry Spaniard at a fair in Seville after being caught kissing the man's girlfriend.

The speculation ended when Philippe was wheeled into the Savoy Hotel on 9 June. Instead, attention turned to the wedding of his younger sister, Princess Hélène, which had been delayed because of his accident. As the new head of the family, Philippe was expected to give her away to the Italian prince, the Duke of Aosta, and the attendance of European royalty had generated great public excitement.

The pomp and ceremony did not disappoint. Thousands lined the route and gathered outside St Raphael's Church in

Kingston as the guests arrived, including the heirs to three European thrones. The Prince of Wales would be a witness alongside the Prince of Naples, heir to the Italian throne, while Philippe was carried into the church by four French game-keepers dressed in Orleans blue livery.

Among the congregation were dozens of princes and prin-cesses, dukes, counts, generals and ambassadors, most of the men in full dress uniform because of the occasion. The lunch-time reception at Orleans House showed off the wedding gifts, including ones from Queen Victoria and the kings and queens of Portugal and Spain. In the evening, guests took a special train back to London for another dinner at the Savoy Hotel where all forty guests were members of royal families.

Nellie, who was staying at the Savoy during the season as usual, was not performing that night but booked to sing Gilda's role in *Rigoletto* the following evening. Given her habit of having a good meal the night before a performance, she would have been in the dining room when Philippe arrived with the wedding party.

Although they would have noticed each other across the room, the occasion and the myriad of eager observers would have ensured that she and Philippe studiously avoided one another.

❧

Nellie had made a spectacular entrance herself a few weeks earlier during her first performance of the season as Marguerite in *Faust*. The French bass Pol Plancon was making his entrance as the demon Mephistopheles, traditionally accompanied by the flames of hell—a real fire in a container that was managed offstage.

Mephistopheles usually appeared via a trapdoor in the middle of the stage but, on this night, he entered from the wings with the flames at his heels. Unfortunately, one of the stagehands had poured too much accelerant into the container and the flames grew too large, lighting a portion of the painted scenery, which quickly caught fire.

Witnesses reported seeing a sheet of flame shoot across the stage as Monsieur Plancon launched into his song. As the audience gasped, Plancon turned, saw the fire and raced to help as stagehands rushed forward to douse the flames.

In that moment, the curtain was dropped and the stunned audience sat silent. There was no explanation and no warning call of 'Fire!' but some in the audience realised the danger as the cry went up and the front rows began moving towards the exits. Behind the curtain, most of the two hundred–strong chorus had also rushed off towards the staircase that led to the stage door.

Theatre manager Augustus Harris, who was seated in the audience, feared there could be a stampede until the curtains suddenly parted and Nellie Melba, dressed as Marguerite, stepped into the footlights and addressed the confused crowd. 'Don't panic,' she called. 'Everything is under control. Please stay seated.'

She then stood there in her white gown while the audience resumed their seats and, when they were resettled and reassured, people erupted into sustained applause that the star soprano herself could calm a potentially dangerous situation.

The applause continued as she disappeared to resume her place with the cast, who had been persuaded to return and reassemble. When the curtain was finally raised, it revealed the seriousness of the situation as the opera continued with a scorched background and water-sodden floor.

'I knew something desperate had to be done for the opera house was crowded from pit to dome,' Nellie would recall some years later.

I nerved myself, walked deliberately across the stage between the fire and the footlights and said to the audience: 'Do not move; there is no danger; I am nearer the flames than you are'. Fortunately those words had the desired effect and the people halted. They cheered me but they did not see me collapse in a dead faint as I reached the wings.

The next morning, papers like *The Graphic* reported not on the quality of the opera, which had continued after the fire was extinguished, but the emergency: 'Through the promptitude and presence of mind of the officials and artists of the theatre, and through the great pluck and presence of mind of Madame Melba, what might have proved a serious panic was averted.'

Despite her onstage heroics, Nellie had to yield the spotlight to another singer. The London season of 1895 would belong to Adelina Patti who, at the age of fifty-two, had announced her intention to retire and was making her last appearances at

Covent Garden. Incredibly, Patti had made her Covent Garden debut on 14 May 1861—five days before Nellie was born—when she sang the lead role of Amina in the Bellini opera *La sonnambula*. The next day *The Times* had described her as a sensation. Now London wanted to pay homage and people scrambled for tickets at four guineas per seat.

♫♫♫

Although Nellie and Patti had come from vastly different backgrounds—Patti from a family of European opera singers and Nellie the daughter of a colonial businessman—they had both challenged norms for women on the stage.

At her peak, Patti commanded $5000 for a performance, demanded star billing and the right to choose her own repertoire and cast members. She always wore real gems rather than paste and was unashamed to use society connections to pursue her career while guarding her position against rivals.

Legend had it that she kept a parrot which she trained to call out 'Cash, cash!' whenever the impresario James Mapleson walked into the room. She dared to manage and finance her own tours of America, travelling across the country in a private railcar, and after her first marriage to a minor aristocrat collapsed in a bitter divorce, which had almost ruined her financially, she never again trusted a man with her money.

Nellie followed a similar path as her career advanced, led not only by comparisons to Patti but the lessons instilled in her by Mathilde Marchesi and learned from the example of her father's hard-headed business ways. David Mitchell was said to have once asked his daughter how much money she had made on the stage.

'Twenty thousand pounds,' she said proudly.

'Never tell anyone what you're worth,' he growled in reply.

Nellie was fierce in protecting her position in the opera (as were her contemporaries), insistent when negotiating her worth in contracts and fearless in risking her reputation to expand her vocal range and musical selection, even though she would not always succeed.

As the years passed, some critics would cast aspersions about her apparent cut-throat grandeur, such as her expectation that stagehands wore noiseless shoes when they were backstage, which was actually a reasonable request. She was considered vulgar in some society circles and known to swear and yet her adoring public, particularly in America, felt connected to her warmth and 'plain speaking'.

Likewise, there were contemporaries like Blanche Marchesi and Emma Eames, who felt Nellie hampered their careers through jealousy. But there were other contemporaries and rivals like Lillian Nordica and Emma Calvé with whom she enjoyed enduring friendships.

More importantly, Nellie would be remembered as a mentor for young singers, many of whom she would steer towards Madame Marchesi for tuition. One such singer was Ada Crossley, a promising contralto from rural Victoria, who would tell of the day in 1894 that she met her heroine at the Savoy Hotel in London.

Not only did Nellie agree to hear her sing but she insisted on escorting her to Paris to be introduced personally to Mathilde Marchesi. 'A letter will not do. Oh, what a glorious voice,' Nellie told the young woman. 'The world wants to hear a voice like that.' In the summer of 1895, as Patti wowed London audiences, Ada Crossley would make her debut on the London stage alongside Melba.

Another young singer from St Louis in America would tell a similar story; of how she had fallen out with Marchesi and then been turned down by other teachers in London. She considered quitting before a friend appealed to Nellie who, after listening to the woman sing, bundled her into a carriage and took her back to Madame. 'I can hardly recognise my own voice,' the unnamed singer would tell the New York media in the midst of Nellie's 1894–95 tour. 'Madame Melba has not only helped to make an artist of me but she positively saved my life.'

∰

It was inevitable, in light of her scandalous affair with Philippe, that there would always be eyes and ears on Nellie's male friendships although it yet again highlighted the double standards in how men and women of the stage were treated.

There was very little speculation, for example, about the private life of male stars like the de Reszke brothers, even when the better known and older brother, Jean, eloped with a married French countess in 1896. That was accepted by society, unlike the constant tittle-tattle about Melba and her relationships.

The rumour mill was at it again in the summer of 1895 as

Nellie prepared to return to America. New York papers began reporting that she intended to marry Timothee Adamowski, a renowned violinist with the Boston Symphony Orchestra who would be among the members of her touring company at the end of the year.

The stories gained credence when Adamowski turned up in London to appear alongside Nellie as a soloist in a concert organised to celebrate the skills of the famous conductor Arthur Nikisch. When Adamowski pulled out of the Melba tour a few months later, the rumours died away.

Philippe's love life was also in the news when he was named as a co-respondent in a divorce case involving a Mrs Wollaston, whose husband was angry that she had been 'living under the protection' of the duc on a houseboat moored on the Thames. The lady was said to be beautiful but it was unclear whether it was Philippe having an affair or, more likely, that he was acting on behalf of a friend, Captain Peters, who was also named as a respondent.

Philippe, who was still in a wheelchair, denied any involvement with Mrs Wollaston, which only excited the newspapers when the case was listed in September, just as Nellie was boarding a boat for New York. But there would be no salacious details as the case died away soon afterwards. Philippe left London to spend the rest of the year in Spain, pondering his next move in the increasingly complex manoeuvrings to reclaim the French throne.

# 28

# OF ENVIOUS MEN

The city of Montreal congratulated itself on the memorable night in October 1895 that Nellie Melba sang to a packed house at the Theatre Royal. It was a financial risk, said *The Gazette* newspaper, to bring such a star to Canada but the city's citizens had repaid the trust and turned out in droves to hear her 'operatic selections'.

Nellie had arrived in New York two weeks earlier where she met Charles Ellis who had assembled a thirty-five-piece orchestra. The musicians had been busy rehearsing with Nellie's support cast of four experienced singers—a mezzo-soprano, contralto, tenor and baritone—who expected they would remain in the shadows.

The Melba Operatic Concert Company had then embarked on a three-month tour during which they would perform forty concerts in two dozen cities and towns, generating an excitement that few had seen before. Without exception, the venues would be sold out as people came from miles around to see and hear the singer billed as the world's finest living soprano. There would be no dispute.

In Rochester the crowd began chanting in unison at the end of the concert, the noise was so deafening that Nellie took shelter in her dressing room, unsure about the response before being reassured and ushered back onstage. The next day, the critic for the local paper felt it necessary to explain that the shout was the highest compliment they could pay her: 'In that shout Rochester was saying: "Mme Melba, you have moved us deeply. We regard you as one of the greatest singers we have ever listened to."'

The full houses continued in Buffalo, Detroit and Portland (Maine), where hundreds were turned away at the door. In Cincinnati there was a momentary lull during one of Nellie's songs and a little boy in the audience was heard to cry out: 'Listen, mama; birdie, birdie.' The crowd erupted in laughter and applause and Nellie had to pause again. 'Nothing has ever pleased me more in all the things said of me in my life,' she later told a reporter.

Philadelphia followed and then Baltimore, Boston and Washington, where a local store launched a new winter coat— The Melba—to cash in on her arrival. It prompted a rash of false advertising, including a corset of which she supposedly commented, 'They certainly improve your figure', while other merchants claimed that she endorsed their cough mixtures and throat lozenges. Nellie fumed and denied it all.

Newspaper stories ahead of her visits spread like forest fires, several revealing that she was carrying a fortune in jewels. Checking into her hotel in Chicago she asked for the same suite she'd stayed in the previous year when touring under the Maurice Grau banner, but it had been booked by a couple who refused to change. It was a decision the couple soon regretted when two burglars, trying to steal the Melba jewels, burst into the room and threatened to shoot the woman, a Mrs Walker, who was alone. After tying her up, they ransacked the suite in a futile search.

Clearly tipped off by a staff member, they tried again the next day and broke into Nellie's room while she was singing in front of four thousand people at the city's theatre, the Auditorium. The men came up empty again because Nellie, concerned about the publicity, had locked the jewels she wasn't wearing in the hotel safe.

The events only added to Melba's publicity and, in the excitement, a second Chicago concert was added. Charles Ellis totalled ticket receipts at $15,000 for the two concerts, the modern equivalent of $500,000.

Nellie brushed off the incident, which only endeared her more to the city's citizens, as the *Daily Chronicle* reported:

Melba delights in America, its instabilities, its youth and its immense stretch of unplowed sentiment. Her tour has been a queenly triumphal march from one charmed town to the other and Chicago packed the great auditorium last night until the dome gapes. The four thousand crowd demanded so many encores between numbers that she had to appear in gauze in the midst of changing costumes.

※

The US Postal Service had been trying to catch up with Nellie ever since her troupe played a practice concert at the Worcester County Music Festival in Massachusetts in late September. A fan had delivered a letter to her hotel the next day hoping to reach Nellie before she left for Montreal but she was already gone. An enterprising hotel clerk decided to post it on to the next concert venue—Rochester—but the letter kept arriving a day or so late, such was the pace of the tour.

The letter finally reached Nellie in Connecticut where the tour had paused while she recovered from a sore throat caused, doctors believed, by the sheer number of concerts. The envelope provoked some mirth. 'Not here. Try Illinois', one hotel manager had scrawled. 'Left yesterday. Going to Chicago', wrote another, and so it went until the letter was delivered to her as she convalesced in the city of Hartford.

The pace did not slow despite her illness. Philadelphia's Academy of Music had only been half-full the previous year but it was sold out as the *Philadelphia Inquirer* trumpeted 'the most remarkable week in the city's musical history'. The three concerts took $25,000 in tickets and the paper's reviewer noted that her popularity stemmed as much from her response to the crowd as her voice: 'She has a gracious manner and attractive personality that have added to her popularity. She strengthened the ties that bound her to her old admirers and made many new friends by last night's performance.'

Likewise in Indianapolis, a reporter for *The Journal* stood watching Nellie as she ate and socialised in the hotel dining room. He was surprised, first, that she was mixing publicly, unlike Patti who would be served in her room 'wrapped in cotton wool'. Nellie's unassuming dress also spoke volumes for her unpretentious ways as she flicked through magazines and chatted with the cigar clerk while Ellis wrote a telegram. Then, instead of waiting for the elevator to go back to their rooms, Nellie hitched her dress and ran up the stairs, prompting the reporter to note:

> Somewhere in some book of advice to vocalists is a warning against climbing stairs or, if stairs are unavoidable, against dashing up them. Melba evidently overlooked that chapter in cultivating her wonderful voice, else displayed recklessness [as] she tripped up the stairs in a manner that would have made a less healthy woman breathless.

The troupe pushed further west in November, through Pittsburgh to Springfield and Minneapolis where the city elders debated where to hold a concert that kept growing in demand. Finally, they decided to spend money and adapt the city's Industrial Exposition Building, normally used for large conventions and indoor markets, to create a theatre space to cater for the thousands who wanted to attend. First, they had to improve its acoustics using sandbags and then bring in furnaces to heat the vast space for a week to ensure it was warm enough in the sub-zero weather. The concert was a triumph.

Finally they reached Kansas City, almost 2000 kilometres west of New York, where on the eve of the concert, the *Kansas City Journal* summed up the tour's success as a great financial surprise:

> Although Melba is generally conceded to be the greatest living soprano, her superlative distinction is still so newly acquired that some of the shrewdest impresarios in the country looked upon the venture as hazardous, especially as it contemplated booking into many cities where the superb voice has never been heard. But everywhere the attendance has been overwhelming, and the enthusiasm lavish.

Interviews invariably centred on Nellie's advice, not only for prospective singers, for whom she was writing a book, but for onstage nerves, which she avoided by a careful diet. She also weighed in on a heated debate about women riding bicycles and wearing bloomers, keen on the first but not on the second as she preferred a sense of feminine modesty.

When she reached St Louis in late November there was another issue on which she felt compelled to add her views. A local woman named Esther Getz had been widowed with two children. Her husband had sold fire insurance and she asked his company if she might take up his position to help feed her family. The company agreed and she was proving to be a good saleswoman until the city's insurance board stepped in and demanded she be sacked simply because she was a woman.

Outrage followed, community meetings were organised and the board pressured to reverse its decision. Nellie, undoubtedly driven by her own experiences, offered her support for Mrs Getz during an interview with the *St Louis Post-Dispatch*:

> Is it possible that . . . anyone has the hardihood to deny women's right to earn a living at any honest avocation? I can scarcely credit a body of presumably intelligent men with such action. I will venture to say that none of these men concern themselves in the least about the thousands of women and girls who eke out a miserable livelihood by hard work in factories and stores. They are not shocked at the idea of women earning their bread by such laborious occupations. It is only when a woman enters into competition with them that they object.

Nellie predicted that working women would increasingly become an important part of society, adding:

> Mrs Getz has taken up the struggle for life where her husband laid it down, and in her honest efforts to support herself and children she has my earnest sympathy. Her example is one for women to follow, and I entertain no fears for her future, in spite of the efforts of envious men.

A week later, faced with increasing public anger and the impact of Melba's opinion, the insurance board relented and Mrs Getz was rehired.

This would not be the last time Nellie spoke out about feminist issues, particularly during the women's suffrage campaign in Britain during which she visited a factory in Manchester and emerged tearfully to insist that women getting the vote would help improve working conditions.

'I suppose the critics will think it awful,' she told Hearst News Service when confirming that she had joined the suffragette ranks.

I have really joined the women who have thrown Cabinet and Parliament into a state of panic, simply because I think their demands are just, and because I am very much interested in the woman of the future. Freedom will surely not rob her of her woman's love of home. The greater use of her brain will spiritualise the future woman. Her face will be alight with intelligence.

She did the same in America, making it known during the 1909 New York opera season that she was attending a Women's Rights Party meeting at Carnegie Hall and announcing that she had registered the green, purple and white of the suffrage movement for her horse racing colours with the Victorian Racing Club. The intention was for her jockeys to wear an olive green jacket, mauve sash and white cap although, despite attending race meetings and expressing a desire to win the Melbourne Cup, she never got around to buying a horse.

In another interview she was asked by the *Evening World* if it was true that she had cooked her own dinner of spaghetti in the hotel kitchen. 'It's perfectly true,' she said, adding that she believed cooking was an essential life skill for young women.

> Yet I am a suffragette. What in the world has that got to do with cooking? People think I cannot sing and cook, and now imagine that I cannot believe in women's suffrage and at the same time know anything about the kitchen. I am an ardent suffragette and yet I think it would be hard to find a woman more interested in her own home than I am.

But she later distanced herself from the tactics of militant suffragettes. 'How foolish of them,' she told the *New-York Tribune* in 1910:

> Anyone who knows the world knows that the woman's way to obtain her end is not by violence. Of course the suffragettes have a portion of right upon their side. I, for instance, employ my butler. Yet my butler has more to say about the taxes I pay than I have. That does not seem to me to be right. I hope that in time a way will be found to change this injustice, but it won't be via the militant suffragette.

Most of all, she believed women should be free to make their own choices, reflecting the regrets of her own childhood, and how close David Mitchell had come to killing his daughter's career before it had even begun. Not only was his daughter a renowned singer but she was now a successful businesswoman.

## 29

# A WAGNERIAN TRAGEDY

When Nellie returned to London from New York in April 1896, Philippe was recovering from another riding accident. He had been thrown from his horse while hunting in forests on the outskirts of Turin, fracturing his right ankle and dislocating a shoulder.

His misadventures were causing great amusement among the Paris journalists and commentators, few of whom thought the Playboy Prince was serious in his endeavours to regain the throne. Some had even questioned whether his younger cousin Prince Henri d'Orleans, who had recently returned a conquering hero because of a two-year exploration of the Far East, might be a better candidate and should replace him as head of the family.

But their views would change in May when the royalist newspapers began reporting that Philippe was challenging the views of party elders and even contemplating submitting his claim to the throne to a public vote.

The royalists held barely 10 per cent of the seats in the Chamber of Deputies and Senate which meant Philippe's political backers faced an almost impossible task to gain a parliamentary majority unless his opponents self-destructed or there was a radical change of course and philosophy that carried public opinion.

But Philippe wanted to modernise the monarchy via the ballot box, 'a policy of adventure' as he told the committee president in a letter that found its way into *Le Gaulois*. 'It is necessary to choose between playing at monarchy and making it a reality,' he insisted.

It was a significant moment, according to mainstream newspapers on all political sides. 'It marks a new chapter in monarchical politics,' editorialised the *Civil and Military Gazette*, which boasted the author Rudyard Kipling among its staff. 'Virtually, the Duc d'Orleans is quietly shelving . . . the theory of the divine right of kings and accepts the Bonapartist principle of the plebiscitium or direct appeal to the people.'

The royalist papers warmly applauded Philippe's sentiments, which they hoped might 'amalgamate monarchical unity and plebiscitary ideals', while Republican titles like *Figaro* remained doubtful whether he could succeed but acknowledged the 'courageous spirit of his manifesto'. It seemed a fanciful proposition, and he would ultimately be denied the right to hold a plebiscite alongside a general election, but Philippe insisted that a democratic monarchy was possible.

As his words and promises were digested, Philippe left for Palermo where his ageing uncle, Duc d'Aumale, had arranged an introduction to Eugenie, wife of the last emperor of France, Napoleon III. The meeting of the seventy-year-old widow and figurehead of the French Imperialists and the 27-year-old Bourbon royalist prompted speculation that the two parties in France were about to form a pact and unite their forces.

After leaving Palermo, Philippe had travelled to Vienna and then Budapest where, keen to get back on his horse, he had accepted an invitation to hunt with Archduke Joseph Habsburg, staying at his castle Alesuth, just west of the city.

But the trip would result in a surprise capture when he announced that he was marrying the archduke's eldest daughter, Maria Dorothea, a cousin to the Austrian Emperor Franz Joseph. Philippe had finally found himself a wife.

The press would spend months analysing the union and whether this was love or, more likely, a marriage of political convenience. Archduke Joseph, the commander-in-chief of the Hungarian Landwehr, or army, was a wealthy man and an alliance between the Austrian and French royal families was advantageous. The only drawback, they concluded, was a superstitious one given that Maria, who used her Hungarian name Maroussia, held the same title as the ill-fated Marie Antoinette.

The wedding would be held in Vienna in early October and hosted by Emperor Franz Joseph. As part of the three-day celebration, the couple were seen around the city at a series of cultural events, including the ballet and two plays.

They would also attend the opera at the Imperial Theatre to see a production starring the tenor Ernest van Dyck, the singer whose outing of Philippe and Nellie four years before had lit the fuse for the scandal that followed.

⚌

As Philippe was preparing to marry, Nellie was making the worst decision of her professional life. Despite her touring success the previous year, or perhaps because of the seemingly endless repeats of the same songs before different audiences across America, she decided to take on a new and controversial role.

Wagner had long been a frustration to her, as many of the German's compositions were considered beyond her range. And in New York, whose opera lovers preferred Wagner to Verdi, it was a weakness, or so she believed. The role she coveted more than any other was as the mythological warrior queen Brunnhilde, who appeared in the opera *Siegfried*, the story of the Germanic mythological hero who slew a dragon.

Mathilde Marchesi was horrified that her prize pupil would want to use her crystal, bell-like chords like a hammer. As Nellie would reveal in her autobiography: 'I had mentioned to Madame this desire, to be met with a horrified expression and great fluttering of the hands, as though I had threatened to cut my throat ... I thought [her] horror was exaggerated.'

Despite Madame's objections, Nellie went ahead and found a language teacher so she could sing in German. The reason for the urgency was that Maurice Grau had indicated he wanted to produce *Siegfried* for the coming New York season with de Reszke in the title role. The only question was, who would play Brunnhilde? Lillian Nordica seemed the obvious choice as she was the company's leading Wagner soprano and would be performing in front of her hometown. Nellie was expected to be cast in a minor, although more suitable role as a forest bird.

Instead, Grau announced that Nellie would sing both roles, which was greeted with surprise by the New York press and tearful astonishment by Nordica, who immediately announced that she was withdrawing from the company for the season and would, instead, tour the country.

Some believed that Nellie had used her dominance to bully Grau into giving her the part, while others insisted it was de Reszke who had lobbied Grau, because he preferred to sing with Melba and feared being dominated by Nordica's voice in a duet towards the end of the opera.

Nordica pinned the blame on de Reszke who, she revealed, had written a letter to Melba during the summer advising her to study for the part. 'This is my own country, and I have made my progress here before my own people,' she said at a press conference to announce her decision. 'They have seen me rise, and it is doubly painful to me that they should see me driven out by foreigners.'

Grau rejected Nordica's allegation, insisting that his decision was actually brought on by her greed, having demanded $1500 for each performance. While de Reszke admitted encouraging Nellie to study Wagner he denied trying to influence Maurice Grau. 'Of course I advised Mme Melba to sing Wagner,' he said.

I wrote that it was possible for a singer like her to learn the Wagner roles, and suggested that, as she had always sung the old repertoire and the lighter music, that she had better commence with such a part as Brunnhilde. She accepted my advice and began to study the role enthusiastically.

Nellie, surrounded by reporters as she got off a train, also denied the accusation. 'I never take part in newspaper controversy and in this case I will only say that Mme Nordica is entirely mistaken in all that she is reported to have said regarding me.'

Opening night was 30 December, and the closer the date came, the more worried Nellie became about her decision. The controversy with Lillian Nordica only served to highlight the high stakes involved. A false step in a single performance could undo all the wonder of the previous season and question the pedestal on which she had been placed by critics and the public across America.

On the night, Nellie waited nervously as the opera progressed. The bird song in the second act went off without a hitch but Brunnhilde did not make an appearance until the last scene of the opera. As she listened, Nellie sensed that Madame had been right and that the music was overpowering, but there was no turning back.

Finally, the curtains rose with Nellie draped across a rock in the centre of the stage, deep in a magical sleep. The script called for Siegfried to discover Brunnhilde and wake her with a kiss before they sang a love duet.

It was a disaster from her first notes, which sounded like a strangled cry. There was no sense of the exaltation she normally felt as her voice floated out to envelop the audience. Instead she felt suffocated, as if grappling with a monster that was beyond her strength. Jean de Reszke's powerful voice beside her only highlighted the problems, as the audience sensed her troubles.

As the curtain fell, she rushed back to her dressing room and shut the door. Charles Ellis found her with a dressing gown over her shoulders, distraught. Outside, the newspaper critics circled: 'Tell the critics that I am never going to do that again,' she told Ellis. 'It is beyond me. I have been a fool.' Ellis confronted the reporters and delivered the message, Nellie waiting for them to leave before venturing out.

She could hardly bring herself to read the reviews the next morning, although they were surprisingly forgiving: 'Madame Melba's Brunnhilde was, all things considered, surprisingly good,' the *New York Herald* concluded. The *Tribune* applauded as admirable 'the sincerity of her effort' and the *Democrat and Chronicle* described it as 'a brave attempt and unmistakably an intelligent effort'.

But the *Brooklyn Eagle* thought her voice 'small' and concluded the obvious: 'In her own line Melba is the greatest singer of her time but that line does not include Brunnhilde.' Later that day a critic found her at the hotel and pleaded, 'Your voice is like a piece of Dresden china. Please don't smash it.'

Still distraught three days later, Nellie put out a statement:

As strong as I find the role of Brunnhilde I do not intend singing it again, at least for some years. My reason for this decision is my belief that in singing it often there would be danger of injuring my voice. My opinion is confirmed by the advice of those whom I consider good authority.

But it would not be the end of the matter. Over the next few weeks Nellie cancelled seven performances, replaced as Brunnhilde by an understudy and even wary of singing parts like Juliet, Violetta and Lucia. Her confidence was shot and her voice strained. A doctor eventually diagnosed a 'severe constitutional depression' and ordered complete rest.

The season would have to continue without her as she sailed for London at the end of January 1897, the newspapers giving little sympathy and some, like the *Democrat and Chronicle*, even predicting she might never return:

Mme Melba staked her artistic rank upon her appearance and lost. Her failure as Brunnhilde must be a terrible mortification to her; must, for a time, make all her former triumphs worthless in her eyes and assume, in her view, the proportions of a final failure, the close of her artistic career.

They were wrong.

# 30

## A STAR-SPANGLED BANNER

It would be almost five months before Nellie sang again in public. She retreated to Paris and into the admonishing but beloved arms of Mathilde Marchesi, who blamed the affair on Maurice Grau, whom she believed had constructed a Machiavellian plot, with the help of Jean de Reszke, to rid the opera of Melba and Nordica.

It was a ridiculous theory, if only because the two women were crowd favourites and money-spinners. More likely, it was a combination of Nordica's demands for more money, Melba's pushy desire for the role and de Reszke's support for Nellie as his partner.

Whomever Grau chose, the other soprano would likely have resigned in protest, and as a business decision, it was better to lose Lillian Nordica than to lose Nellie Melba. In hindsight, of course, he made a bad choice because Nellie's failure and subsequent withdrawal badly affected takings for the season.

With little to do in Paris, Nellie's thoughts turned to George and her family in Australia. 'I am very miserable and blue,' she wrote in one letter to her sister Belle, asking that she arrange for a photo to be taken of their father, who was approaching seventy years of age. But it was the company of children she most desired. 'I love both your kiddies,' she wrote to her sister. 'I think they are beauties. I wish you would lend me one of them.'

Although she was confident that her voice would be restored, Nellie was less convinced that her Wagner mistake would be quickly forgotten or forgiven by audiences and critics. Had her ego wrecked her career just as she had reached the pinnacle?

She was still reticent in May when her doctor, Felix Semon, gave her the all-clear. The London season had already begun and there was a clamour for her to return to Covent Garden in time for the celebrations planned for the sixtieth anniversary of Queen Victoria's reign. Initially she refused to sing when asked to front a royal gala performance but relented at the behest of the Prince of Wales.

Any concern about her voice and friendship with Jean de Reszke was put to rest on this night when she appeared with him to sing the third act of *Romeo et Juliette*. The next day *The Stage* remarked: 'Nothing need be said of Madame Melba's delightful embodiment of Juliet. Her rendering of Gounod's sweet music was as free and brilliant as ever.'

Relieved and encouraged, she returned a week later to sing the entire opera and then two performances of *Faust* in July. The critics welcomed her return. Covent Garden wasn't the same without Melba. 'The absence of Melba this season has been severely felt,' said *The Graphic*. '*Faust* was chosen for her re-entry and one needs hardly record how brilliantly the jewel song was rendered or with what seductive beauty she sang the love music of the garden scene,' added *The People*.

The summer social scene was also a useful distraction. She hosted a dinner at the Savoy to celebrate her return to the stage and had frequent weekend parties at a house she now rented in Richmond by the banks of the Thames River.

Among the guests was Haddon Chambers, an Australian dramatist and playwright whom she had met the previous summer when he had offered himself as a drama coach. She accepted and they formed a close friendship. He was a year older than her and engaging company, with an undeniable physical similarity to Charlie—a blond, blue-eyed horseman with a carefree attitude to life. His one drawback was that he was married, although estranged from his wife.

There was a second man with whom she had become close. Joseph Joachim was a celebrated Hungarian violinist who, despite being thirty years her senior, had tried to woo Nellie when they first met at a concert some years before. They would meet again in the autumn of 1897 when they were both invited to the Italian city of Bergamo, whose citizens were celebrating the centenary of the birth of its most famous son, the composer Gaetano Donizetti.

Although neither man swept Nellie off her feet as Philippe d'Orleans had done, their relationships were clearly close and, in Haddon Chambers' case at least, might have been sexual. The hint lay in her autobiography in which Joachim was mentioned but Chambers was not. On that basis, Nellie and Haddon Chambers might well have been lovers.

But neither man could hold a candle to Philippe, as Nellie would hint at many years later. The reference was contained in a memoir *People in Glass Houses*, written by Adelaide Lubbock, daughter of the former Governor of Victoria, Sir Arthur Stanley, and based on hundreds of letters written by her mother, Margaret, who was a close friend of Nellie Melba.

In one letter, Margaret Stanley recounted a weekend she spent with Nellie during which the singer spoke about the difficulties of her first marriage.

'She came into my room one morning before I was up and said she would like to tell me about her early life and her marriage and what happened after it,' Margaret wrote.

She said she just wanted me to know everything there was to know because she valued my friendship ... and couldn't bear to be in doubt as to whether it might make any difference. I wish I could tell you all she told me. You couldn't help admiring the way she tackled the crashing smashes she got into when she was [young] and I am glad that the man she sacrificed everything for then is still as true to her as when they first met, and is the one rock in her life to which she clings with all the passion and intensity of their first love. You can imagine that I satisfied her that what she had told me could not possibly make any difference and that I should probably have done the same if I had been her.

Philippe's financial fortunes had changed since his marriage but little else. Not only was his wife from a wealthy family but his ageing uncle, the Duc d'Aumale, died in 1897 leaving him the vast majority of his estate, including the house Wood Norton in Evesham where the couple would move. But the change would not save a marriage that was clearly hasty and ill-matched. The union would last barely two years before Maria moved back to her family's estates in Hungary.

Philippe then concentrated on his wildlife museum, which continued to grow and eventually became the largest collection of taxidermy in the world. And he continued to probe weaknesses in the French political maelstrom, tussling in court for the right to use the French royal arms and signing himself Philippe, head of the House of France, and lobbying a prominent Paris theatre, the Théâtre du Châtelet, to produce a series of plays 'favourable to the royalist cause'.

But his main hopes were pinned on the fallout from a scandal surrounding a French army officer named Alfred Dreyfus, which would have ramifications for French politics for more than a decade. Captain Dreyfus, an artillery officer of Jewish descent, had been convicted in 1894 of divulging military secrets to the German Embassy in Paris and sentenced to life imprisonment.

Two years later evidence emerged of a cover-up, and that the espionage had actually been committed by another officer, a major named Ferdinand Esterhazy, who was acquitted after a two-day trial during which senior officers suppressed evidence of the forgery that had implicated Dreyfus, who remained in prison on Devil's Island in French Guiana.

The case was reopened in 1898 after a newspaper published an open letter, written by the novelist Émile Zola and titled *J'accuse*, which revealed the forgery. As the city, divided by pro and anti 'Dreyfusards', prepared for a new trial, Philippe and his supporters could sense a political opportunity. It was further enhanced when the embattled Prime Minister Felix Faure had a stroke and died while having sex with the notorious society figure Marguerite Steinheil, a woman half his age.

Cobbling together a disparate group of political movements including nationalists, Republicans and royalists, Philippe's associates planned a series of protests and riots which they hoped would be backed by the army, whose senior officers felt under siege over their handling of L'Affaire, as the Dreyfus Affair would become known.

In the confusion, and with the backing of the army, Philippe would be smuggled into the city and then revealed as the uniting voice who could calm public unrest and form a stable leadership group that would then re-form government and restore the monarchy in the process.

There were ten thousand medals struck with his image and embossed with a rally cry to pass out among the crowds. Around its circumference he had vowed *I will only avenge the insults done to the country*; and across its face—*I will replace my country in the first rank of nations with the help of all true French people.*

Inevitably though, hints of the plot emerged and it was rumoured that Philippe was already in Paris and waiting in hiding. It wasn't true but when he was spotted in Genoa, the French government began shadowing his movements, only to have their awkward attempts revealed by the press.

The next day the Central News Agency reported that Philippe had left Genoa aboard his steam yacht 'in order to avoid unwelcome attentions of the authorities'. Instead, he would cruise his yacht in the waters of the Riviera while he waited and watched events unfold in Paris.

The excitement would last a few weeks but eventually the protests were quelled and some of the leaders arrested, including a Monsieur Andre Buffet, who was one of the duc's representatives in Paris. In their searches, police found copies of several telegrams sent to Philippe, who was in Turin at the time: 'All our men are ready', one read, followed a few days later by dejection: 'Useless to come. Attempt failed.'

At his trial, Dreyfus would be convicted once more but pardoned because of public sympathies. However, the matter still did not die as he pursued justice and was finally exonerated in 1906 and his army rank restored.

But Philippe's last chance of re-establishing the monarchy appeared to have disappeared.

⌖

On 9 May 1898, a reporter from *The Chronicle* couldn't quite believe his eyes as he stepped aboard a carriage near the back of the Northern Pacific train that had just arrived from Seattle. The usual bench seats had all been removed and replaced with soft couches, armchairs and nests of small tables. This was a reception room on a train, a bijou grand piano set up in the far corner at which sat the 'queen of song', Nellie Melba, who welcomed him with a firm handshake.

'No other prima donna, not even Patti, has ever dreamed of travelling like this,' he would write after being shown around the five carriages that made up the *Melba*, the name emblazoned on the side in gold by the Pullman company, which had built the carriages for the star.

Next door there was an observation carriage with overly large windows from which Nellie and her guests could watch the countryside flashing by, then a kitchen and dining car staffed by her own chef, and waiters to tend the tables set in white linen, silverware and crystal glasses. The last two carriages were Nellie's private apartments, furnished with the comforts of home brought from Paris.

The cost of $11,000 to run and staff the carriages during the two-month tour seemed exorbitant, and a huge slice of the expected profits. But, as the reporter observed:

there is economy in this, and a sound business sense and judgement. The danger of sickness and the thousand trifling ailments which may be of no importance to the ordinary mortal but which may injure the greatest and most fluent singing voice of all time will be reduced to a minimum.

Nellie, once again, had broken away from the comfort of the New York opera season, where she now commanded $1500 a night, to take her own company with its financial risk even further across the vast continent, over the Rocky Mountains to the Pacific coast and back again.

San Francisco had been a revelation, the sunny climate and vegetation a reminder of Australia, which she had left more than a decade before. But there was danger in the visit, too. America and Spain had been at loggerheads over the sovereignty of Cuba and tensions were high in California, a former Spanish territory, with frequent street demonstrations and an expectation of war.

As chance would have it, Nellie was due to open on 26 April with a performance of the Rossini opera *The Barber of Seville* in which she would sing the part of Rosina, the heroine—'an intensely Spanish opera in a city where the very name of Spain was an anathema', as she would later write.

Then war was declared the day before the opening, which led to a frantic discussion with Charles Ellis about whether they should cancel. Eventually it was decided to continue as there was a full house and they did not want to disappoint the audience. Nellie, who had watched departing seamen—'the boys in blue'—from the harbour during the afternoon, made a statement to the press to explain her dilemma, saying she expected to be hissed at in her Spanish outfit but insisting that 'I am with America's heart and soul in this'.

The first act passed without incident, although Nellie and the other cast members could sense the unease in the stands. In the second act, Rosina appears at a piano where she is giving singing lessons during which she plays a song. Rossini had not stipulated the song to be played, leaving it to the discretion of the performer. It was an oversight that Nellie considered lazy but it turned out to be fortuitous.

As she approached the piano, Nellie had an idea. Instead of playing an aria, she began to play and sing the opening bars of 'The Star-Spangled Banner'. 'The effect was miraculous,' she would write in her memoir. 'As my voice floated out I could hear the sound of the vast gathering rising to their feet. By the end of the first few lines every man and woman in the audience was shouting their national anthem and my own voice was drowned out.'

The *Los Angeles Evening Express* described the scene:

> Those who witnessed the enthusiastic outpouring of patriotism will never forget when the beautiful Australian seated herself at the piano and gave forth with astonishing clearness the first notes of 'The Star-Spangled Banner'. You may imagine the tremendous cheering, the rising of the house en-masse, the sea of handkerchiefs which fluttered through the auditorium, the fragrant flowers waved in the air by the beautiful and enthusiastic women, and in fact the utter abandonment of the vast audience to a veritable pandemonium of patriotism.

Far from being run out of town, the response and demand for more forced Charles Ellis to announce an extra performance. When the performance sold out the next day there were still seven hundred people lined up at the ticket office.

Nellie was back on top.

# 31

# DIVORCE, TEXAS-STYLE

Judge William H Stewart of the tenth judicial district court in Texas was not a man of high culture, or at least not a fan of opera. He admitted as such on the morning of 9 April 1900, to a reporter from the *Tribune* newspaper, as he sat behind his oak desk in the Galveston courthouse, overlooking the local port, where he administered his form of justice.

The reporter asked if the judge knew that Nellie Armstrong, a defendant in a case on which he had just ruled, was one of the most famous women in the world. 'I don't know,' he said. 'There was, I remember, some testimony introduced to the effect that she was on the stage and that she is now in Paris.' His response struck the reporter as disingenuous.

The testimony to which the good judge was referring was in the case *Armstrong v Armstrong*, heard in front of an all but empty courthouse a few days before, which resulted in him granting Charlie a divorce and full custody of George, now aged sixteen, on the basis that they had been callously abandoned without cause by an uncaring wife and mother who had repeatedly ignored requests to attend the court.

The newspaper revealed the next day that it had only known about the case after being tipped off by another member of the Galveston bar. 'The *Tribune* is reliably informed that the Nellie Armstrong mentioned is Melba, one of the greatest operatic stars the world has ever known,' the reporter wrote rather pointedly. 'The man who got the divorce is the owner of the Buena Vista Ranch in Karnes County.'

Charlie Armstrong had emerged from his self-imposed exile to finish the job he had begun nine years before, only this time residency was on his side because he was appealing to a court that was happy to acknowledge him as a Texan and his errant wife as a foreigner.

Judge Stewart, aged eighty-two, was just the man for the job. A former major in the Confederate Army during the Civil War, he had then enjoyed a lengthy political career in the Texas legislature before taking a lifetime appointment on the bench. He'd had plenty of experience with divorce as well, having fathered six children with four wives.

Charlie's motives were a mystery. He had no plans to remarry and lived as a single man on his ranch, bought with funds from the Armstrong family, or so his court declaration said. He'd also had effective custody of George for seven years, even though he had promised to return the boy to his mother after one.

Perhaps that was his reason—to avoid a legal confrontation—although that was highly unlikely given that the British courts had no jurisdiction in America. And Nellie had no idea where they were living, continuing to send letters to the post office address in the town of Murphy where they went uncollected, George never knowing that his mother cared.

The testimony also shed light on Charlie's movements since leaving his cousin's plantation. Repeating his lifestyle from Queensland, he had moved around North Carolina taking piecemeal jobs before using his share of the Armstrong inheritance to buy into a 208-acre property outside Galveston where he resorted to his first love—horses.

He had also recently sunk money with two local businessmen into a fishing operation. The Galveston Red Snapper Fishing Company had three schooners which harvested seafood from the rich fishing grounds of the Gulf of Mexico. His activities meant he had become well known around the city where he was regarded as a quiet but 'pleasant enough fellow'.

Charlie's affidavit would have enraged Nellie for its lies. In it, Charlie claimed that Nellie had travelled to America with him and George and they had lived together 'as husband and wife' until 1894 when she had suddenly 'left his bed without cause' and abandoned him.

The statement, which Judge Stewart accepted as true in absence of any rebuttal from Nellie, went on to state:

> The plaintiff has invited the defendant to live with him as his
> wife and she has refused to do so, and has refused to keep her

marital obligations. The plaintiff has observed all his marital obligations and always supported the defendant in good style and conducted himself lovingly toward her.

It was little wonder that the judge denied knowing that Nellie Armstrong was a famous and wealthy opera singer who didn't need her estranged husband's financial support, or that Charlie had been accused of extortion, bullying and acts of violence which had been widely reported in newspapers across America, including Texas.

Instead, he noted that Charlie was a 'bonafide' Texan who had tried to notify his estranged wife, a 'non-resident', that he wanted a divorce. She had ignored all attempts, the judge concluded, and therefore he was releasing him from 'the bonds of marriage' and granting Charlie sole custody of George.

⁂

The story had swept the country within days. The mysterious tale of an aristocratic Texas rancher who had apparently been abandoned by Nellie in her search for fame fuelled a renewed interest in the scandal of Nellie and the Duc d'Orleans.

But the interest would reach new, farcical levels when stories emerged that Nellie was planning to remarry two different men in two different countries. First she was linked to Joseph Joachim. Nellie had been singing in Germany in front of the Kaiser and wildly enthusiastic Berliners, who openly wept when she was sidelined for a week with influenza. In the intervening period, rumours had sprung up that she and Joachim, who was her concert accompanist, had struck up a personal friendship that had become something more.

Nellie, fully recovered from the flu, had scotched the rumours but they would not die, even when American newspapers began reporting the divorce and announcing that the singer was due to wed a different man—Haddon Chambers.

A reporter from the *San Francisco Examiner* claimed to have confronted Nellie in a Paris street where she confirmed the rumour. The wedding would be held in a fortnight. 'My divorce from Mr Armstrong delights me,' she was reported to have said.

I am immensely relieved. It is what I have hoped for. I have never had any time to live in those awful Dakota and Texas places. Now all is done. As for me, I will marry Haddon Chambers. I never thought of marrying Herr Joachim. Why, he is eighty. I have already bought a house in Great Cumberland Street, London, where I expect to be very happy as Mr Chambers's wife. After the London season, we shall spend some time on my new steam yacht.

The report was fabricated. Nellie and Chambers were close friends but he was still a married man, as his sister pointed out angrily when the claims of an imminent marriage were published back in Australia.

Nellie, angry that Charlie's lies were being ignored and she was being made out as the villain, issued a statement through her management. 'All reports representing me as contemplating marriage are entirely without foundation, including the report that I would marry Haddon Chambers. Any further tales of this kind will be equally unfounded, even if the most prominent newspapers should publish them.'

'I hate the American press, it is too shocking,' she told her sister Belle in a letter written soon afterwards. 'I shall never marry again. I could never put up with a man bossing me. I should kill him.'

Her anger at the surprise, one-sided divorce proceedings and marriage tittle-tattle was tempered by the excitement that at least she knew where Charlie had taken George, or at least the nearest city—Galveston in Texas. She hoped it might be possible to make inquiries when she returned to America later in the year and perhaps be reunited with her son who would now be a young man.

But her hopes would be dashed four months later when a hurricane swept in from the Gulf of Mexico, creating a tidal wave that smashed into the city of Galveston and laid waste to the nearby countryside, killing an estimated twelve thousand people. The storm and its devastation made headlines around the world and, more than a century later, remains the biggest natural disaster in American history.

When Nellie heard the news she panicked. Had Charlie and George survived or been injured? She appealed for help from Alfred Harmsworth, owner of the influential *Daily Mail* newspaper. Harmsworth, better known by his later title Lord Northcliffe, was able to use his American publishing contacts to confirm that neither her son nor her recently divorced husband were among the listed dead. Nellie breathed a sigh of relief.

Behind the scenes, Charlie's fishing operation had played an integral role for the city's survivors in the first days after the storm. The Red Snapper Fishing Company's storehouse was among the few waterfront buildings to survive the sea surge and, when morning broke, it had the city's only supply of ice, which was badly needed in the late summer, and quickly distributed.

Two days later, three of the company's boats returned safely, having chosen to remain at sea and ride out the storm while many others that returned to harbour were smashed to pieces. The Red Snapper schooners had not only survived but were laden with fish, all of which was given away to the hundreds of people, most hungry and thirsty and many sleeping on wooden boards, who flocked to the port.

Despite the heroics, Charlie Armstrong did not fare as well as his fishing fleet. In years to come he would say only that he had barely survived the storm, perhaps on the docks as the furious winds struck. Whatever happened that night, soon afterwards he sold out of the business and put his land, also impacted by the storm, up for sale. It was time for Charlie and George to move on again, but where would they go?

Nellie's concern had turned to anger. 'I have had frightful accounts of the way Georgie is being brought up,' she wrote to her sister Belle. 'I am heart-broken about it; the solicitors say there is nothing to be done. I can only hope that God will one day punish that bad man—surely he must be punished someday.'

She then went one step further and changed her will. Her

growing fortune would now be diverted to Belle's daughter, Nellie, at least until George came of age and out from under Charlie's custody and influence. As she wrote to her sister:

> You can imagine how sad it is for me to write this but my heart
> is breaking and I must talk to someone I know and I know
> I can trust you and Tom. Under the circumstances it would
> never do for my Boy to have too much money so I am taking
> care of every details. Do not mention this to Pater please. God
> bless you dear. I am <u>very sad</u> and wish you were here with me.

## 32

# AUSTRALIA FINALLY

It was an unusual route to approach Australia by ship, from the northern hemisphere, across the Pacific and down the east coast of the continent rather than across the Indian Ocean to Perth and then along the southern coast to Melbourne and Sydney, but perhaps it was an appropriate passage for Nellie's return after sixteen years—via Queensland where, years before, she had vowed to break free from male expectation.

The *Miowera*—Hawaiian for 'weary mother'—was aptly named as she struggled in the tropical heat, breaking down several times and causing those waiting ahead in Brisbane to begin to worry about the safety of her precious cargo. On the late afternoon of the third day of watching, the *Miowera* finally appeared on the horizon and everyone breathed a sigh of relief.

Now, as she steamed across Moreton Bay, Nellie stood alongside a reporter from the *Sydney Morning Herald*, an ostrich feather flopping lazily over the brim of her hat as she leaned, wistful, on the railing and looked back up the coast which glowed red in the evening light from numerous bushfires.

'My native land,' she exclaimed, laughing lightly. 'Yes, that's my country. I bowed three times to it for luck when I saw it in the distance half an hour ago.'

Nellie fell silent again, a moment of reflection clear on her face as her eyes filled with tears: 'I am very proud of my father,' she offered as explanation, unable to express the conflict of emotions about David Mitchell, a man she loved dearly but who believed that her only role in life was as a wife and mother.

Then the tears were gone as suddenly as they appeared, smoothed over by Melba merriment as she told a story about an American critic who wrote apologising that his paper had omitted a report about a performance because he'd been delayed at a race track and missed the concert.

It was typical Melba, a reporter noted, 'the very embodiment of a brilliant, intellectual and also intensely womanly woman, frankly unaffected and utterly unspoiled by success; in fact, just the very woman of whom Australia has every reason to be proud'.

He had boarded the *Miowera* from the pilot boat to conduct Melba's first formal interview as she arrived in Brisbane on the evening of 17 September 1902, but there was nothing formal about Melba. She was a mad conductress as the conversation ebbed and flowed, from Marchesi to *Madame Butterfly*, and from the devotion of the kings of Sweden and Norway to the defiance of a hotel maid who refused to clean her room because she was simply a 'singing actress'.

She was excited and anxious, almost childlike, as she hoped Australia would 'like me' and worried about the power of the media who wrote without fear of libel. Once, when she had refused to be interviewed, a reporter had simply made up a story about her knocking down an old woman on a bicycle.

It seemed ludicrous that the world's great soprano, who had conquered London, Paris, Milan and New York would feel such anxiety, but so high were her emotions. Yes, she had triumphed across the world but this was different; this was a desire to show that she had been right to endure the slings and arrows and to pursue her dream against the odds. 'I am not nervous in the slightest, but something rises in my throat and almost chokes me when I think of coming back again after all these years to sing to the Melbourne people and especially my own dear father.'

The reporter could see the gathering throng of media as they approached the dock. Nellie was surrounded by the hungry mob as soon as she stepped ashore, fielding shouted questions before the Mayor and Mayoress of Brisbane intervened to welcome her with a bouquet while porters struggled with the thirty-seven trunks in which Nellie had brought the various costumes she might wear onstage over the next six months of her stay.

It was a low-key welcome compared to the stops her train made on its way to Sydney the next day. Crowds gathered along platforms and sidings of small towns as the train whistled past.

At larger stations the train stopped and she descended from her carriage to meet people like an arriving monarch on a royal tour, accepting bouquets and listening graciously to flowery speeches.

The closer she got to the city of Sydney, the larger the gatherings, causing inevitable delays that only added to the anxiety of her promoters about the concert schedule. At Hornsby she met her brother Charlie, whom she hadn't seen since her departure in 1886, and then her sister Belle boarded as they neared Central Station in Sydney where two thousand people jostled to catch a glimpse of the diva. A police cordon ushered her through the cheering crowd.

Jack Moore was among those who lunched with Nellie at the Australia Hotel during her stopover in Sydney. He had been surprised to receive a telegram in which he was invited to meet her. It seemed that the Darling Point party all those years before had been a pivotal moment in Melba's life, and she wanted to see the attendees again and invite them to a concert so they could see for themselves the woman they'd encouraged to strike out for Europe.

But amid the joy and celebration, there were two pieces of bad news. Because of the travel delays and the arduous journey, promoter George Musgrove had decided to postpone her first concert, scheduled for 24 September, by three days. It was a risky decision given the public's anticipation, and the fact that all four Melbourne concerts had been sold out, but it was worse to risk Nellie's voice and wreck the tour before it had begun.

The other news was personal and devastating. David Mitchell, who had been waiting in Albury, on the NSW–Victoria border, to escort her back to Melbourne, had suffered a stroke. He was alive but gravely ill. After much thought, Musgrove decided to keep the news from Nellie until she arrived in Albury the next day.

Nellie had left Sydney the same night and slept on the train as it steamed down the east coast. She woke in time for breakfast before the train pulled into Albury then panicked when she couldn't see her father on the platform.

The news was then broken to her by a doctor and she was led away to a nearby house where the 73-year-old David Mitchell was resting in a darkened room. It was a distressing scene on what should have been a joyous reunion. Her father had seemed indestructible and now Nellie was being told that it was her delays that might have caused the stroke.

The train was delayed while she stayed by her father's bedside, weeping and vowing to cancel her concerts. It was only when David Mitchell told her to go on without him that she agreed to continue the journey to Melbourne, where thousands gathered patiently at Spencer Street Station.

'Lass, do not disappoint,' he called after her, the first time he had ever verbally encouraged his daughter.

And so she left, reluctantly, and now she could see the size of the crowd who wanted to welcome her home. Sydney had seemed enormous but Melbourne was overwhelming as police helped her through the masses to a carriage that would take her through the city and on to Toorak where she had rented a house for her stay. There was a women's choir and a brass band playing along Collins Street, and yet more speeches by dignitaries eager to be associated with a returning heroine.

She brightened a little as the carriage passed Allans Music Shop, where she had taken lessons as a child, rebuilt although recognisable among the swathe of new buildings erected as the city had grown. Then, egged on by the crowd, she tore apart a bouquet of violets and flung the petals and stems through the window where they were passed around as 'Melba memorabilia', just as her borrowed pencil had been shared among the crowd in the St Petersburg square after the opera for Tsar Nicholas.

Nellie Mitchell was home.

⁂

Although they had all bought tickets, the audience began gathering in the Town Hall almost two hours before Nellie's first concert. Such was the occasion that everyone wanted to see and hear the woman who'd left Melbourne as fledgling singer Mrs Nellie Armstrong and returned as opera diva Madame Melba.

The previous few days had been a rush of events and appearances: a reception hosted by the city mayor, dinner with the governor-general and a theatre performance where, much to her dismay, her arrival almost overshadowed the performers. A pair of police constables were hired as bodyguards when *The Argus* published a story valuing her jewellery at £100,000 and the other papers reported with awe that her friend the Prince of Wales, now King Edward VII, who had ascended the throne the year before at the death of his mother, had asked that she receive 'every attention'.

Nellie's favourite event was a luncheon at her old school, the Presbyterian Ladies' College, where she blushed as the school band played 'See, the Conquering Hero Comes' and laughed while mingling with old friends. Requests to autograph a school photograph initiated a rush of requests from the bonneted gathering, who put down their cups of tea and offered up anything they could find—cards and even cake plates—for signing.

But tonight was special. Electric lights festooned the front of the grand building, the late spring evening warm with anticipation. It might have reminded Nellie of her debut in Brussels when she stood in wonderment at the sight of her name in lights above the door of Monnaie.

This time she could not pause as she was led through a sea of people in the street who had waited for her arrival and would be there when she left several hours later. Some even shrieked as she passed by, such was the fervour. There had never been scenes like this and it would not happen again for another sixty-two years, until The Beatles arrived.

Inside, the hall was packed to its edges, the crowd a mix of finely attired society men and women, who could afford the three guinea ticket price for the best seats, and hundreds more who struggled to pay for seats at the back and yet did so because they simply had to be there. It was a 'leavening' of people, the reviewer for *The Herald* observed, adding that Nellie appealed not just to music patrons but also 'the man in the street'.

Those inside would have to wait until almost the end of the first part of the program to see their goddess but when Nellie finally appeared the audience rose to applaud and flutter a sea of white handkerchiefs. They cheered in a volume and enthusiasm normally associated with an encore.

She was dressed triumphantly but simply in white silk, veiled in chiffon, silver sequins and outlined with white roses, and stood blowing kisses for several minutes until the crowd settled back into their seats. Then she sang, her emotions tangling with her voice at first before soaring through the mad scene from *Lucia di Lammermoor*. When she finished the audience rose again, this time casting flowers and wreaths onto the stage. Outside, the crowd cheered along.

The scene would be repeated when she returned twice more during the evening, even the man tapping his feet to the beat forgiven by the purists either side as she sang the touching lyrics of the ballad *Home Sweet Home*:

Mid pleasures and palaces though we may roam

Be it ever so humble, there's no place like home

Nellie had given the crowd what they wanted, and when she finished with the aria 'Ah! Fors' e lui' from Verdi's *La Traviata*, which she had sung at her last concert before leaving Australia, the encores seemed to last forever. Finally, they let her go and she descended the steps, the cries still ringing in her ears. A reporter waited at the bottom for her. Shouting over the noise of the crowd, he asked how she felt at that moment.

'I am a very proud woman tonight,' she replied.

The reviews would come thick and fast, the sage words of the main city newspapers reprinted in dozens of country titles across the state, and the country. This was not the night to question her performance but to thrill at what Australia had produced, as the report published in the *Bendigo Advertiser* concluded:

> It would seem, of course, absurd to offer any criticism in regard to Melba's singing. She has long passed that. Suffice it to say that she possesses a beautiful, soft, soprano voice, of the true velvety texture, and that her execution is marvellous to a degree, every note being absolutely perfect. The selection chosen was accompanied by a flute obligato, and it was at times difficult to say which was the instrument and which was the human voice.

But praise for her talent was no longer important to Nellie, instead she was looking for an acknowledgement that she had succeeded despite other people's belief that she wasn't talented enough to make it on the world stage. Or to prove wrong those who questioned why a woman would strive for anything more than a husband and children. A report in *The Age* set the record straight. It began:

> When Nellie Melba went away some sixteen years ago to 'prosecute her studies' in Europe, with a beautiful voice and unbounded self-confidence as her chief stock in trade, it is a

matter of history that she left behind her very few who had any great faith in her success in the career she had chosen, or who looked upon her as a singer much out of the ordinary. It was only when this rash Melbourne girl came to be talked about in the art centres of Europe as the brightest particular star of the musical firmament, and when the unexampled rapidity of her rise to the top-most rung of the ladder of fame proved the precursor of an evident intention to keep that exalted position all to herself, seemingly secure against any and every rival, that her compatriots began to see the enormity of the blunder they had made in not recognising her capabilities earlier.

Nellie Mitchell's belief in herself and her right to pursue a professional career had finally been vindicated.

## 33

# THE BRUTAL *TRUTH*

Nellie revelled in the remaining four Melbourne concerts. She enjoyed entertaining in her rented Toorak mansion while the audiences and newspapers continued to swoon in admiration. It had been a difficult arrival but Nellie dared not have hoped for a better reception.

There was one particularly poignant moment when her father, still frail but determined, made his way to the front row of the second concert to see his daughter perform. It was said that he had once asked promoter George Musgrove if the stories were true about his daughter's success, as if he could not quite believe her letters or the media coverage from Europe, but this reception had shown him how wrong he'd been.

Nellie had sensed her father's emotions and sung 'Comin' thro' the Rye' for him. It was a ballad he had taught her as a child and the pair exchanged winks across the stage to hide the tears that otherwise might have flowed.

She and her troupe now moved to Sydney where audiences adored her even more, in part because, unlike Melbourne, they had encouraged her to seek fame and sent her on her way to Europe with a specially struck gold medal. Her return as the all-conquering heroine had vindicated their confidence.

'Let it always be remembered to the credit of Sydney that although Mrs Armstrong's debut at the Theatre Royal was that of an absolute unknown student, her talents were at once recognised,' the *Sydney Morning Herald* correspondent wrote after the first concert on 11 October. 'There is a world of heart interest between her and our audiences . . . cheered her as a favourite and a friend.'

There was a hiccup when she was forced to reschedule her third and fourth concerts because of a 'relaxed' throat, which had a knock-on effect on two concerts that were to follow in Brisbane. She apologised in a letter to the editor, explaining that her doctor had insisted she not sing for a few days:

'I deeply regret the inconvenience which this change of plans will entail upon concert-goers,' she wrote.

I am obliged to ask the public, who have been so kind to me, to forgive me for a short but absolutely unavoidable postpone- ment of my two remaining concerts. I, above all things, am anxious that the public shall hear me at my best, and I feel that it would not be fair either to the public or myself for me to sing again until I have had a few days' rest.

The tickets returned by those who could not attend the new dates were quickly snapped up and the last two concerts went ahead without incident, with more than four thousand filling the Sydney Town Hall for her last concert while five hundred more listened outside. Immediately afterwards, she boarded a train to return to Brisbane for the two rescheduled concerts before travelling to Adelaide where there were two more concerts.

But it was not enough. The concerts so far had been a mix of her singing arias and general ballads, mixed in with performances by other artists. Nellie was desperate to present opera and managed to put together a fifty-piece orchestra and hire a handful of singers for supporting roles in a program made up of a selection of acts from *La Traviata*, *Rigoletto*, *Lucia di Lammermoor* and *Faust*.

There were six sell-out concerts, three each in Sydney and Melbourne, and by mid-December she was exhausted but planning a regional tour through Victoria before crossing the continent to Perth in the new year.

But the gloss had started to wear off and there were rumblings of discontent among the adulations, not about her performances but an uneasiness about ticket prices. When she arrived in September, the media was enamoured with her glamour and success but the stories of wealth were beginning to rub raw, some even believing that Nellie was not only charging too much but should be singing for free, as if in gratitude for her home crowd, as one columnist in the *Newcastle Herald* proposed. 'First, she was going to sing merely in order that her fellow country men and women should have an opportunity to hear her voice, but the prices . . . show that the commercial instinct is the predominating one.'

There were quibbles about her hiring police at 10 shillings a day each to guard her jewels. Eyebrows were also raised at the frequent appearance at her side of Lord Richard Nevill, a handsome aristocrat employed as the aide-de-camp and private secretary to Baron Tennyson, the new governor-general. It gave some scribes the opportunity to rehash the Duc d'Orleans story. Nellie may have been divorced and single but being seen in public with a man, however innocent, was vulgar in the eyes of some.

It was clear to Nellie and George Musgrove that they needed to counter the perception of greed, particularly as Australia was in the midst of its worst drought since white settlement. Nellie had seen the devastation herself, from the window of the train as it returned to Melbourne from Brisbane: 'I've seen the skeletons of cattle and sheep dotting the paddocks and the signs of desolation and starvation everywhere,' she wrote in another letter to the editor. 'I have read in the newspapers the accounts of suffering endured by the settlers . . . and I feel that I must do something to help them.'

She proposed a special fund, the Melba Fund, which she would kick off with £200 and then grow by asking thirty of her powerful and wealthy friends in Europe and America to contribute. But the idea backfired. The offer was 'gracious and warm-hearted', the government said, but it was misguided and created the impression overseas that Australia, so recently unified as a federation, was not capable of fending for itself.

Nellie withdrew, instead giving hundreds of pounds to a series of good causes like the Women's Hospital in Sydney, the Adelaide Children's Hospital and the Civil Ambulance and Transport Brigade. She also made appearances at places like the Victorian Institute for the Blind and the city's general hospital where she gave an impromptu performance and donated £100.

There were other acts that occurred spontaneously and without fanfare, like the day she stopped at a small allotment on the outskirts of Sydney after noticing three cows in desperate condition. Nellie spoke to the destitute farmer and then ordered feed and chaff to be delivered to the farm, enough to last the next month.

But it was not enough. Where America loved Melba for being a down-to-earth star who arrived in a gilded train carriage, the Australian media began to see her as a tall poppy who needed chopping down.

Nellie feared the newspapers and their unfettered power. She had learned to accept the occasional bad review but the personal slights—what she called 'Dame Rumour'—had taken their toll over the years. She feared being called a loose woman and being blamed for the failure of her marriage to Charlie Armstrong. Most of all, she fretted about what would be said about the loss of her son, George.

She had resisted all media attempts to lure her into discussing the Duc d'Orleans, most notably when two reporters from rival newspapers agreed to work together during interviews onboard the train from Brisbane. She had dismissed their questions by mentioning white cockatoos every time the duc was raised and they went away disappointed, but the threat was ever-present, as she would later write.

> Would they say, for instance, that I took too much drink? I decided against that because I concluded that nobody would be quite so imbecile as to imagine a singer could keep her voice for a month under such circumstances. Would they discover that I was a morphia maniac? Looking at my exceedingly healthy face in the glass, I smiled that supposition away. I supposed, therefore, that they would content themselves by telling each other that I was in love with my baritones and my conductors.

As her concert schedule grew into the new year, so too did the pressure on her physically. She was exhausted by the grand opera concerts and was forced to reschedule one concert in Perth when the temperatures peaked at over 37 degrees Celsius. In February she travelled to New Zealand via Tasmania where she had to cancel her Launceston appearance on doctor's orders because of the rough crossing of the Bass Strait, which threatened her throat with a swollen lymph node. This time, the locals were not so forgiving.

Success in New Zealand softened her disappointment but the cumulative impact of the delays and continued concern about ticket prices was about to explode.

John Norton was a vindictive, violent drunk with a history of domestic cruelty and adultery who once hid the death certificate of a man who had died in his house because he feared being charged with killing him. Norton was also regarded as a megalomaniac. He owned the *Truth* newspaper and used its pages as a weapon against rivals he thrashed with verbose tirades.

Like a Donald Trump of yesteryear, he was worshipped by his readers and was elected to the NSW Parliament and city council on numerous occasions, a supposed champion of the masses and opponent of the political class. He was so despised by his contemporaries that one man horsewhipped him in the middle of Pitt Street.

As her tour wound to an end, Nellie came into the spiteful sights of John Norton and the vile contents of his three thousand–word 'Open letter' would have far-reaching consequences, simply because, once flung, mud sticks and congeals.

Norton had been a Melba fan when she arrived in Australia, one of the chorus of admirers for her first concert, but by March 1903 Norton had adopted a new stance. This was how he began his column on 29 March:

Madame,—Marvellous Melba,

Mellifluous Melba, Supreme Singer, Crowned Cantatrice, and Monarch of Matchless Music though you be, your public and private conduct during your short six months' sojourn in Australasia makes it compulsory that you should be told the truth ... Your scandalous breaches of public faith and private propriety are no longer to be borne without protest. That protest I now make.

Norton went on, and on, and on. He was angry about high ticket prices, that she had missed or delayed performances, and questioned whether her father had even been ill. He accused her of being a vulgar bully, spat about her private life and laid the blame for her failed marriage at her feet, a 'grass-widow' who put her career ahead of her husband and child and had an unseemly affair with the Duc d'Orleans.

Worst of all, he claimed, without evidence, that Melba was a sad drunk who was destroying her own talents:

Your powers are ripe; your reputation is made. All the world asks of you is the privilege of paying to hear you, and applauding you. What more could woman wish or desire? What woman with a heart or soul would rashly risk such rich gilts and golden opportunities as yours by wantoning in wine?

The invective was greeted with stunned silence by the other newspapers editors, unsurprised at such an attack by Norton, who enjoyed chopping down tall poppies, but shocked by its intensity. They were also cowed, as much by Norton's repu-tation as anything else, and so chose to ignore his words and continue to cover Nellie's appearances as if nothing had been written.

But the fact that his words went unchallenged only served to instil a sense that they were true, at least in part. In fact, some of the criticisms might have been valid. Ticket prices were high and Nellie had upset concert-goers, particularly in Tasmania, when she cancelled events even as many made long journeys to see her. In Paris or London a last-minute cancellation could be covered by an understudy, or audience members could choose to turn their carriages around and go home. But this was colonial Australia and many travelled long distances to see their famous countrywoman.

Snippets of Norton's vicious attack appeared in some social newspaper columns where his accusations were not challenged. The *Mudgee Guardian* was typical: 'John Norton publishes in *Truth* a brutally candid open letter to Madam Melba imploring her to drink less champagne and use less bad language, and reminding her of her treatment of her husband and the bestowal of smiles on the Duc d'Orleans.'

Even positive reports in Nellie's final few days in Australia could not heal the hurt, and when she left on 14 April aboard the steamship *Orontes*, the wharves filled with well-wishers, Nellie felt only sadness. It was unlikely that she would return to sing, she told assembled reporters, adding that she hoped the public would not believe what had been written about her.

A few weeks later John Norton entered Dr O'Hara's hospital for the inebriates in Melbourne.

## 34

# 'I AM FIVE FEET ELEVEN INCHES'

It was by the banks of the Lost River outside the Oregon town of Klamath Falls that Charlie Armstrong made his way in early 1901, having sold his storm-flattened business interests in Galveston. What brought him to this lonely place, more than 4000 kilometres from Texas, was unclear, as was the route he took. It is likely that he and George had gone north first, as far as Kansas, and then joined the Oregon Trail, the great east–west pathway across America created by frontier pioneers more than half a century before. Charlie was probably following it towards the Pacific in search of the only thing he knew—cheap land.

Whichever route they took, the two must have made the arduous journey by horseback because it would be nearly a decade before the railroad came to Klamath Falls, a neat settlement of four hundred or so residents perched on the edge of a large lake flanked by the Cascade Mountains and surrounded by forest. There was fertile land here, although much of it would have to be drained, but Charlie saw what he must have thought would be his last opportunity.

The forced sales at Murphy and Galveston meant that his share of the Armstrong fortune was all but gone; but there was enough left to buy what was called 'a meagre stretch of range' near Lost Gap, a dozen or so kilometres from the town. It was land that must have reminded him of the mangroves in the long-abandoned thoroughbred stud north of Mackay because 'meagre' was probably a kind description, according to a later report which assessed the land and its condition in detail as 'one of the most desolate sage bush and alkali wastes in the country' fronting a lake so shallow that it wasn't navigable.

But Charlie pressed ahead and by 1902, just as Nellie was preparing for her triumphant return to Australia, he had managed to convince a group of local investors that although his land was too marshy to plant crops, it was ideal for running cattle and sheep. The Olene Livestock Company was incorporated, with an office in the town while Charlie managed the property. A year later the partners chipped in again, this time to construct a dam in the vain hope they could corral and harness the swamp so that crops could be planted.

George was Charlie's lone offsider, now a lean and strapping teen who had adopted the American cowboy hat and followed baseball instead of cricket, while his father remained steadfast to English clothes and saddles. No one questioned why the boy was not in school, not out here in the American West. As for his mother, it was assumed she was dead or gone.

Despite the challenges of the new property, the enterprise was a modest success and Charlie slotted into his now familiar role around town as the handsome, rugged horseman who was known as a polite if slightly gruff man of few words. He had a fearsome reputation as an amateur boxer, and was a favourite drawcard at exhibition bouts, frequently held in one of the town's three saloons, in which he was able to dispatch most opponents even though he was now aged in his mid-forties.

But, as had happened so often in the past, Charlie was also prone to disputes and, almost inevitably, he argued with his business partners and they decided it was best to sell out and leave him alone to run the operation—the Armstrong Ranch—in his own way.

Around the same time, rumours began to emerge that there was more to Charlie's story than met the eye. It began when staff at the post office noticed letters arriving for him embossed with coronets, signs that he was somehow connected to English nobility, and gained traction when he began replying to the letters. Eventually, someone plucked up the courage to ask him, only to be met with a terse stare. 'He has never gratified their curiosity,' a local reporter offered when the story emerged some years later.

In the early winter of 1904 another secret emerged as the local newspaper, the *Klamath Republican*, reprinted a feature story written by a city paper in nearby Portland of the arrival in America of the songstress Nellie Melba. There was particular excitement because Madame Melba might, for the first time, venture to the city. According to the story, the singer had an ex-husband named Charles Armstrong.

This time he could not ignore the questions of his neighbours: Charlie Armstrong, the quiet rancher and boxer, had to admit that he was the ex-husband of the world's most famous opera singer and that their son, George, was spending his days in the American wilderness tending sheep.

❀

George's twenty-first birthday, on 16 October 1904, was on Nellie's mind as she prepared for her latest American tour. She had written to him the year before but had received no reply and wondered if she could go through the heartache again. There was no way of knowing if he had even received the letter—perhaps stopped by his father—let alone read its contents, but she desperately wanted her 'Georgie' to know she was thinking about him on the day he was becoming a man.

Winifred Rawson also wanted to write to wish her godson well on his landmark birthday. The Armstrong family had given her a new address in Oregon, which she promptly passed on to Nellie. In her letter to George, she also mentioned that his mother was on her way to America and wanted to meet up with him. It was less likely that Charlie would intercept her correspondence and at least George might read the message, even if he didn't respond.

In the weeks before she embarked for New York, Nellie decided to send her own letter, more in hope than in expectation. She was arriving on 12 November, she told him, and was staying at the Manhattan Hotel.

A fortnight later she boarded the steamship *Luciana* for

yet another rough Atlantic crossing, arriving in the midst of a freezing New York winter, thawed slightly by celebrations of Theodore Roosevelt's presidential victory four days earlier. Among the fan mail waiting at the hotel was a letter for which she'd only dared to dream. It had been penned just six days earlier, in handwriting that she could not have recognised, given that George was a nine-year-old child when she had last seen him. It read:

Nov 6, 1904

My darling mother,

I received your dear letter today, so overjoyed to hear from you that tears came into my eyes. Your letter that you wrote last year, if I had, dear mother, I would certainly have answered. I have thought of you every day of my life since I left you, and why I have not written is more than I can tell.

I will come and see you as soon as it can be arranged. Now that I am of age I am my own master, but, of course, before I could not come without my father's consent. Father is away at present but will be home in a few days, and I will tell him I intend going to see you. Of course I will spend half the year with you. To think that we have not seen one another for eleven long years, but that shall never be again.

I am five feet eleven inches now and I weigh 145 pounds, when we parted I was a little boy but I love you now better than ever. I lived in Galveston, Texas, for a few years, and know some very nice people there. The Byrne family,

318

especially Mrs Byrne who was very good to me and I will tell
you all about her when I see you.

I will have to say goodbye for the present. Hope that you
will reach New York safely.

I remain your loving son George

PS: Please excuse poor writing, but I am so overtaken with joy
and cannot write well.

Overwhelmed with emotion, Nellie read and re-read the letter.
How sad that a young man had to describe himself physically
to his mother, as if to show that he had survived the ordeal
and was okay. She had always feared that George might have
believed the stories that she had abandoned him, but it seemed
that he knew the truth and had felt her absence as much as
she had his. And there were hints that, even though Charlie
had not turned the boy against her, he had somehow blocked
any communication between them. She wondered what might
have happened if Charlie had been at home and intercepted
this letter. Four days later a second letter arrived.

Nov 10, 1904

My dear mother,
I am writing again to say that I am starting in a few days.
Father returned home yesterday and is delighted to have me
come and see you and wants me to start as soon as possible.
He will drive me to the railroad, which is seventy miles. There

will be no need to send any money. A man is just moving into our ranch today, he has rented it for a year, so we will be all straight in a few days. I will send a telegram, from Portland the day I leave here. It won't be long before we see one another again so do try and be happy till I come. I will have to say goodbye, Mother. Hoping to see you soon.

With much love, I remain

Your loving son George

Charlie had accepted the inevitable and accompanied George as far as Portland where the boy caught a train to New York, which would take several days. The reunion of mother and child a week later was emotional and held in private but the story would soon become public when George accompanied his mother on her American tour, travelling with her in her private rail coach.

According to eager newspaper reports, George heard his mother sing in public for the first time on 5 January 1905 in the Convention Hall in Kansas City. He spoke to reporters afterwards about standing amid the cheering crowd giving his mother ovation after ovation: 'To say that I was pleased would be putting it lightly. Of course I knew what the public thought of my mother's singing, but it never came home so forcibly to me before.'

More significantly, the shy young man also acknowledged the difficulty in re-establishing a relationship that both had been denied for so long: 'We are hardly acquainted as yet, and I can hardly realise the relationship in which I stand to this woman, whom the public seems to worship. She has always been a fairy godmother.'

Newspapers cast Charlie as the victim in the saga. Given that he was unlikely to discuss his life publicly, papers felt emboldened to create their own versions and most took the misogynistic view that it was he who had driven Nellie's career, discovering a young woman with potential in Melbourne, sponsoring her travel to Europe and then paying 'lavishly' for her lessons in Paris. In return for his generosity, Nellie had simply cast her husband and young child aside, leaving them to live hand-to-mouth in a wooden hut. Worse, it was said that George had grown up never knowing his mother as she was indifferent to his existence.

Nellie, busy on her tour and with George by her side, was thankfully ignorant of the coverage, as was Charlie who was readying to quit the property and the town of Klamath Falls. The departure of George was a blessing in many ways. They had grown apart in recent years as it became more impossible to bat away his questions about Nellie. Charlie was better on his own; he'd always been more comfortable as a solitary figure who could pick and choose when and where to seek company.

The land here had finally defeated him, the marshland making it impossible to run enough stock or grow crops in abundance. But an opportunity to sell out at a profit had emerged during the first months of 1905. The government was keen to fund the millions required for drainage works to turn the area into thriving agricultural land and attract thousands into the region, providing the impetus for the long-awaited rail line.

Charlie's land was suddenly valuable, not for farming but as the site for a potential new town. He sold out to real estate developers who laid out grand plans for a new town called White Lake City that would emerge from the marshes. They convinced hundreds of small investors across the Midwest to pay $15 each for a housing plot, then built and opened two grocery stores, a hardware shop, butchers and even a newspaper to give the project some credibility. But the promises would amount to little. Few homes were built and the businesses failed. The buildings were eventually razed and the land returned to nature.

By then Charlie was long gone, headed north in search of the next, lonely adventure while Nellie and George went back to London. Mother and son had to get to know one another again.

# 35

# A LONG FAREWELL

With George back by her side Nellie had reclaimed the mother-
hood that had been taken from her. The vengeance of Charlie
Armstrong would leave permanent psychological scars for his
wife and son but, for now at least, the world seemed a calmer
place. On her return to Europe she told Madame Marchesi
that she planned to step back from the frenetic pace of performances to concentrate on her son, who she felt needed her full
attention after his experiences.

She was right. George not only had the tall and lean look of his
father but also his introspection and shyness, which made it difficult for him to find a place in the social whirl of London society.
His lack of schooling during the years he'd spent roaming the
American wilds only added to the problem and, despite private
coaching, it was clearly impossible to even consider that he might
attend the place at Oxford that had been reserved for him.

Instead, Nellie found him a commission with the Royal Berkshire Militia which, she hoped, might turn into a military career. But George's interests lay in a different direction, and in the late summer of 1905 he became engaged to nineteen-year-old Ruby Otway, the only child of a wealthy Mayfair art collector.

Nellie was against the marriage on the basis that they were both too young and immature but, mirroring her own youthful defiance, George was determined, and in December 1906 he and Ruby married, the church filled with the wealthy, famed and titled, although there was no sign of his father, who did not make the journey from Canada where he now lived on a remote island near Vancouver, and where he would die in 1948 at the age of ninety.

It appeared to wedding guests that Nellie had a beau on her arm as she made her way around the room at the Ritz. Lord Richard Nevill, whom she had met during her tour of Australia, had been frequently identified as a suitor and likely new husband but, like other men with whom she had been and would be romantically linked, it did not come to pass.

Nellie's professional career was also about to take a turn. She was at the peak of her powers as a singer, proclaimed critically and adored publicly on both sides of the Atlantic, but the world was changing. There would be young challengers to her throne and new male partners with whom to forge partnerships. Jean de Reszke retired to teach and she was paired with the up-and-coming Italian tenor Enrico Caruso. The partnership was a sensation onstage, particularly when they were singing the parts of Mimi and Rodolfo in the opera *La Boheme*, which had become a rare and important addition to Nellie's repertoire in the second half of her career. But the relationship was problematic offstage in many ways and lacked the genuine camaraderie Nellie and de Reszke had shared.

The human voice was being recorded around this time and Nellie was among the first to release a gramophone record, although the technology was both a blessing and a curse. It gave her access to a much bigger audience—by 1905 an estimated one million had listened, according to advertisements of the time—but the initial, scratchy technology could not capture the dimensions and power of her voice as it would for those who came later.

There was also a new challenge with the arrival in Paris of Oscar Hammerstein, a German-born cigar-maker and inventor turned theatre impresario who was building a new opera house in New York in an audacious bid to break the dominance of The Metropolitan and its wealthy establishment benefactors.

Hammerstein, unconventional and quixotic, was convinced that Nellie held the key to his success because of her popularity with the masses, and came knocking at the door of her apartment one day offering to pay her $2000 per performance.

Ever the opportunist, Nellie replied by demanding $3000 and Hammerstein agreed. The next day he returned with $20,000 in cash as a guarantee, which he tossed on the table. Nellie promptly swept the notes from her desktop into a drawer without bothering to count them. She later called him 'the only man who ever made me change my mind'.

Her debut season at the new Manhattan Opera House in the first months of 1907 seemed to take public adulation to new heights, if that were possible, beginning in January with *La Traviata* to a packed house and ending two months later with a performance of *La Boheme* that was met with wild scenes of excitement and thirty-four curtain calls. Asked if he would rather make cigars or manage opera, he replied, 'It's much more fun to make Melba sing than it is to make cigars.'

Despite her vow not to return to Australia, she would venture back home towards the end of the same year, not to sing but to see her siblings and her father, who was about to turn seventy-nine.

She also hoped the warmer climate would give some respite to a bronchial problem she had carried ever since her reunion with George, who faced problems of his own. The marriage with Ruby, although less than a year old, was clearly in trouble as Nellie watched them argue aboard the ship on the way out to Australia, a sharp reminder of her own troubles with Charlie on the way to Europe so many years before. It would not be the only similarity.

Although she had not planned to sing in Australia, Nellie yielded to public demand and gave two concerts, one in Melbourne and the other in Sydney. The Melbourne concert, in particular, was an emotional moment and helped repair the ill-feeling of five years before. There were eight thousand in the audience; one critic, concluding, 'No matter what comes and goes, Melba is ours, yours and mine.'

But as much as the trip helped Nellie reconnect with her homeland, the return to Europe would bring her face to face with the inevitable appearance of new, young rivals. Among them was the Italian soprano Luisa Tetrazzini, whose career until now had been confined to the opera houses of Italy and South America but whose Covent Garden debut in the autumn of 1907 had been hailed by critics as the emergence of a new star.

Nellie's appearance at Covent Garden in 1908 was delayed by several weeks as she sat by Madame Marchesi's side while her old teacher mourned the death of her husband. It was significant because, in the interim, Tetrazzini was performing what had traditionally been Nellie's roles, such as Gilda in *Rigoletto* and Violetta in *La Traviata*, while her own performances that season were cut back to mainly *Othello* and *La Boheme*.

In public, Nellie remained cool and seemed to accept her younger rival but in private she fumed, unhappy that one critic dubbed the Italian as the next Melba. 'Many are called but few are chosen,' she responded.

Lady de Grey, her hold over the opera loosened somewhat by new management, wrote to Nellie sympathising about the unhappy season but reminding her that no one could take away her achievements: 'You must not be knocked down by the want of appreciation of a few people—when you are Melba!'

To complicate matters, George and Ruby had separated after their return from Australia and, while in Paris, George had begun an affair with a Mrs Hoffman. He confessed and begged Ruby to return to him but she refused. The affair was merely the last straw in a marriage that, despite its luxurious ceremony, had always struggled. George's frustrations with life bubbled over into fits of anger, which had occasionally ended in a level of violence. He had once pushed Ruby into the sea at the beach and, on another occasion, locked her in a room when she wouldn't kiss him. It seemed he was repeating the violence he had witnessed as a child.

Nellie, trapped between the love of her only son and concern about Ruby's safety, announced she would not be appearing in London for the 1909 season and would instead tour Australia and New Zealand, taking George, now divorced, with her. Her uninterrupted run at Covent Garden was drawing to a close as she sold her house in Great Cumberland Street and boarded the ship for Melbourne.

❈❈

Despite her success in the great cities of the world, Nellie was hankering for what she called the *backblocks* of her home-land—'a breath of fresh air, far away from the clever men and great musicians, from vast cities and easy comforts'.

She began her tour in Ballarat, wondering if the country folk were interested in hearing her voice or whether they preferred something simpler. The answer was a resounding yes, as she would write years later: 'At every stopping place the village halls were packed, and at each place where I arrived they gave me a reception of which even royalty could not have complained.' Many travelled hundreds of miles, by train, on horseback and even on foot. People sat on iron rooftops to watch and listen, and in north Queensland, where buildings were on stilts, they crouched beneath the floorboards.

Back in Melbourne, she bought a property at Coldstream in the Yarra Valley with views of the mountain ranges. She would call it Coombe Cottage after an English house she had rented the memorable summer after being reunited with George. The farm was within comfortable reach of the city where she established free *bel canto* classes at the Conservatorium of Music at Melbourne University, teaching students for two hours every Wednesday.

Her departure, planned for February 1910, was delayed when George fell ill, prompting a pained letter to her friend Lady Susan FitzClarence: 'I have so many triumphs and so little happiness—I am sick to death of it all.'

The long tours across America were beginning to take their toll, and she embarked on another at the end of the year. Travelling in a purpose-built train was once thrilling but now it seemed monotonous as did the singing night after night.

Her one joy was Australia, her long estrangement now repaired as she returned again in 1911 for a full tour, this time with twelve operas that she hoped would be a significant cultural event, as she told reporters gathered on the Fremantle docks: 'It has always been my ambition to present grand opera in Australia—grand opera such as it is given in Covent Garden—and I trust that the people here will all be pleased.'

She would get her wish. The concerts were all sell-outs, people camping out waiting for the box office to open. Touched by the enthusiasm, Nellie insisted that those in line should get free tea while they waited and she would appear occasionally to sing to the crowd.

Her performances were greeted with ovation and acclaim but the stress of performing, as well as managing the tour and even set designs and costumes, began to have an impact on her, not only mentally and emotionally but physically as she developed an ear and throat infection.

When she began to miss performances there were those who chose to believe that she was 'drinking again' because, although the journalist John Norton was silent, his vitriol had become folklore and she was an easy target for lazy journalists. Ticketholders were known to phone the theatre before a concert to ask if she was sober enough to perform.

'The muck clung,' wrote Therese Radic in her 1986 biography *Melba: The voice of Australia*.

For the rest of her life Melba was pursued by Norton's malice. It was useless to protest that no singer who was drunk could perform a schedule as Melba did. Even now, when the idiocy of such an accusation has long since been established, the rest of the mud splashed by Norton is still visible on Nellie's tarnished image.

Ann Blainey, who published *I am Melba* in 2008, observed: 'How people could continue to believe that a singer so hard-working and self-disciplined was an alcoholic was beyond her understanding.'

Once again Nellie would delay her planned return to Europe, this time for several months because of her father's ill-health, which meant she was again missing from Covent Garden. The silver lining was that George was in love again, with a young Australian singer named Evelyn Doyle. Nellie approved the union and the couple were wed in London in February 1913, this time without the fanfare of royalty and publicity.

But the year would end in more sadness. Mathilde Marchesi died in November at the age of ninety-two. Nellie was away on yet another American tour when the news came through. The previous year she had visited her old teacher in Paris and been shocked at her frailty, later writing: 'She whom I had known as trim, strict and alert, with a brain as keen as steel, was now only a sad, shrunken figure, almost lost to the world.'

There would be more bad news, first that fellow soprano and friend Lillian Nordica had been shipwrecked in far north Queensland on the way back to America after completing an Australian tour. She would be rescued along with the passengers and crew but, already in failing health, would linger in hospital and die a few months later from pneumonia.

And there were growing concerns about the health of Nellie's father who was now eighty-five. Nellie was taking no chances, forgoing most of the London season to travel home and be beside the man who had wanted his daughter to be a mother and housewife instead of one of the world's great musical artists. For all his faults, she still regarded him as her greatest supporter:

He and I have always been more to each other than ordinary father and daughter. I have always had great admiration of him . . . he realises it and understands although he is never demonstrative . . . so when I think of losing him, it is as though I were losing my life's mate.

The unscheduled journey back to Australia would be serendipitous. Not only would David Mitchell's hardy nature keep him alive but, within weeks of her arrival in Melbourne, World War I broke out and Nellie found herself in the safety of Australia, along with George and Evelyn who had travelled with her.

Fundraising and teaching would become her salvation. She held concerts and raised an estimated £100,000, driven in part by her own family's sacrifice when five male relatives were killed when Australian troops made their ill-fated landing at Gallipoli. Privately, she was thankful that George's ill-health meant he couldn't sign up.

Although cut off from Europe, she made several tours of America and Canada. She was there in March 1916 when told that her father needed bladder surgery. This time she couldn't get back home and David Mitchell died on 25 March. 'My heart broke. I lost my all,' she wrote.

The one joy for her was the birth in September 1918 of her granddaughter, Pamela. A month later, with the war at an end, Nellie, who had been made a dame for her war charity work, received word from King George V that he wanted her to reopen Covent Garden.

𝄋𝄌

It was snowing when Nellie landed at Liverpool in March 1919. The journey across the Atlantic, cold and uncomfortable aboard a vessel scratched and torn from war, was forgotten in the magic of the moment, snowflakes drifting down from a desolate sky evoking fond memories of riding in a hansom cab to her first Brussels concert through a snowstorm.

But the harsh reality of war struck home by the time she reached the city—'this new, untidy, haphazard metropolis, so grey and strange from the London which I had known,' she would write. When she visited Buckingham Palace, Queen Mary asked her if she found London dirty. 'I was forced to admit that I did.'

The joy of war's-end celebrations was long forgotten in sombre streets filled with returning soldiers, many injured or homeless and searching for work. There were signs of the effects of war even in her own, rarefied social circle where sugar and butter, once simple pleasures taken for granted, were now smuggled into restaurants in small silver pots by aristocratic women, forcing waiters to dig out sugar spoons that had been hidden away.

Far worse was the human toll. In May 1914, when she turned fifty-three years old, Nellie had held a party for a select group of London friends before she departed for Australia. Her memories of that joyful night were of couples dancing, among them Lady Juliet Duff and her husband Sir Robert, the second baronet of Vaynol Park. They were young and happy, laughing as they twirled around the floor. But five months later Sir Robert was dead, killed by a sniper's bullet a few days after arriving at the Belgian front.

He would be the first of many. Nellie thought of the other men at the party, listing their names in her head. There were twenty from memory, sixteen of them young enough to go to war. Only six had returned alive.

Gladys de Grey was also gone, from cancer in 1917. The great society hostess had spent her last days raising funds for the King George Hospital, her stunning gowns and jewels exchanged for simple cotton dresses as she took her stint most days tending the wounded. The obituaries were numerous and generous, all pointing to her beauty and impact on London culture, especially the introduction of Nellie Melba to London.

Nellie thought of Gladys on her first night back at Covent Garden when she sat in her dressing room and felt the ghosts of the past. '"It's not you," I said to myself as I peered into the glass. "It cannot be Melba. It is somebody else. So many have gone, so many new faces have come—it cannot be that you have remained."'

The concert was a triumph and there would be eighteen more appearances that summer. But not everyone was enamoured with her. She clashed with the new manager, Thomas Beecham, whom she thought was a bumptious upstart, while he considered her a pampered prima donna as they fought over the colour of her dressing room. 'It will probably be my last season in London,' she told her daughter-in-law Evie in a letter, adding: 'So I intend to have a jolly good one for the last and then exit Melba.'

She was right, and in January 1920, when she was told her services were not required for the coming season, Nellie again wrote to Evie. 'I don't suppose I shall get a word of thanks for all I have done for thirty-one years—just the order of the boot . . . I am most indignant and don't quite know what to do. But I think I shall tell the king.'

Although she would perform in England in the interim, Nellie would not appear again at Covent Garden until 1923 when she sang eight times, free of charge, for the struggling British National Opera, with which Beecham had no involvement.

Instead, she toured Australia in 1922 and 1924, her health increasingly frail as she struggled with diabetes, bronchial infections and colitis among other ailments. It became obvious that her voice was, inevitably, wearing with age and she embarked on numerous farewell concerts, including one at Monnaie in Brussels where it all started. It was time to retire, and do so gracefully.

On 8 June 1926, Nellie farewelled Covent Garden in a night of ovation, floral tributes and royal ascent from George V and Queen Mary as she sang acts from *Romeo et Juliette*, *Othello* and *La Boheme*.

This was not a night for review but of tribute, many in the audience expecting that, at the age of sixty-five, Melba would no longer thrill. They were wrong as the critic for London's *Daily Telegraph* would observe:

It would be stupid to say that time has not had an effect. It certainly has; but even so, if a little of its old mellowness is gone, no singer, not even the youngest of the day, is steadier in tone, or hits the notes more precisely or accurately . . . A colossal night of music and a glorious exhibition of the noble art of singing.

John Brownlee, a young Australian baritone discovered by Nellie after he won a singing contest in Ballarat, made his debut that night alongside his mentor. 'The auditorium was a sea of gowns and tiaras and uniforms and decorations and white shirtfronts,' he told biographer Joseph Wechsberg years later.

> The atmosphere was charged almost beyond endurance. Melba's ordeal became Melba's triumph . . . In all my life at the opera I've never heard another ovation that had such overtones of love, affection and adoration. Only the supposed cold English can bestow such a tribute upon an artist whom they worship.

Nellie's speech was understandably tearful. 'It is such a great and glorious evening, but you can imagine what a terrible feeling it is for me to think that I shall never again perhaps sing within these beloved walls. Covent Garden has always been my artistic home and I love it . . . but all things must end.'

# EPILOGUE

Nellie and Philippe would remain in touch after their emotional reunion but their time as a couple had long passed. 'His letters show a dignified and grateful devotion,' Nellie's granddaughter Pamela observed in her loving 1996 biography of her grandmother.

But their paths rarely crossed, at least in a public sense. There were occasional notes in the theatre press that Philippe had been seen in the boxes at the opera admiring a Melba performance, but little else. Their affair had been characterised by romantic, carefree youth which neither was able to repeat with anyone else nor recapture with one another in later life.

Love had passed them by as Nellie spent more and more of her time in Australia, and Philippe, still in exile, explored the world to build his collection of wildlife. He might have failed to retrieve the French throne but he hoped to at least leave this legacy.

His journeys included crisscrossing Africa and the Subcontinent as well as four Arctic expeditions, travelling between Norway and Greenland, where he not only discovered and named new lands and hunted for specimens to add to his museum but collected vital scientific data that helped ocean-ographers understand the Arctic waters.

In 1926 Philippe spent several months travelling through Ethiopia and the Blue Nile, during which he celebrated his fifty-seventh birthday. But on his return to Palermo, he became sick, was diagnosed with smallpox and died on 28 March. He was holding a small silver box filled with French earth, having not set foot in the country since the provocative escapade of 1890 that led to him meeting Nellie.

The death of the Duc d'Orleans was greeted with sadness across France. He was described as the 'stormy petrel' of his country. The French government accepted the duc's animal bequest and a new wing was added to the Museum National d'Histoire Naturelle in which his collections were displayed. Many remain today, although scattered throughout the museum.

Nellie was at her apartment in Paris when she heard on the radio that Philippe had died. At the time, she was sponsoring a young American singer named Elena Danieli who watched as Nellie walked slowly from the room, paused at the doorway and sighed, 'Ah, Philippe.' It was the lament of lost love.

Nellie's last charity concert was at the Park Lane Hotel in May 1930, after which she would spend several months travelling through Europe, ending up in Switzerland where it is believed that she had a facelift.

She became ill on the voyage home to Australia, and after

several months convalescing at Coombe Cottage, it was clear that her condition was serious. In mid-January 1931 she was admitted to St Vincent's Hospital in Sydney where, despite a brief rally, she died on 23 February. The official cause of death was septicaemia.

Perhaps the most poignant moment of her many farewells came in October 1924 when she stood on the stage at His Majesty's Theatre in Sydney after what was billed as her final Australian operatic concert. *The Argus* carried her words the next morning:

> I have done my best. I have tried to keep faith in my art. For all that Australia has done for me, for all the beauty that she has shown me, for all the love she has offered, I wish to say, thank you from the bottom of my heart. I never was prouder than I am tonight to be an Australian woman.

Australia's first real international superstar was dead. Thousands filed past her coffin as she lay in state inside Scots' Church, and thousands more stood, heads bowed, outside along Collins Street as the hearse, draped in an Australian flag, began its journey to Lilydale. The procession took most of the afternoon, slowed by mourners who lined the 40-kilometre route, and it was almost sundown before 'the greatest of Australia's daughters' was buried, as requested, next to her father in the local cemetery.

The words on her headstone are ones she sang many times as Mimi in *La Boheme*:

> *Addio, senza rancor*
> Goodbye, without rancour.

# ACKNOWLEDGEMENTS AND
# NOTES ON SOURCES

The fact that Dame Nellie Melba adorns Australia's $100 banknote shows the esteem in which she is held by her countrymen and women, alongside other greats like war hero Sir John Monash, Antarctic explorer Sir Douglas Mawson and astronomer John Tebbutt whose images have also graced the note.

And yet somehow Nellie's story and achievements as one of the world's greatest ever sopranos remain muddied in a sea of misunderstanding, rumours, jealousies and downright journalistic thuggery.

For most of us, Helen Porter Mitchell, as she was born in Melbourne in 1861 is of an older, squarish woman whose celebrated voice on scratchy early recordings sounds thin and doesn't sit easily with modern music trends. But this image, left when she died, suddenly and awfully in 1931 just before her seventieth birthday, ignores the impact she had on the world stage as Australia's first real superstar.

It is hard to fully appreciate her fame at the peak of her career, from the thousands of ordinary folk who crammed into town hall theatres across rural America to cheer 'the nightingale' to the demanding audiences of Europe's great concert halls and the crown heads in royal boxes at Covent Garden that she kept spellbound for more than two decades.

Nellie was fierce and independent, at times arrogant and ruthlessly competitive; the same attributes as a champion Olympic athlete or prosperous businessman or woman would possess to become, and then remain, successful.

But she was also generous with her money and time for young singers, unapologetic for her plain speaking and belief in issues such as women's suffrage, although she drew the line at discussing her private life and suffered in silence for more than a decade when her only son, George, was kidnapped by his angry father.

Nellie's life has been examined by many writers and opera lovers over the past century. My take concentrates more on the woman behind the performer and is focused on her youthful rise in the last decade of the nineteenth century, a career initially pursued against the wishes of a puritan father, negotiated in spite of a bad and violent marriage, and achieved despite the challenges of being a single parent on the far side of the world from the support of family.

It also follows more closely and in more detail the love affair with Philippe, the Duc d'Orleans and would-be King of France, that threatened to sabotage a career almost before it had really begun. While many writers have previously dismissed this as youthful flirtation, I believe they loved each other and were forced apart by the expectations of others. Certainly, a lone surviving letter from Philippe to Nellie points to a shared longing as does the fact that both struggled to find love with others.

I would like to acknowledge the many biographies that have come before, in particular the fine work of Therese Radic (*Melba: The voice of Australia*, 1986) and Ann Blainey (*I am Melba*, 2008) which were invaluable resources, as were others such as *Melba: A family memoir*, written in 1996 by Nellie's granddaughter Pamela Vestey, while Nellie's autobiography *Melodies and Memories* published in 1925 sits as a counterpoint, important as much for what it doesn't say as for what it reveals, and demonstrating very real fears that her actions could be misconstrued or, in some cases, deliberately twisted by vitriolic journalists that marked Nellie as an early example of tall poppy syndrome. Thanks to the Nellie Melba Museum for the help with the photos.

I am indebted to Richard Walsh, whose enthusiasm created the opportunity to write about Nellie, as well as senior executives at Allen & Unwin in Australia and Atlantic Books in the UK. I feel privileged to have a career writing books. It is a notoriously difficult industry and I have always had amazing support from people like Patrick Gallagher, Clare Drysdale, Annette Barlow, Tom Gilliatt and Will Atkinson, not to mention my in-house editor Tom Bailey-Smith and copyeditor Deonie Fiford.

Finally, thanks to my wife, Paola, who has never doubted my endeavours and with whom I continue to share an eventful, mad but fulfilling life journey.

# BIBLIOGRAPHY

**Books and published material**

Achard, JB, *Le duc d'Orleans*, 1890

Anonymous, *Fifty Years of London society, 1870–1920*, London: Eveleigh Nash, 1920

*Australian Dictionary of Biography* online, Canberra: Australian National University, 2020

Barr, W, 'The Arctic Voyages of Louis-Philippe, Duc d'Orleans', *Polar Record*, 41(1), pp. 21–43, 2010

Benson, EF, *As We Were: A Victorian peepshow*, London: Longmans, Green, 1930

Blainey, A, *I am Melba*, Melbourne: Black Inc, 2008

Calvé, E, *My Life*, New York: D Appleton, 1922

Casey, M, *Melba Re-visited*, Melbourne, 1975

Colson, P, *Melba: An unconventional biography*, London: Grayson & Grayson, 1932

Cornwallis-West, Mrs George, *The reminiscences of Lady Randolph Churchill*, London: Edward Arnold, 1908

Craik, J, *Mathilde Marchesi: A study of her life and work in vocal pedagogy, including historical and modern implications*, Florida Atlantic University: MA thesis, 2011

Eames, E, *Some Memories and Reflections*, New York: Appleton, 1927

Escoffier, A, *Memories of My Life*, 1955

Escoffier, A, *A Guide to Modern Cookery*, London: Heinemann, 1907

Ganz, W, *Memories of a Musician: reminiscences of 70 years of musical life*, London: John Murray, 1913

Hetherington, J, *Melba: A biography*, Melbourne: Cheshire, 1967

Klein, H, *The Golden Age of Opera*, Abingdon: Routledge, 1933

Kolodin, I, *The Metropolitan Opera 1883–1939*, Oxford University Press, 1940

Leslie, A, *The Marlborough House Set*, London: Doubleday, 1973

Leslie, A, *Some Players: Personal sketches*, Chicago: Herbert & Stone & Company, 1899

Lord Rossmore, *Things I Can Tell You*, London: Eveleigh Nash, 1912

Lubbock, A, *People in Glass Houses: Growing up at Government House*, Melbourne: Nelson, 1977

Marchesi, B, *Singer's Pilgrimage*, London: Grant Richards, 1923

Marchesi, M, *Marchesi and Music: Passages from the life of a famous singing teacher*, New York: Harper & Bros, 1905

Melba, N, *Melodies and Memories: The autobiography of Nellie Melba*, London: Butterworth, 1925

Moran, WR, *Nellie Melba: A contemporary review*, Westport: Greenwood, 1985

Mordden, E, *Opera Anecdotes*, New York: Oxford University Press, 1985

Murphy, A, *Melba: A biography*, London: Chatto & Windus, 1909

*Musical Courier*, New York, April 1895

*Musical Courier*, New York, January–June 1900

Neill, R, *Divas: Mathilde Marchesi and her pupils*, Sydney: NewSouth, 2016

Nichols, B., *Evensong*, London: Jonathan Cape, 1932

Nicolson, J, *The Perfect Summer: England, 1911*, London: John Murray, 2008

Pascoe, CE, *London of Today: An illustrated handbook for the season*, London: Simpkin, Marshall, Hamilton, Kent & Co., 1890

Radic, T, *Melba: The voice of Australia*, Melbourne: Macmillan, 1986

Rodmell, P, *Opera in the British Isles, 1875–1918*, Abingdon: Routledge, 2016

Rosen, B, *Victorian History*, vichist.blog.com, 2008

Shaw, GB, *London Music in 1888–89*, London: Constable and Co, 1937

Sherard, RH, *Twenty Years in Paris: Being some recollections of a literary life*, Philadelphia: George W Jacobs & Co, 1906

Shigo Voice Studio, www.shigovoicelessons.com

Somerset-Ward, R, *Angels and Monsters: Male and female sopranos in the story of opera 1600–1900*, New Haven: Yale, 2014

Vestey, P, *Melba: A family memoir*, Melbourne: Phoebe, 1996

Wechsberg, J, *Red Plush and Black Velvet: The story of Dame Nellie Melba and her times*, London: Little, Brown and Co, 1961

**Archives**

Ancestry.com

Archives Nationales (Royal)

Australian National Archives

British Library

British National Archives

British Newspapers archive

Centre of Diplomatic Archives in Nantes

Comtedeparis.com

Lilydale and District Historical Society

National Archives France

National Library of Australia

Newspapers.com

New York Public Library

Proquest

Royal Opera House Covent Garden collection

State Library NSW

State Library of Queensland

The Twickenham Museum

Trove.com.au